W9-DCU-873

THE WORLD'S 100 BEST
ADVENTURE TRIPS

TEXT BY JASMINA TRIFONI

PROJECT EDITOR VALERIA MANFERTO DE FABIANIS

EDITORIAL STAFF LAURA ACCOMAZZO
GIORGIO FERRERO

MAP PRODUCTION GEO4MAP s.r.l. - Novara

GRAPHIC DESIGN CLARA ZANOTTI

SUMMARY

ON FOOT

ON THE ROAD

SUMMARY

BY SEA

ON 2 WHEELS AND 4 PAWS

FRESH WATER JOURNEY

ADRENALINE

INTRODUCTION

Adventure is itself worthwhile, said Amelia Earhart

In a much more prosaic way, Roald Amundsen, one of the most intrepid explorers in human history, defined adventure as a synonym of bad organization. In reality, between these two extremes, the term "adventure" is not perfectly definable because it is terribly subjective, like all adventurers are. From the "active" adventurer who is happy just to travel toward the unknown, to "passive" ones who just like to take journeys in their minds. With the help of a good book.

Although it is true that, today, the era of great adventures and discoveries is irremediably over (even if it would be great if someone surprised us tomorrow with a new breakthrough) – there isn't a single place on our planet that has not been explored, photographed or mapped by Google – the sense of liberty that only traveling gives us is still the same for everyone. Awaking the adventurer's spirit in us all. This is the goal of this book as we present 100 adventurous journeys in every corner of the globe, on foot or by bike (or motorcycle), on horseback, on a sailboat or aboard a – not necessarily comfortable – cruise ship, driving off-road, on a train or even more "exotic" transportation. To immerse yourself in the wild nature right up close with its fauna and live the experience of extreme climates or come into contact with peoples and cultures that are quite different from our own. Or even testing our limits and facing our fears by playing extreme sports.

Some of the adventures contained in this book last only one or two days, others can take us on epic itineraries - deep into the South American Amazon, along the Grand Trunk Road, the "travelling continent" between Pakistan and India, in the surprisingly varied desert dunes of the Egyptian Sahara or the Gobi in Mongolia, or on the ices of the North Pole and the coasts of the Antarctic Peninsula - that you will remember as the experience of a lifetime. Naturally, the adventures listed here are for many different kinds of adventurers. We know that some readers will call certain journeys presented here "unexciting" and too close to home to be able to arouse interest and passion for another place. Then there are those who, on the other hand, will ignore some of these trips for being too excessive for their cultural inclinations, physical capacities, the amount of time required, age or economic investment (even if often you can organize these vacations with local agencies, reducing the cost more than you may realize). But remember, almost all of our proposals could be broken down into smaller parts – for example, it would be impossible to horseback across the entire Australian Bicentennial Trail, which cuts the country in half for over 5000 kilometers, unless you took at least a year long sabbatical, but the itinerary is just as fascinating even if you only see one of its sections – and remember that often the goal of a journey isn't the destination.

There's a Zen proverb that says: "Traveling is better than arriving." While a Confucian precept declares: "No one gets as far as he who does not know his destination." Remember these maximums when you choose the itinerary for your next adventure and be ready and open to appreciate every moment along the way (there's even something special about the boredom of long trips in the monotonous landscapes!), to stop and change routes, if you think, impulsively, on a whim, that you want to.

The particular story of each of these very special journeys is, in the end, merely a rough outline for a journey that you are free to follow to the letter or, alternatively, change, mold and twist according to your own personal desires. Here, in this volume, we would simply like to give you a little taste to stimulate your imagination, accompanying each proposal with splendid pictures, and providing you a little bit of practical information along with some friendly advice from previous travelers. Because, God rest Amundsen's soul, the perfect adventure is always the intelligently organized (or unorganized) one.

HOW TO USE THIS GUIDE

EVERY CHAPTER OPENS WITH AN INTRODUCTIVE STORY THAT ILLUSTRATES THE ADVENTURE'S ITINERARY, DESCRIBING ITS GEOGRAPHICAL CONTEXT, LANDSCAPES, FAUNA AND/OR CULTURE AND ANY POSSIBLE DIFFICULTIES.

EVERY ADVENTURE IS ACCOMPANIED BY AN ILLUSTRATION TO MAKE FINDING IT EASIER AND, IF NECESSARY, BY A MAP THAT SHOWS THE ITINERARY IN DETAIL. IN ADDITION, AT THE BOTTOM OF THE PAGE, YOU WILL FIND SYMBOLS THAT INDICATE THE DISTINCTIVE ELEMENTS OF THE JOURNEY (FOR EXAMPLE, AN ETHNOGRAPHIC EXPERIENCE OR WILDLIFE SPOTTING) AS WELL AS THE RELATIVE MEANS OF TRANSPORTATION USED.

IN THE IN-DEPTH PARAGRAPH COLUMN, DIVIDED INTO POINTS, WE NOTE THE MOST IMPORTANT STOPS ALONG THE JOURNEY, DIGRESSIONS OFF THE "MAIN ROUTE" THAT OFFER PARTICULARLY INTERESTING ACTIVITIES, OR OTHER POSSIBLY TO ENRICH YOUR EXPERIENCE USING ALTERNATIVE TRANSPORTATION.

NEXT, THE BEST SEASONS FOR EXPERIENCING THE ADVENTURE (OR, SOMETIMES, THE MOST TRADITIONAL MOMENT FOR THEM) AND THE MINIMUM AMOUNT OF TIME NEEDED, EXCLUDING ARRIVAL AND DEPARTURE, ARE NOTED. PLUS, UNDER "ORGANIZATION", YOU'LL FIND INFORMATION FOR A DO-IT-YOURSELF VACATION AS WELL AS THE MOST TRUSTED TOUR OPERATORS IN THE ZONE.

DON'T FORGET TO READ THE ADVICE WE PROVIDE AT THE END OF EACH SECTION OF PRACTICAL INFORMATION: SOMETIME THEY REGARD SANITARY NORMS, OTHERS ARE SUGGESTIONS FOR EQUIPMENT OR LITTLE HINTS THAT WILL HELP YOUR TRIP.

FINALLY, THE MOST LENGTHY CHAPTERS ALSO INCLUDE THREE CURIOSITIES, SOMETIMES ABOUT THE NATURAL, HISTORICAL OR CULTURAL ASPECTS, AND THEY WILL HELP STIMULATE YOUR CURIOSITY TO LOOK DEEPER AND DISCOVER SOMETHING THAT WE DON'T KNOW YET...

MAP LEGEND

- ITINERARY
- LOCATION OF THE SUGGESTED ITINERARY
- AIRPORT
- CHURCH, ABBEY
- CASTLE, TOWER
- MOUNTAIN SUMMIT
- MOUNTAIN PASS
- CAVE
- NATURAL CURIOSITY

Ethnographic journey

Wildlife spotting
Wildlife watching

Caving

Trekking

Rockclimbig, Škraping

Bungee Jumping

Snowmobiling

Ski

Bicycle,
Mountain bike ike

Motorcycle

Off-road, automobile

Bus

Train

Airplane

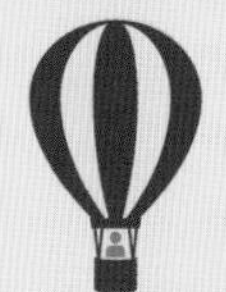
Hot air balloon

Ship, boat,
ice-breaker

Sailing

Motorboat

Canoe, kayak, rowboat

Rafting

Diving

Fishing

Whale watching

Camelback

Elephant

Horseback

USEFUL INFORMATION

	ART AND CULTURE	LANDSCAPE	WILDLIFE SPOTTING	GASTRONOMY	SHOPPING	DIFFICULTY	PRICE-QUALITY VALUE
Italy, France, Switzerland - Mont Blanc Tour	••	•••	••	••		••	•••
Italy, Switzerland - The Monte Rosa Tour	••	•••	•	••		••	•••
Germany - Along the König Ludwig Weg	•••	••		••	•	•	•••
France - The Grande Randonnée in Corsica	••	•••		•••		•••	•••
Italy - On Etna							
Mali - Along the Dogon Cliffs	•••	••			•••	•	•••
Rwanda - Virunga, the Gorilla Mountains		••	•••			••	••
Tanzania - On the Peak of Kilimanjaro		•••	•			•••	••
Zambia - Walking Safari in Luangwa		••	•••			•	••
Kyrgyzstan - Trekking in Tien Shan	•	•••	•		•	•••	••
China - Pilgrimage on Mt. Kailash	••	•••			•	••	••
Nepal - The Annapurna Circuit	•	•••			•	••	•••
Nepal - Trekking in Mustang, the Last Tibet	•••	•••			•	••	••
Bhutan - Taktsang Monastery	•••	•••			••	•	••
India - At the Spring of the Ganges	••	••			•	••	••
Japan - On the Japanese Alps	••	•	•••	•••	••	•	••
Japan - Pilgrimage to Koyasan	•••	••		•••	••	•	••
Papa New Guinea - Among the Papua Natives	•••	••	•	•	••	••	••
Australia - The Great Ocean Walk		•••	••			•••	••
New Zealand - In Fiordland		•••	•			••	•••
Vanuatu - Ambrym, the Black Island	•••	••		•	••	•	••
United States - On the Lava of Kilauea		•••				••	•••
United States - The John Muir Trail							
Peru - Atop Cordillera Blanca	•	•••	•	•	•	••	••
Argentina - Trekking in Parque Nacionál Los Glaciares		•••	•	••		•	•••

	ART AND CULTURE	LANDSCAPE	WILDLIFE SPOTTING	GASTRONOMY	SHOPPING	DIFFICULTY	PRICE-QUALITY VALUE
Egypt - From Cairo to Gilf Kebir	•••	•••		•	••	•	••
Ethiopia - In the Omo Valley	•••	•	•		•••	••	•••
Tanzania, Kenya - The Great Wildebeest Migration		•••	•••			•	•••
Madagascar - On the Fianarantsoa-Côte Est Railway	•	••		•	•	•	•••
Pakistan, China - Along the Karakorum Highway	••	•••		••	•••	••	•••
Pakistan, India, Bangladesh - On the Grand Trunk Road	•••	••		•••	•••	•	•••
Laos - Among the Ethnicities of Luang Nam Tha	•••	••	•	••	•••	•	•••
Mongolia - In the Land of Genghis Khan	••	••	•	•	•	•	••
China - In the Kingdom of the Lugu Hu Women	••	••		•	•	•	••
Japan - Wild Hokkaido	••	••		•••	•	•	••
Russia - Chukotka, the Last Frontier	••	•••	••	•	•	••	••
United States - On Kodiak Island	•	•••	•••	•		•	••
Canada - In Churchill, with Polar Bears		••	•••			••	••
Mexico - A Train Ride through the Barrancas del Cobre	••	•••	•	••	•••	•	•••
Bolivia - In the Salar de Uyuni	•	•••		•	•	•	••
Greenland (Denmark) - In the Ilulissat Icefjord	•	•••	••			•	••
Norway - Cruising to Spitsbergen	•	•••	•••	•		•	••
Norway - Fishing in Lofoten	••	•••	•	••	•	•	••
United Kingdom - Kayaking the Outer Hebrides	•	••	•			••	••
Sudan - Diving Cruise in Port Sudan		••	•••			••	••
Madagascar - Kayaking Masoala	•	•••	•••			••	••
Myanmar - In the Mergui Archipelago	••	•••	•	•	•	•	••
Indonesia - Komodo, the Island of Dragons		••	•••			••	•••
Indonesia - Diving Safari in Raja Ampat		•••	•••			••	••
Russia - On the Ring of Fire	•	•••	••			••	••

USEFUL INFORMATION

	ART AND CULTURE	LANDSCAPE	WILDLIFE SPOTTING	GASTRONOMY	SHOPPING	DIFFICULTY	PRICE-QUALITY VALUE
United States - The Humpback Whale of Frederick Sound	•	•••	•••	•	•	•	••
Canada - Along the Coasts of Baffin Island	•••	•••	•••	•	•	•••	••
Mexico - Whale Watching in El Vizcaíno		••	•••	•	•	•	••
Belize - Diving the Great Blue Hole		•••	••			••	••
Ecuador - Galápagos Cruise		•••	•••			•	•••
French Polynesia - Cargo Boating the Marquesas Islands	••	•••	•	•	•	•	••
Australia - Sailing the Whitsunday Islands		•••	••	•		•	••
Palau - Diving Cruise through Rock Islands		•••	•••			••	••
Argentina, Antarctica - Cruising Antarctica	•	•••	•••			••	••
Iceland - Mountain Biking Geysers and Volcanoes	•	•••		•		••	••
Norway - Along the Rallarvegen	••	•••		•	•	••	•••
France, Spain - Pyrenees Tour	•••	•••		•••	•	•••	•••
Namibia - On Horseback in the Fish River Canyon		•••	••			••	••
Russia, Kazakhstan, Mongolia - On the Altai Mountains	•••	•••	•	•	•	••	••
China - In the Taklamakan Desert	••	••	•	•	•	••	••
Thailand - Whith Elephants in the Golden Triangle	•	••	••	•••	•••	•	••
Vietnam - Along the Ho Chi Minh Trail	••	••		•••	•••	••	•••
Australia - The Bicentennial National Trail		•••	••			•••	•••
Australia - Western Australia by Motorcycle	••	•••	•••	•	•	••	•••
United States - In Monument Valley	•	•••		•	••	•	•••
Cuba - The Far West of Pinar del Río	••	•••		•		•	••
Argentina - In the Pampa with the Gauchos	•••	••		•••	••	••	•••
Ireland - Ireland's Waterways	•••	••		•	•	•	••
India, Bangladesh - In the Labyrinth of the Sundarbans	••	••	•••	•	•	•••	••
Vietnam, Cambodia - In the Mekong Delta	•••	•••	•	•••	•••	•	•••

	ART AND CULTURE	LANDSCAPE	WILDLIFE SPOTTING	GASTRONOMY	SHOPPING	DIFFICULTY	PRICE-QUALITY VALUE
Indonesia - With the Orangutans of Kalimantan		••	•••	•	•	•	••
Canada - On the Nahanni River		•••	•			•••	••
Botswana - In the Okavango Delta	•	•••	•••	•	•	•	•••
Guatemala - Sailing the Río Dulce	••	••	•	••	•	•	••
Honduras - In a Cayuco at La Moskitia	••	••	••	••	•	••	••
Venezuela - Canoeing Salto Ángel	•	•••	•	•	•	•	••
Brazil - On Rio Negro	•••	•••	•••	•	•	•••	•••
Brazil - In the Pantanal	•	••	•••	•		••	••
I S A - Cross-Crossing Skiing the North Pole		••	•			•••	•
Finland - Emotions in Lapland	•••	•••	•	••	•	•	••
Switzerland, France - At the Portes du Soleil		••		•••	•	•	•••
Croatia - Škraping in Dalmatia		••		•	•	••	•••
Zambia, Zimbabwe - Rafting the Zambezi		•••	•			••	•••
South Africa - Caged up in Shark Alley		•	•••			••	••
Jordan - Hot Air Ballooning the Wadi Rum	••	•••	•	•		•	••
Russia - On Lake Baikal	••	•••	•••	•	•	••	••
Thailand - Rockclimbing in Krabi		••		••	•	••	••
Malaysia - Down the Gunung Mulu Caves		•••	•	•		••	••
The Philippines - The Underground River of Puerto Princesa	•	•••	•			•	••
New Zealand - Bungee Jumping in Queenstown		••		••	•	•	••
Canada - Heliskiing the Rocky Mountains		•••		•		•••	••
United States - Rafting the Grand Canyon							
Mexico - In the Mayan Cenotes	•	••	•	•	•	••	•••
Costa Rica - "Air Trekking " in Monteverde							
Costa Rica - Sharks at Isla del Coco		•	•••			•••	••

ON FOOT

"IF YOU ARE A FREE MAN, YOU ARE READY FOR A WALK." THUS SAID HENRY DAVID THOREAU, THE PROPHET OF THE WILDERNESS.

"The real miracle is not to walk either on water or in thin air, but to walk on earth." Written in the middle of the 6th century – and therefore way before the invention of the airplane – this Chinese aphorism speaks a great truth. Going on foot is the journey with a capital "J", in the most primitive and universal form possible that, more than any other thing, allows you to immerse yourself in, even touch the landscape that surrounds you, discovering its pure essence.

Traveling on foot is necessarily a slow adventure and the pace of our steps is both the right one for truly meeting other wayfarers as well as for living in nature, be it rocks, flora or animals. Plus, there is no better occasion than walking for appreciating solitude and freedom, learning to better know yourself.

The foot adventures presented in this section range from going around Mont Blanc, Europe's ceiling, and the one on Mt. Kailash, the world's most sacred summit, to the long crossing of the John Muir Trail between Yosemite and Sequoia National Park in the United States and, above all, in the places where the awareness that the nature of our planet is a treasure to protect.

ETHNOGRAPHIC JOURNEY
WILDLIFE WATCHING
CAVING
TREKKING
SKI
TRAIN
MOTORBOAT
WHALE WATCHING
HORSEBACK

YOU ONLY HAVE TO CHOOSE
YOUR DESTINATION,
FROM THE ALPS TO THE ANDES,
FROM THE HIMALAYAS
TO THE EXTREME SOUTH OF
THE PRIMORDIAL NEW ZEALAND.

ON FOOT

CHOSE THE RIGHT EMOTION

JOURNEY	PG	TIME ZONE	WHEN TO GO	NOT TO MISS
Italy, France, Switzerland - Mont Blanc Tour	20	GMT +1	May-October	*Mer de Glace Glacier*
Italy, Switzerland - The Monte Rosa Tour	24	GMT + 1	May-October	*Walser Ecomuseum, Gressoney La Trinité*
Germany - Along the König Ludwig Weg	28	GMT +1	May-October	*Neuschwanstein Castle*
France - The Grande Randonnée in Corsica	31	GMT +1	June-October	*Mt. Paglia Orba*
Italy - On Etna	34	GMT +1	All Year	*Valle del Bove*
Mali - Along the Dogon Cliffs	36	GMT	November-February	*Festa del Bulo*
Rwanda - Virunga, the Gorilla Mountains	39	GMT +2	June-September	*Sabyinyo Silverback Lodge*
Tanzania - On the Peak of Kilimanjaro	42	GMT +3	Jan-Feb/September	*Lago Chala*
Zambia - Walking Safari in Luangwa	44	GMT +2	April-October	*Safari under the Stars*
Kyrgyzstan - Trekking in Tien Shan	48	GMT +6	June-September	*Inylchek Galcier*
China - Pilgrimage on Mt. Kailash	50	GMT +8	May-September	*Darchen*
Nepal - The Annapurna circuit	52	GMT +5:45	All Year	*Barga Monestary*
Nepal - Trekking in Mustang, the Last Tibet	55	GMT +5:45	June-October	*Tiji Festival*
Bhutan - Taktsang Monastery	58	GMT +6	Sep-Nov/Mar-May	*Ugay Tsemo Temple*
India - At the Spring of the Ganges	60	GMT +5:30	May-June/Aug-Oct	*Gaumukh Cavern*
Japan - On the Japanese Alps	62	GMT +9	June-October	*Onsen di Matsumoto*
Japan - Pilgrimage to Koyasan	64	GMT +9	All Year	*Kongobuji Temple*
Papua New Guinea - Among the Papua Natives	66	GMT +10	May-October	*Goroka show*
Australia - The Great Ocean Walk	68	GMT +11	September-December	*Twelve Apostles*
New Zealand - In Fiordland	70	GMT +12	October-April	*Milford Sound*
Vanuatu - Ambrym, the Black Island	74	GMT +11	May-October	*Back to the Roots Festival*
United States - On the Lava of Kilauea	76	GMT -10	All Year	*Kilauea Visitor Center*
United States - The John Muir Trail	78	GMT -8	June-September	*Half Dome*
Peru - Atop Cordillera Blanca	82	GMT -5	May-September	*Lagunas Llanganuco*
Argentina - Trekking in Parque Nacionál Los Glaciares	84	GMT -3	December-February	*Perito Moreno Glacier*

| 18-19 *The trek along the Annapurna Circuit provides high altitude emotions.*

DON'T FORGET	A CLASSIC BOOK FOR EVERY JOURNEY
Trekking Poles	*Mary Shelly*, Frankenstein
Binoculars	*Starr Hoyt Nichols*, Monte Rosa, the Epic of an Alp
Wagner	*Frances A. Gerard*, The Romance of King Ludwig II of Bavaria
Swimsuit	*Alexandre Dumas*, The Corsican Brothers: Corsica - Paris
Flashlight	*T.V. LoCiero*, The Obsession
Sleeping Bag	*BambaSuso*, Sunjata
Camera	*Dian Fossey*, Gorillas in the Mist
Sun Screen	*Ernest Hemingway*, The Snows of Kilimanjaro
Anti-Malaria Pills	*Norman Carr*, Return to the Wild
Compass	*Ella Maillart*, Turkestan Solo: A Journey Through Central Asia
Book for Meditation	*Colin Thurbon*, To a Mountain in Tibet (P.S.)
Big Backpack	*Majushree Thapa*, Forget Kathmandu
Notebook	*Ferd Mahler*, Under the Painted Eyes: A Story of Nepal
Incense	*Eric Weiner*, The Geography of Bliss
Snacks and Energy Bars	*Eric Newby*, Slowly Down the Ganges
Swimsuit	*Yasunari Kawabata*, Snow Country
Raincoat	*Eugen Herrigel*, Zen in the Art of Archery
Camera	*Lawrence Osborne*, The Naked Tourist
Tall Socks	*Robert Hughes*, The Fatal Shore
Rainproof Clothing	*J.K. Tolkien*, Lord of the Rings
Camera	*Joseph Conrad*, Twixt Land and Sea
Flashlight	*James Michener*, Hawaii
Bear Box	*John Muir*, My First Summer in the Sierra
Medicine for Altitude Sickness	*Manuel Scorza*, Drums for Rancas
Warm Clothing	*Henry James*, The Patagonia

MONT BLANC TOUR

Discovering the mountain with a capital "M", between legendary landscapes and splendid places that are the global cradle for alpinism and trekking.

With its clear, majestic profile and its excessively bright colors (many more than just white...), Mont Blanc was an impregnable castle in terrifying legends: for our ancestors, the nightmarish glaciers and the rumble of avalanches hid an Olympus that was said to be the home of unfathomable and sinister beings. So much that it wasn't called "White Mountain" in French, Italian or Patois. For villagers it was "the cursed," Monte Malet or Mont Maudit (the latter is still a toponym for one of its peaks). This is all hard to imagine today now that the summit of Europe's giant – that extends over three nations in the shape of an almond 59 kilometers long and between 8 and 15 kilometers wide with an altitude of 4810 meters at its highest point – can nearly be touched from the panoramic platform built on the splendid spire of Aiguile du Midi, at the celebrated Chamonix cableway, and that the long history of its conquest marked the birth of Alpinism tout court. For this, we have to thank the Genevan scientist Horace-Bénédict de Saussure who, in 1760, offered a reward to whomever found a way up to the summit of Mont Blanc when he visited Chamonix.

On August 8th, 1786, Jacques Balmat and Michel Gabriel Paccard managed to finally do it. Still, we owe De Saussure for the birth of trekking, that brought the joys of the mountain to us "mere mortals." He himself, for scientific and

| **20** *From Col du Brevent, northwest of Chamonix, you can see the eternal snows of Mont Blanc.*
| **21** *The ibex, endangered ever since the 19th century, owe their survival to the Savoy.*

NOT TO MISS

- NOT FAR FROM CHAMONIX, **SAINT-GERVAIS-LES-BAINS** MERITS A STOP FOR ITS VIEWS OF THE MASSIF AND FOR ITS HOT SPRINGS, FOUNDED IN 1808. THE SPA THERMAL DU MONT BLANC IS MARVELOUS AND THEIR TREATMENTS WILL GIVE YOU ENERGY TO CONTINUE YOUR JOURNEY.
- LEAVING FROM CHAMONIX, THE TRAIN TO CREMAGLIERA DEL MONTENVERS TAKES YOU TO THE FOOT OF **MER DE GLACE** (1913 METERS), THE LARGEST FRENCH GLACIER. FROM HERE, ACROSS A PATH, YOU CAN SEE AN CAVE CARVED INTO THE ICE THAT IS HOME TO AN EXPOSITION ON THE HISTORY OF MONT BLANC FROM THE 19TH CENTURY UNTIL TODAY.
- IN **MORGEX,** IN VAL D'AOSTA, TAKE A BRIEF DETOUR FROM THE TMB TO WALK ALONG THE **BAREFOOTING PATH** THAT WILL PUT YOU IN DIRECT CONTACT WITH NATURE. WALKING BAREFOOT, THIS PATH HAS SECTIONS MADE OF MATERIALS LIKE STONE, WOOD, SAND AND MOSS.
- IN THE VAL FERRET, IN SWITZERLAND, BOOK THE **ALPAGE DE LA PEULE A LA FOULY** REFUGE: IT OFFERS THE TRADITIONAL EXPERIENCES OF SLEEPING ON HAY, CHEESE TASTINGS AND DEMONSTRATIONS OF ARTESIAN CHEESE PRODUCTION.

| 22 *The Tour du Mont Blanc has excursionist trails through fascinating landscapes.*

touristic reasons, went around the circumnavigation of the rock 3 times between 1767 and 1778, marking the excursionist trail now called the Tour de Mont Blanc, i.e. the most spectacular and gripping high altitude walking adventure on the continent. In truth – and ironically – the first Tour du Mont Blanc guide, written in English by John Ball and published in London in 1863, describes this itinerary as "suitable for less adventurous travelers," "viable on mule... often followed by the women." But Ball was above all an alpinist and so he was a bit snobby about any experience that couldn't be classified as an epic journey. The great thing about the Tour du Mont Blanc is also the fact that this 170 kilometer circular route (or a bit more, depending on the variations), divided into 12 parts, is accessible to anyone in good shape. And, winding up to a maximum altitude of 2665 meters in Swiss territory, you can admire the "thin air" landscapes as well as experience the nature and culture of the valleys plowed around the massif.

Although the part of the trail halfway around Val Ferret, in the Italian Val d'Aosta and starting from the Courmayeur Basin is the most stunning panoramic balcony over the snow and peaks of the Blanc range – from Aiguille Noire de Peuteurey to the summit of Mont Blanc, from the surly Dent du Géant up to the Grandes Jorasses and Mont Dolent – the whole trip is a succession of valleys flowering with rhododendrons, conifer forests that extend up to 2000 meters in altitude and green pastures studded by chalets that are magnificent examples of mountain architecture. During the walk you can touch glacier tongues, enjoy the crystal-clear Alpine lakes (Champex Lake perfectly reflects the homonymous city, a pearl of the Helvetian side of the massif and the Grand Combin group) and have close encounters with the rich Alpine fauna that includes ibex, deer, foxes, marmots and golden eagles. In addition, the stops along the Tour du Mont Blanc are just as exciting: surrounded by the most authentic mountain atmosphere in the refuges, all part of the legend of Europe's ceiling, just like the alpinists who give them their names, you can even savor an elegant worldliness because the little burgs around Mont Blanc are the same ones that have kept high altitude tourism alive until today. Among these, an honorable mention goes to the French Chamonix that, with its magnificent, traditional hotel-chalets that seem like castles from a fable, still holds the title as the global capital of mountain vacations. Both skiing and ice-skating were born here and, in 1924, the first Winter Olympics were held here. In the main square, obviously, Chamonix pays tribute to De Saussure with a statue of him pointing to the summit of Mont Blanc.

Internet site www.autourdumontblanc.com

When to go *From May to October, with the opening of the lifts and the mountain huts.*

How long to stay *In order to go all the way around the trail, it takes 8 to 12 days, depending on how in shape you are.*

Organization *Well marked, the Tour du Mont Blanc can be taken both clockwise and counter-clockwise leaving from each of the places along the path. It is a good idea to book the refuges in advance: a complete list with contact information can be found on the official TMB site. If you prefer to be accompanied by a guide, contact Compagnie des Guides et Accompagnateurs de Chamonix Mont-Blanc in France, l'Associazione Guide Escursionistiche Naturalistiche della Valle d'Aosta in Italy and Les Guides de Verbier in Switzerland.*

Advice *To recover from the fatigue of walking and better enjoy the experience of Europe's ceiling, take some time to stop a day or two along the way, possibly in Chamonix, Courmayeur or Champex.*

Curiosities

- *Chamonix was the first Alpine city in the world to regulate the profession of Alpine guide. The now legendary Compagnie des Guides was founded in 1821 with already 200 members.*
- *The first woman to reach the summit of Mont Blanc was Marie Paradis in 1808. She was a servant in a Chamonix inn. However, she herself admitted that she had to be carried up to the summit, so the aristocratic Henriette d'Angeville - who accomplished the task in 1838 - is considered the first female alpinist. She is now known as "Blanc's girlfriend."*
- *The etymology of the French term "chalet" is derived from "cale," a word that defined rudimentary shelters for animals in high altitudes, nothing more than a heap of rocks with a fireplace between two boulders. Nothing further from what modern chalets are, with their suggestive and often luxurious presences that represent the dream mountain vacation.*

| 23 *The Réserve Naturelle des Aiguillles Rouges facing Mont Blanc.*

THE MONTE ROSA TOUR

A journey through four Italian and two Swiss valleys, experience the nature of the most extensive massif of the Alps and the culture of the Walser people.

| **24-25** *The Capanna Margherita is the highest refuge in Europe: 4554 meters.*

Today environmentalists would be horrified, but in 1893 the leaders of the Club Alpino Italiano showed no remorse when they leveled the rock obelisk of Punta Gnifetti, thus reducing the summit of Monte Rosa by a few meters, to build a small refuge. For them, it was a question of honor to take the prize for the highest building in Europe from the French, who had erected one on the crest of Mont Blanc a few years earlier at the altitude of 4350 meters. Over 100 years later, sitting at 4554 meters, the prized Capanna Margherita – named in honor of the Queen of Italy who visited it on its inauguration, carried up on a sedan chair along with her poodle – is still the champion, even if a new, bigger refuge took its place in 1980 which now also home to a scientific laboratory. Getting there from Alagna Valsesia on a strenuous 2-day walk isn't for everybody and an Alpine guide is needed: from here, on a clear day, the panorama stretches from the Maritime Alps to the Bernese Oberlad, all the way to the Dolomites. To admire Monte Rosa – that boasts 29 peaks over 4000 meters, the highest being Punta Dufour at 4634 meters and being the vastest massif of the Alps (its celebrated east face is the only one on the continent that can be com-

| 26 *The Alagna Valsesia territory was colonized by the Germanic Walser people in the 13th century.*

pared to the Himalayas) – one of the most suggestive, varied and exciting trekking itineraries in the whole Alpine range has been traced around it.
Over 190 kilometers through 6 valleys, 4 of which are in Italian territory (Valsesia and Valle Anzasca in Piedmont, Val del Lys and Val d'Ayas in Val d'Aosta) and 2 on the Swiss side (Saastal and Mattertal), even if the ideal starting and ending point is the Helvetic Zermatt, its circular path makes it accessible from any of these valleys. Broken up into 9 parts, it gives you a chance to cross a glacier, an immense stone quarry studded with limpid Alpine lakes, breathtaking landscapes and an extraordinary wealth of Alpine flora and fauna: the latter includes species like deer, ibex, chamois, marmots and red foxes. Along with nature's incantation, the Monte Rosa Tour offers excursionists the discovery of a particular mountain culture, the Walser. This Germanic community established itself throughout most of the valleys that surround Rosa between the 11th and 14th centuries, where they created completely self-sufficient villages. Still faithful to their traditions and their language, the Walser are also noted for having created the most complex and refined Alpine architecture: resting on a sort of stone "mushroom," the stadel are both wooden barns, stalls and houses, gifted with very practical solutions for resisting the rigorous winters and embellished with decorative elements that testify to an uncommon aesthetic sense. Even if many Walser have emigrated over the past 2 centuries – some becoming esteemed carpenters, others going even as far as Lyon where they have become famous pastry chefs – some of the villages along the Monte Rosa Tour are still quite populated and very active. Among the worthwhile stops are Macugnaga, in Valle Anzasca, Gressoney-St-Jean and Gressoney-La-Trinité in Val del Lys.

Internet site www.monterosa4000.it

NOT TO MISS

ZERMATT HAS NOT LOST ITS STRONG ALPINE CHARACTER WITH ITS DELICIOUS TUDOR STYLE CHALETS. OFF LIMITS FOR AUTOMOBILES, IT IS THE STARTING POINT FOR ONE OF THE MOST PANORAMIC TRAIN RIDES THROUGH THE ALPS ABOARD THE **GLACIER EXPRESS** THAT CONNECTS IT TO ST. MORITZ AND DAVOS.

IN VAL D'AYAS, THE **COLLE SUPERIORE DELLE CIME BIANCHE** LEADS TO THE LAKE OF THE SAME NAME, A DIAMOND TUCKED AWAY IN A LANDSCAPE OF RARE BEAUTY WITH THE MATTERHORN IN THE BACKGROUND.

THE **WALSER ECOMUSEUM** IN GRESSONEY-LA-TRINITÉ HOUSES A SERIES OF ARCHITECTURE EXHIBITIONS, WALSER CUSTOMS AND, IN THE SECTION DEDICATED TO MONTE ROSA, PHOTOS OF THE EVOLUTION OF THE GLACIERS, THE HISTORY OF ALPINE CONQUESTS AND RESEARCH DONE IN THE SCIENTIFIC LABORATORY IN CAPANNA MARGHERITA - ALL IN TRADITIONAL *STADELS*.

IN A MARVELOUS 18TH CENTURY WALSER HOME IN PIEDMONT, IN THE FRACTION OF ALAGNA VALSESIA, THE **MONTAGNA DI LUCE** IS A TRADITIONAL HOTEL: HOUSED IN A BARN, THE RESTAURANT SERVES SPECIALTIES LIKE POLENTA AND SAUSAGE RAVIOLI, TAROZ WITH LAMB AND, FOR DESSERT, APPLE TORTELLI.

When to go *From May to October, with the opening of the lifts and the mountain huts.*

How long to stay *The tour takes 9 days.*

Organization *Well marked with signs with "TMR" on them in big yellow letters, the Monte Rosa Tour can be taken independently. Along the itinerary, a wide selection of well-equipped refuges can be found and, in the burgs, numerous structures offer hospitality in various categories. To reduce the fatigue of the walk, it is possible to use a series of lifts so it is also a vacation fit for families with children. If you prefer a guided tour, contact the guide associations found at every step along the way. The Compagnie des Guides de Champoluc-Ayas, for example, organizes classic walking circuits, trips along the railways, canyoning and rock-climbing.*

Advice *The Monte Rosa Tour is a very popular destination, in particular in July and August, so you should book ahead for places in the refuges.*

Curiosities

It would be too easy if this mountain was called Rosa *due to the color of its snow at sunrise: in reality, its name is derived from rouja, which means "ice" in Valle D'Aostian Patois.*

For centuries a mountain pass between Italy and Switzerland, the Passo di Monte Moro owes its name to a group of Saracens who arrived here in the 10th century from Provence and settled, then imposing levies. According to some scholars, the name of a peak on the Swiss side of Rosa, Allalinhorn, also comes from the Arabic "Allah's Crown."

On Monte Rosa the vegetation reaches higher altitudes than in all the rest of the Alpine range.

| **27** *The term Monte Rosa comes from the Patois rouése or rouja and means "ice."*

ALONG THE KÖNIG LUDWIG WEG

Was he crazy or one of the greatest utopians of all time? Discover the story of King Ludwig of Bavaria in an itinerary through the places he loved.

The poet Paul Verlaine considered Ludwig II of Bavaria "the only true king of his century." The nicknames attributed to him were numerous, from "the Fairytale King" and "the Swan King" to "Mad King Ludwig." He probably deserved them all, but the truest definition, regarding his explosively eccentric life (and prophetic death), he gave to himself, affirming: "I wish to remain an eternal enigma to myself and to others." Crowned in 1864, shortly before his 19th birthday, he immediately displayed his misogyny, his reluctance to be seen in public, his refusal to contact anyone outside his close circle of favorites and functionaries – and the composer Wagner, for whom he admired so much that it bordered on idolatry – preferring to abandon Munich, his capital, to flee reality in the romantically utopic Bavarian countryside that took him back to the legendary origins of his people, and to construct (only for himself) absurdly timeless fairytale castles. In hindsight, however extravagant, Ludwig II's architectural, artistic and cultural legacy has generated touristic interest that represented – and still represents – one of the most economically profitable areas that have rendered Bavaria the richest German state. Although the Neuschwanstein Castle, the craziest and most famous of his palaces, and the Wagner festival in Bayreuth that he inspired are the most desired destinations for tourists the world over, the deepest and most poetic approach to the Fairytale King's Bavaria is walking the 8-9 day König Ludwig Weg Trail, an easy 120 kilometer path that crosses all the places he loved and explored by carriage, often at night, dressed as the hero Parsifal. Marked by signs with a "K" topped with a crown, the itinerary begins... at the end, in Berg, the village on the banks of the Steinberger See where, on June 13th, 1886, the king was found drowned together with his doctor in mysterious circumstances: it isn't know if it was suicide, a tragic fatality, or homicide. Whatever it may be, this is a romantic walk that leads to the votive chapel that commemorates the event, from which it continues (covering no more than 15 kilometers per day) through perfect cultivated fields and villages with cute little houses decorat-

Internet site www.bavaria.by

| **28-29** *The Neuschwanstein Castle is seen every year by 1.3 million people.*

NOT TO MISS

● ON LAKE STARNBERG, TAKE A BOAT RIDE TO THE **ROSENINSEL ("ISLAND OF ROSES"),** THAT WAS ONCE ONE OF LUDWIG II AND PRINCESS SISSI'S FAVORITE SPOTS. BEYOND THE ROSE GARDEN WITH OVER 15,000 EXEMPLARS, HERE YOU WILL FIND A SPLENDID RESIDENCE IN POMPEIAN STYLE THAT IS HOME TO A MUSEUM DEDICATED TO THE NOBLES WHO CAME TO THE LAKE, NOT BY CHANCE NICKNAMED FÜRSTENSEE, "LAKE OF PRINCES."

● IN THE ZONE KNOWN AS PFAFFENWINKEL, "THE PRIESTS' CORNER" DUE TO THE ABUNDANCE OF CHURCHES, THE **WESSOBRUNN** VILLAGE DESERVES A VISIT FOR ITS LOCAL ABBEY. YOU CAN SLEEP IN THE GUESTROOMS AND THE MONK'S BREAKFAST IS A DELIGHT. INSTEAD, IN WIES, VISIT THE **WIESKIRCHE,** WITH ITS SUPERB ROCOCO INTERIORS. PROTECTED BY UNESCO, IT IS OFTEN HOST TO CONCERTS.

● THE **NEUSCHWANSTEIN CASTLE** IS, LITERALLY, AN ONEIRIC VISION WHEN YOU SEE IT, IN ALL ITS SPLENDOR, AT THE END OF THE WILD POLLATH GORGE.

● AT THE END OF THE ITINERARY, DEDICATE ONE DAY TO DISCOVERING THE TREASURES OF **FÜSSEN** (AND RELAXING IN THE PLEASANT BIERGARTEN) AND THE **HOHENSCHWANGAU CASTLE,** BUILT BY LUDWIG II'S FATHER. THEN, ON A LIFT, GO UP TO TEGELBERG'S 1800 METERS TO ADMIRE THE PANORAMA OF THE LAKES AND THE AUSTRIAN ALPS.

ed by explosions of geraniums, through the wild scenery heard in Wagner's operas – like the Hohenpeissenberg Hill that, at 988 meters high, is the most beautiful panoramic balcony in all Bavaria, or like the wild Ammersee River and the numerous beech and fir forests – and towns and villages with medieval hearts that are home to masterpieces in baroque architecture. Among the treasures along the König Ludwig Weg Trail, things that deserve special mention are the magical town of Diessen, on the Ammersee River, with its splendid baroque Marienmünster Cathedral, and Rottenbuch, the tiny village at the foot of the Alps, home of the Rottenbuch Abbey of Augustan monks whose sober gothic exterior hides the rococo cascade of gold inside. And, naturally, the Neuschwanstein Castle, near the end of the itinerary that concludes at Füssen, the wonderful little town on the Forggensee that borders Austria where Ludwig II spent his childhood basking in the romantic mountain landscape.

When to go *From May to mid-October.*

How long to stay *9 days.*

Organization *Well marked and, thanks to the ease of the path, also fit for those who travel with children, the König Ludwig Weg is perfect for a do-it-yourself vacation. If you prefer an organized excursion, with or without guide, including transportation in train from Munich to Berg and from Füssen to Munich with hotels, we recommend Alpenland Touristik.*

Advice *In July and August, and above all during Munich's Oktoberfest, book well in advance for rooms along the way.*

Curiosities

- *You will recognize the Neuschwanstein Castle even if you have never seen it: Disney totally copied it for the castle in Cinderella (an there is one in every Disneyworld on the planet). In any case, there have been more than 60 million visitors, with over 2 million coming each year.*
- *The construction of the Neuschwanstein Castle nearly bankrupted the Bavarian state: over 465 tons of Salzburg marble, 400,000 bricks and 2030 cubic meters of wood were used to build the immense structure. Despite its dimensions, the castle doesn't have any rooms for the court because it was conceived as a theatrical scenery and a temple to the friendship between Wagner and the King. Ludwig lived there for only 173 days.*
- *Not only King Ludwig: a short deviation from Starnberg See will take you to the tiny Ess See where the naturalist and Nobel Prize winner Konrad Lorenz studied the phenomenon of imprinting by observing wild geese. Today his residence is an Ornithological Center run by the prestigious Max-Planck-Institüt. And Lorenz' famous geese crowd the lake and its banks in idyllic scenery.*

| 30 *The Hohenshwangau Castle was built in the 12th century.*

THE GRANDE RANDONNÉE IN CORSICA

It takes 15 days of difficult walking to cross the granite heart of the island along one of the most beautiful exclusionist paths in all Europe.

Bastia
Calvi
Calenzana
Monte Cinto
Paglia Orba
Corte
Vergio Pass
Restonica Valley
Monte Rotondo
Vizzavona
Parc Naturel Régional de Corse
Ajaccio
Bavella Pass
Conca
Porto Vecchio
Bonifacio

NOT TO MISS

- IN THE NORTH, THE **RESTONICA VALLEY** IS CHARACTERIZED BY THE SPLENDID GORGE DUG BY THE RIVER OF THE SAME NAME FLOW FOR ABOUT 15 KM UNTIL REACHING THE SERENE LANDSCAPE OF PASTURES OF SHEEPFOLDS GROTTELLE, PARTICULAR STONE CONSTRUCTIONS, AND FINALLY EMPTYING OUT INTO MELO AND **CAPITELLO LAKES.**

- ONCE YOU REACH VIZZAVONA, THE HALFWAY POINT, TAKE A REST AT HOTEL **MONTE D'ORO:** HIDDEN IN THE BEECHES YOU'LL FIND THE ISLAND'S OLDEST MOUNTAIN INN. IT HAS A MARVELOUS 1800S ATMOSPHERE AND THE RESTAURANT SERVES SPECIALTIES WITH BOAR AND TYPICAL CHEESES LIKE *BROCCIU* AND *BRIN D'AMOUR.*

- FROM THE VIZZAVONA FOREST, GO UP TO THE **CASCADES DES ANGLAIS:** THESE ARE A SERIES OF CLEAR WATER POOLS AND HAVE THE DESERVED FAME OF BEING ONE OF THE MOST IDYLLIC PLACES ON THE ISLAND.

- NEAR THE END, YOU'LL HAVE TO OVERCOME THE **PAGLIA ORBA** MOUNTAIN CLIMB. ONCE ON TOP, STOP TO ADMIRE THE PANORAMA OF THE **GULF OF PORTO VECCHIO,** ANTICIPATING SOME REST ON THE MOST BEAUTIFUL BEACHES OF THE MEDITERRANEAN.

| 31 *To reach the Colle della Bavella, you must climb to 1243 meters.*

In Corsica, granite is everywhere. Pillars like prehistoric menhir (or contemporary art sculptures), walls and slabs accompany those who come ashore in Bonifacio, those who go down the coast between Ajaccio and Calvi, those who climb the main ridge of the Vergio, Vizzavona and Bavella passes. To really discover the marvels and oddities of this grey-red rock, however, you have to foot the Grande Radonnée – or GR20 according to its official acronym – that crosses all of Corsica's mountains from north to south and is considered one of the most beautiful and challenging paths in Europe, just under 200 kilometers long with over 10,000 meters of slopes in total. The history of the path that the Corsicans call *Tra i monti* (Between the mountains) is closely tied with the Parc Naturel Régional de Corse that, extending over 40% of the island's territory, was instituted in 1972 by the French government as an act of reconciliation following the years of lead for the Independent Corsica Movement. Its birth, and the consequent development of the GR20 – including a network of easier trails that follow the traditional pastoral transhumances – plus constant maintenance by volunteers from the *Fédération Française de la Randonnée Pedestre* has favored green tourism, bringing earnings to the mountain villages and thus preventing depopulation.

The itinerary of the Grand Rondonnée diagonally cuts Corsica from northwest to southeast and starts in Calenzana, near Calvi and its splendid gulf, Porto Vecchio. To cross the entire island, it takes 15 days, in just as many parts that take 6-8 hours each: if the challenge seems excessive, remember that each part is subdivided into two sections, in correspondence with the Vizzavona train station, called GR20 Nord and GR20 Sud, each taking about 1 week to walk, with the first being a more difficult than the second. Although the trail is barely visible in some parts, hidden by rocks, the trail markers are some of the best in Europe, so much that the adventure of crossing Corsica is possible without a guide. Plus, over the last few years, the number of agencies specialized in supporting excursionists has boomed, offering luggage transport services from one stop to the next and mule rentals. Today, after a rough start, the network of refuges is also good – with picturesque names like Ciottolu di i Mori, Carrozzu and Tighjettu – where resting and restoring yourself with delicious typical plates and pasture cheeses. So, all you have to do is put a little effort into overcoming the adversities of the walk through extraordinarily varied mountain landscapes, with glacial lakes, dense larch pine forests – the ones in Vizzavona-Valdo-Niello and Bonifato are breathtaking – and high altitude valleys where wild orchids and blankets of crocuses and daffodils bloom in summer. And the granite creates masterpieces everywhere, with spires and towers that stand out against the blue sky with edges as sharp as knives that litter the trail. The prize in the category of the best giant rocks that give this landscape a surreal air is, without at doubt, the Cirque de la Solitude (to get to it you really have to deserve it, after coming up the most tiring rises of all the GR20), an amphitheater dominated by Monte Cinto that slopes down to the Girolata and Galeria gulfs. But the big loaf of Monte Rotondo, shocking red at sundown, and the enchanting Paglia Orba Mountain, cut every few meters by the so-called "tafoni," circular holes dug out from millenniums of wind and water erosion, are also quite exciting to see. Surprising to see, especially if you keep in mind the harsh landscapes of the nearby Sardinia, is the constant presence of water along the path: every part is cut through by creeks,

| 32 *Lake Nino, along the GR20, is glacial in origin and the Tavignano River flows from it.*

| 33 *From the summit of Capo D'Orto, in the Parc Naturel Régional de Corse, you get a great view over the Mediterranean.*

falls and lakes that, on hot summer days, become wonderfully refreshing stops for a quick swim, with your thoughts turning to the island's beaches, so close geographically yet so far below... Moreover, you can feel the Mediterranean in the vegetation, with green blotches that reach the highest points of the mountains, made up of juniper bushes bent over from the wind where flocks of goats, cows and wild pigs graze, the latter actually becoming a bit invasive. Instead, you need a little luck to see the eagles, peregrine falcons and deer reintroduced a few years ago from Sardinia. And you need a lot of it to see a muflon, the only European species of wild goat. The proud Corsican people have chosen this resistant animal as the symbol of their island.

Internet site www.parc-corse.org

When to go *From June to mid-October.*

How long to stay *2 weeks.*

Organization *Of the many tour operators that propose guided itineraries along the GR20 and offer reservation services for the refuges and luggage and food transportation, we recommend Corsica Adventure, Corsica Trek and Corsica Rando Evasion.*

Advice *The GR20 can be very crowded in summer: book refuges in advance or, better yet, bring a tent.*

Curiosities

- *The record for the fastest GR20 is held by the Catalonian marathoner and mountain skier Kilian Jornet i Burgada who, in June 2009, completed the journey in 32 hours and 54 minutes.*
- *There is no better way to start the GR20 Sud than arriving at Vizzavona aboard the ancient train that runs from Bastia to Ajaccio through 32 tunnels and 51 viaducts. Jokingly, Corsicans call it their TGV (High Speed Train), but in this case the acronym means High Vibrations Train. You can also take the train to complete the GR20 Nord...*
- *The territory of the Parc Naturel Régional de Corse is characterized by large chestnut trees. Not by chance, the chestnut – defined by the patriot Pasquale Paoli as "Corisca's bread" – is the island's most typical product and every year over 300 tons are sold. In the refuges, a wonderful chestnut flour polenta will be served to accompany Brocciu cheese and figatelli, typical Corsican sausages.*

ON ETNA

Trekking the most majestic (and capricious) mountain in Europe, on a magical journey that includes an adventure in a dark lava cave.

Internet site
www.parks.it/parco.etna

Sicilians call Etna "a muntagna," rigorously feminine, because they don't consider it an evil volcano but a mother who, like all women, has a forgivably capricious character. Then the Sicilians – and actually not only them, because Etna's charm captures everyone as soon as they see its size and the smoke from the plane windows before landing in Catania – have a kind of fatal, almost religious attraction to it, above all when she shows her power. Between ancient and modern eruptions, divided by a catastrophic one in 1669 that destroy a good portion of the city of Catania, the most notable eruptions number around 200, spectacularly displaying incandescent magma fountains, each time with new cracks and new craters and the consequent variation of the volcano's height, currently at 3340 meters. Protected as a national park, Etna's territory is extraordinarily varied, from Monti Sartorius' so-called eccentric craters, surrounded by

| 34 *You can do winter sports on Etna.*

| 35 *You can safely watch Etna erupt.*

clearings rich with endemic species and white birch forests in the high craters, often blanketed in snow, to Alcantara gorge to the Bove valley, an enormous basin on the east side nearly 7 kilometers wide and 5 deep, with rock walls reaching 1000 meters high. While this valley is one of the most surreal landscapes during the volcano trek, you are sure to be amazed by flashlight and helmet excursions into one of the 200 lava flow caves where the magma has channeled in past eruptions and where ancient populations buried their dead. The most famous one, at 2000 meters up on the north side of the volcano, is the Grotta del Gelo, home to Europe's southernmost glacier.

When to go *All year (volcanic activity permitting).*

How long to stay *Excursions to the volcano can last 1 day, but itineraries that include visits to local towns are organized for between 2-7 days.*

Organization *There are plenty of agencies that have guided treks on Etna, varying in length and difficulty. We recommend Etna Avventura, Etna Experience and Etna Trekking.*

Advice *Etna is also a big business and the products from its blackened lands represent the best of Sicily, from great wines to Bronte pistachios, from extra-virgin olive oil to fruit (prickly pears, cherries and pears) to cheeses. After trekking to the volcano, give yourself a break with an enogastronomic tour.*

NOT TO MISS

- IN THE VILLAGE **NICOLOSI,** VISIT THE **ETNA NATIONAL PARK CENTRE,** ACCOMMODATED IN AN ANCIENT BENEDICTINE MONETARY, THAT HOSTS AN INTERESTING MUSEUM ON ETNA'S GEOLOGICAL HISTORY, ERUPTIVE ACTIVITY AND CAVES AS WELL AS A RECONSTRUCTION OF THE MOUNTAIN'S RURAL WORLD.
- IN THE **BOVE VALLEY** THERE IS A TIRING CLIMB (UP 700 METERS) THROUGH THE BLACK SAND THAT LEADS TO THE MONTAGNOLA, ETNA'S MOST SPECTACULAR ADVENTIVE CONE, FORMED AFTER AN ERUPTION IN THE MID 1700S.
- FOLLOWING THE TRAIL THAT GOES TO THE CENTRAL CRATER, YOU WILL REACH THE **TORRE DEL FILOSOFO** AT 2900 METERS IN ELEVATION (THE HIGHEST EXCURSIONISTS ARE ALLOWED TO GO), A REMINDER OF THE ADVENTURE OF EMPEDOCLES, AN *ANTE LITTERAM* SCHOLAR WHO WANTED TO THROW HIMSELF INTO THE CRATER 2 MILLENNIUM AGO TO PROVE THAT HEPHAESTUS, THE GREEK GOD OF FIRE, DIDN'T REALLY LIVE THERE. HE NEVER CAME BACK.
- TAKE INTO CONSIDERATION TREKKING UNTIL SUNDOWN. FROM UP THERE, THE PANORAMA WILL TAKE YOUR BREATH AWAY AND WHEN NIGHT FALLS THE VOLCANIC ACTIVITY IS EVEN MORE VISIBLE. THEN IMAGINE THE EXCITEMENT OF WALKING DOWN THROUGH THE SULFUR MISTS WITH ONLY A FLASHLIGHT...

ALONG THE DOGON CLIFFS

Designating the border between Sahel and the plains of Niger, the Bandiagara Cliffs hide the magnificent villages of the "people of words."

"God brought you! How's it going?" "Well." "And your family?" "Well." "And the harvest?" "Well." "Good, may God keep you well!" This is the way that the Dogon greet each other when they meet along the inaccessible trails in their territory. And, after these pleasantries, they then sit on a rock to talk for hours, apparently forgetting about their errands at hand. This comes at no surprise since, in their language, *dogon* means "those who have been given the word." Their world is the Bandiagara Cliffs, a fracture – geologic and symbolic – between the arid Sahel and the plains of the Niger River. Next to this 150 kilometers long red rock wall, live around 400,000 Dogon who speak about 20 dialects and, despite their close contact with the local Muslim populations, most Dogon have remained deeply tied to their ancestral animist beliefs. Here, every rock, every baobab, every animal has a spirit. And, constructed in

Internet site www.dogoncountry.com

| 36-37 *The Dogon village Teli, at the foot of the Bandiagara Cliffs.*
| 37 *For the Dogon, dance has a profound religious connotation.*

banco (a mix of clay, hay and dung), their villages are full of symbols, meant to resemble the human body: the head is the home of the *hogon,* the main spiritual leader and oldest member of the community who lives in an observed solitude, cared for by a pre-pubescent little girl; the heart is the *togu-na,* literally the "house of words," a shelter composed of 8 carved poles that represent the mythical ancestors topped by thick layer of millet bundles; the arteries and veins are the *ginna,* the homes of large, extended families, each with its poles and millet with roofs that look like the long pointy hats of fairies. This people, for whom daily life is directly tied to the supernatural and where spirits are actually a "tangible" reality, is celebrated for their extremely interesting artesian masks, from the splendid *kanaga* that looks like a flying bird to the majestic *sirige,* a 4 meter high symbol of the *hogon.* Even if you need a bit of luck to see them worn during a ritual ceremony, a trek along the Bandiagara Cliffs will get you closer to one of the most mysterious cultures of Africa that, actually, follows its own calendar determined by the position of the stars. Some fanatics of alien civilizations have even speculated as to whether the Dogon came from another galaxy but, since we prefer to keep our feet on the ground, it's interesting enough to know that their week has 5 days, cadenced by the market that, every day, is held in a different village: under enormous baobab, the Dogon exchange agricultural products and meet to drink *kadjo,* a slightly alcoholic drink made from fermented millet. As for the stars, they seem close enough to touch when, in the vast silence of the African night, you are camped out on the roofs of their houses: sleeping outside, protected by the relaxing heat radiating from the cliffs hot rocks, makes sleeping in the land of the Dogon an experience that, by itself, makes the trip worth it. We guarantee you won't be disappointed.

NOT TO MISS

FOR THE DOGON, THE MOST SACRED PLACES ARE THE INNUMERABLE **CAVES** THAT STUD THE IMPOSING VERTICALITY OF THE CLIFFS. ONLY REACHABLE WITH A SYSTEM OF BAOBAB FIBER ROPES AND MOBILE WOODEN PINS, THEY ARE USE AS BURIAL GROUNDS AND SHOULD BE ADMIRED FROM AFAR.

ENDÉ IS ONE OF THE MOST FASCINATING VILLAGES. FAMOUS FOR ITS ARTISANS, IT IS THE PLACE TO BUY **BOGOLAN,** THEIR CHARACTERISTIC INDIGO COTTON FABRIC. HERE, IT IS ALSO POSSIBLE TO GET A TRADITIONAL DOGON MASSAGE.

AT THE EXTREME SOUTHERN EDGE OF THE CLIFFS, **KANI KOMBOLÉ** HAS A PICTURESQUE **MUD MOSQUE** WITH DECORATIONS THAT REPRESENT THE SYNCRETISM BETWEEN ISLAM AND ANIMISM. THE VILLAGE HAS THE AIR OF AN OASIS AND NEARBY YOU CAN ADMIRE A SPECTACULAR WATERFALL (DURING THE RAINY SEASON).

BETWEEN MAY AND JUNE THE DOGON CELEBRATE **BULO,** A FESTIVAL THAT MARKS THE BEGINNING OF THE RAINY SEASON. YOU CAN WATCH ANIMIST RITUALS AND DANCES WITH ELABORATE MASKS ALSO BETWEEN FEBRUARY AND APRIL DURING DAMA, THE CEREMONIES IN HONOR OF THE DEAD.

When to go *The coolest season (highs near 30° and lows near 15°C) is between November and February. But if you're not afraid of the heat, the village is enjoyable in October and from March to May too.*

How long to stay *From 3 days to 1 week.*

Organization *In Bandiagara, the little town on top of the cliffs and the most populated Dogon center (with a Tourism Office), it is easy to find guides and interpreters for trekking independently to the villages. Among the Mali operators that organize guided tours with experts in Dogon culture, we recommend Mali Adventure and Afric Vision Tourism.*

Advice *Before descending along the cliffs, in Bandiagara or Mopti (the main city for tourism in Mali), buy a bag of cola nuts to give as a sign of respect when you are invited into Dogon houses.*

Curiosities

According to Dogon mythology, the cliff caves were inhabited by their ancestors, a tribe of giants with supernatural powers. In reality, those caves were inhabited by Tellem, semi-nomadic pigmies that were driven away by the Dogon in the 16th century.

Coinciding with the passing of the star Sirio B (once every 60 years), the Sigi is held. It is the most important Dogon festival that lasts many weeks and culminates in the Awa initiation rite: a group of men who will perform the funeral rites in the years to come. The next Sigi is in 2027.

The Dogon are farmers: the base of their diet is millet, but they also cultivate sorghum, rice and tiny, super sweet onions. Chopped, shaped into balls and left to dry in the sun, these onions are the main "exportation" and are sold throughout Mali and even in Cote d'Ivoire.

| 38 *Dogon villages are built in human forms and the barns represent arteries and veins.*

VIRUNGA, THE GORILLA MOUNTAINS

It is expensive and lasts just an hour. But the experience of observing the mountain gorillas in the Parc National des Volcans is priceless.

39 *A baby gorilla at the Parc National des Volcans.*

In our collective imagination, King Kong is the gorilla, the terrifying beast that beats on his chest climbing through the skyscrapers of New York in the 1933 Hollywood colossal, or maybe in the even more famous remake. In reality – and for those who have seen another successful film, *Gorillas in the Mist,* that tells the story of the tragic life of the great primatologist Dian Fossey – gorillas are one of the 4 species of great primates similar to man and, even if their sheer size can be intimidating, they are a peaceful and sociable herbivore that lives in harem-communities led by a dominant male, the silverback (who derives his name from the silver stripe down his back), tall 170 centimeters on average and weighing 160-200 kilograms. The species is subdivided into two subspecies, the western or planes kind (Gorilla gorilla) and the eastern or mountain kind (Gorilla beringei). Of the second – that lives in the Virunga forest, the massive rugged volcanic peaks reaching nearly 5000 meters spread throughout Rwanda and the Democratic Republic of the Congo, and Bwindi, the impenetrable forest of Uganda – only 786 exemplars still exist. The place to observe mountain gorillas in their natural habitat is the Parc National des Volcans – founded in 1925, it was the first protected area in Africa – on the Rwanda side of the Virunga and home to the research center Gorilla Fund, that has been working and studying to protect the species ever since it was started by Dian Fossey.

NOT TO MISS

- RECENTLY, IN THE PARC DES VOLCANS, A TRAIL THAT LEADS TO THE SUMMIT OF THE VISOKE VOLCANO (3711 METERS) HAS BEEN OPENED. HERE, ON THE SHORES OF THE CRATER LAKE, YOU CAN FIND **DIAN FOSSEY'S GRAVESITE.**
- WITH A LITTLE PATIENCE, IT IS POSSIBLE TO OBSERVE ELEPHANTS AND FAMILIES OF VERVETS, ENDANGERED PRIMATES WITH GOLDEN-BLUE FUR DISCOVERED ONLY IN 2007, **IN THE VIRUNGA FOREST.**
- NOT FAR FROM THE PARK'S VISITORS' CENTER, IN A DREAMLIKE LANDSCAPE, THE **SABYINYO SILVERBACK LODGE** OFFERS LUXURY ROOMS IN THE HEART OF AFRICA.
- AFTER TREKKING - IF THE BORDER BETWEEN RWANDA AND THE CONGO ISN'T CLOSED DUE TO WAR - VISIT **GOMA,** THE CITY ON THE CONGOLESE SIDE OF LAKE KIVU. NOTED AS THE AFRICAN POMPEII, IN 2002 IT WAS DESTROYED BY THE ERUPTION OF THE NYIRAGONGO VOLCANO, IMMEDIATELY REBUILT ON TOP OF THE LAVA, AND IS NOW EVEN MORE POPULATED THAN BEFORE.

| **40 and 41** *Mountain gorillas risk extinction.*

Even if most extraordinary, the experience of meeting these great primates is not an adventure in the normal sense of the term, but a carefully organized trek with draconian rules that comes at a considerable price. Every day, only 56 visitors, subdivided into 7 groups, are lucky enough to obtain permission to participate in the Gorilla Trek, corresponding to the same number of gorilla families that are in the park and that are all wearing radio collars and quite used to having guests around. Before taking off on the trek, each group is "assigned" a family and the trek through the forest immersed in fog can last anywhere from 30 minutes to 6 hours – and therefore be rather taxing since the trail is often inexistent, blazed by rangers using *panga,* a blade similar to a machete, and always at an altitude between 2500 and 3500 meters – depending on where the lucky gorilla family is. But your efforts are amply repaid when you suddenly find yourself in the presence of these noble forest giants. Speaking softly and moving slowly, you can even come within 7 meters of them and observe their human-like behavior: they eat leaves with a peaceful air, milking their babies, playfully chasing each other through the trees, poking a stick into an anthill and then pulling it back out, covered with ants, to lick like a lollypop, or look at you with what seems like an annoyed air of superiority. Since interaction between visitors and gorillas doesn't have any sensible effects on their natural behavior, you can observe them for exactly one hour. And, believe us, each minute is one of the most intense experiences you will ever have.

Internet site www.igcp.org and http://gorillafund.org

When to go *Between June and September, during the dry season.*

How long to stay *The "classic" trek to observe the gorillas last just a few hours, but you need at least a week for a trip around Virunga.*

Organization *The international tour operators that propose trips to Rwanda, Congo and Uganda take care of obtaining permits for Gorilla Trekking. The price for one hour of gorilla observation is $750 dollars: this is, obviously, an expensive trip, but this money finances the hard work of protecting one of the most endangered species on the planet. The Dian Fossey Foundation organizes an 8 day Gorilla Expedition into the Parc National des Volcans four times a year, guided by experts and includes a visit to the Karisoke Research Center, founded by the celebrated primatologist.*

Advice *Closely follow the ranger's directions when you are near the gorillas. It is prohibited to speak loudly, use flash photography or make movements that could be considered aggressive. If a gorilla comes close enough to touch you (and this happens often), stay still.*

Curiosities

- *It has recently been observed that gorillas use a few tools: rocks as hammers for breaking branches, sticks for measuring the depth of puddles and waterways and even leaves as napkins.*
- *The main threat to gorilla survival is the loss of habitat (the slopes of the Virunga on the Rwanda side are under an anthropogenic pressure judged unsustainable) and poaching.*
- *Gorilla families are usually made up of 10-15 individuals and it has been observed that their behavior varies depending on the personality of the dominant male. The female – just like chimpanzees – has a much stronger and better articulated sense for raising offspring than found in other primates.*

ON THE PEAK OF KILIMANJARO

Climbing to the roof of Africa is for (almost) everybody. And it lets you experience a "world tour" in 8 days, from the tropics to the arctic.

"As wide as all the world, great, high, and unbelievably white in the sun" wrote Ernest Hemingway in his story The Snows of Kilimanjaro, spellbound by the size and magnificence of Africa's roof. It is the perfect mountain (better yet, it is a dormant stratovolcano) that rises from 900 meters of the high plains to 5895 meters at Uhuru or Kibo, the highest of its three volcanic cones. And, at just 325 kilometers from the equator, its perennial white snows contradict all logic. The bad news is that, due to global warming, according to estimates they will no longer be perennial snows sometime between 2022 and 2033. Instead, the good news is that Kilimanjaro is the world's easiest mountain to climb: anyone in good shape can try, armed with a walking pole, adequate clothing and a good dose of determination. Every year around 25,000 people reach the peak, after a surreal voyage in a landscape and climatic sense that goes from the Tropics to the Arctic.

Internet site
www.tanzaniaparks.com/kili.htm

| **42** *Climbing Kilimanjaro allows you to see numerous habitats: from rain forests to moors, from high altitude deserts to perennial glaciers.*

| 43 *Seneca grows on the slopes of Mt. Kilimanjaro.*

There are 6 official itineraries that lead to Uhuru - Shira, Lemosho, Machame, Umbwe, Marangu and Rongai - blazed by guides and by indigenous porters from Moshi, the village at Kilimanjaro's base. Among them, Yohani Kinyala Lauwo is a legend: he accompanied the Austrian mountaineers Hans Meyer andLudwig Purtscheller on the first summit climb. After having repeated the task more than ten times, he died at a record 125 years of age, when his mountain had already become a "mass" tourist destination.

When to go *It is possible to climb Kilimanjaro year round. The best (and most crowded) months are January, February and September, when the climate is dry and not too hot.*

How long to stay *The minimum for a climb to the peak is 5 days, but your chances for success rise to 85% if you follow an 8 day itinerary.*

Organization *Contrary to other, more technically difficult mountains around the world, the Tanzanian authorities prohibit individual climbing on Kilimanjaro, so it is obligatory to go through one of the many companies that organized guided expeditions. Among these, we recommend Kilimanjaro Climbing Company, Ultimate Kilimanjaro and Team Kilimanjaro.*

Advice *Besides the effort needed, the biggest difficulty is the anything but remote possibility of suffering from serious forms of altitude sickness, so it is advisable to proceed slowly in order to acclimate yourself and, before leaving, get a complete check-up. Cases of death - for hypothermia, dehydration or edema - are extremely rare in excursionists, more often involving the indigenous porters who lack food and adequate equipment. When selecting the tour operator who will lead you up Kilimanjaro, privilege those adhering to the Kilimanjaro Porters Assistance Project.*

NOT TO MISS

- MAKE SURE THAT THE FATIGUE OF THE CLIMB DOESN'T DISTRACT YOU FROM THE BEAUTY OF THE FOREST THAT, UP TO 2700 METERS, IS HOST TO **ANTELOPES AND LEOPARDS.** A BIT HIGHER, THE LANDSCAPE IS DOMINATED BY SPLENDID GIANT **CARDINAL FLOWERS WHILE,** JUST BEFORE THE ICE-CAPPED PEAKS, ONLY MOSS AND LICHEN GROW.

- ON KILIMANJARO'S EASTERN SLOPES, **LAKE CHALPA** OCCUPIES A VOLCANIC CALDERA AND ITS TURQUOIS WATERS LOOK LIKE TANZANITE, THE RARE GEM EXTRACTED FROM THE NEARBY MINES. AFTER YOUR MOUNTAIN ADVENTURE, TAKE A COUPLE OF DAYS TO RELAX IN THE NATURAL SURROUNDINGS OF **LAKE CHALA SAFARI CAMP.**

- FEW SUPERMEN ARE ABLE TO PARTICIPATE IN THE **KILIMAN ADVENTURE CHALLENGE,** THE WILDEST TRIATHLON IN THE WORLD THAT INCLUDES CLIMBING TO THE PEAK IN 6 DAYS, COMING DOWN ON MOUNTAIN BIKE (160 KM) AND A MARATHON. JUST WATCHING IT IS THRILLING!!

| 44 *The Luangwa River, after a long, torturous journey, flows into the Zambezi.*

WALKING SAFARI IN LUANGWA

Experience the real Africa on a "safari wakale," following in the footsteps of the savannah tribes and a hunter that became a pioneer of conservation.

The desire of anyone on an African safari is to see up close – and photograph – the Big Five, i.e. an elephant, a lion, a rhinoceros, a buffalo and a leopard that, in our collective imagination, are the animals that represent the essence of a savannah adventure. However, few know that in Africa's southern animal sanctuaries there are also the Small Five: the shrewmouse elephant (a macroscelide with a trunk), the ant lion (an adult exemplary can get up to 4 cm wide), the rhinoceros beetle (with powerful horns) and the leopard tortoise (weighing 23 kilos and has a spotted shell). The privilege of a close encounter with the smallest and most curious species of the bush is the exclusive perk for those who experience what the indigenous call a safari wakale, an expression that can more or less be translated as "traveling in the traditional way." We admit it: absorbing African nature sitting more or less comfortably in a jeep has become a commonplace thing. Much different – and more ethical – is instead following the footsteps of the people of the savannah.

In the literal sense of the word: on foot. The first to have the idea of building a safari camp in Africa was, in 1951, the British Norman Carr, a reformed hunter who reached the conclusion – revolutionary at the time – that hunting animals with cameras could be more exciting than with a rifle. Today his name is shrouded in legend: he fought for the creation of national parks in Rhodesia (now Zambia and Zimbabwe), he was a pioneer in the fight against poachers who killed elephants to sell their horns and in 1980 instituted the Rhino Trust, a project to protect the rhinoceros, now a shining example of the WWF's work. The territory that Carr chose for his new hunting method was the Luangwa River Valley, in Zambia, that runs a torturous 700 kilometers south to Lake Malawi, marking the end of the great Rift and feeding a territory that, due to its enchanting landscapes and concentration of fauna, is now considered the very symbol of "true Africa." Carr was a pioneer also because he was the first one to involve the members of the Kumba tribe in his "non-violent safari." They have always lived in the valley and he relied on them both for building the safari camp as well as for guiding visitors, thus inventing the community tourism that sustains the indigenous populations. Today the South Luangwa and the North Luangwa National Park are the two administrative entities that protect the territories adjacent to the western riverbanks: in the first there are around 20 safari camps, while the second part is still mostly wild. It goes without saying that in both the Kumba guides' know-how is fundamental for experiencing the formidable safari wakale during which, moving silently through the bush, you find yourself enchanted just a few meters from a pride of lions or a large parade of

NOT TO MISS

- UNDER THE BRIDGE THAT MARKS THE ENTRANCE TO THE **SOUTH LUANGWA NATIONAL PARK,** THERE ARE ALWAYS BETWEEN 30 AND 70 HIPPOPOTAMUSES LAZING AROUND. NOT UNUSUAL, CONSIDERING THAT THEIR POPULATION IS ESTIMATED TO BE AROUND 50 EXEMPLARS FOR EVERY SQUARE KILOMETER.
- THE MOST "EXTREME" STARTING POINT FOR A *WALKING SAFARI* IN NORTH LUANGWA IS **KUTANDALA SAFARI CAMP,** ACCESSIBLE BY PLANE. IT OFFERS FASCINATING LODGINGS THAT HOST UP TO 6 PEOPLE AND A CANDLELIGHT DINNER ON THE BANKS OF THE MWALESHI IS A PRICELESS EXPERIENCE.
- ALTHOUGH IT IS ALREADY AN EMOTIONAL EXPERIENCE TO FIND YOURSELF IN THE PRESENCE OF A HERD OF ELEPHANTS OR WATCHING LIONS HUNT, DURING A **WALKING SAFARI UNDER THE STARS** YOU CAN SEE ANIMALS WITH NOCTURNAL HABITS, LIKE LEOPARDS AND GALAGOS, SMALL PRIMATES KNOWN AS "BUSH BABIES" DUE TO THEIR CRY.
- GO AS FAR AS **MUCHINGA ESCARPMENT,** A WALL THAT MARKS THE RIVER'S FLOODPLAIN, RISING NEARLY 1000 METERS. HERE THE VEGETATION CHANGES AND YOU CAN SEE THE RAREST CARNIVOROUS SPECIES LIKE THE CARACAL AND THE WILD AFRICAN DOG.

| **45** *A herd of buffalo going to drink from the Luangwa River in South Luangwa National Park.*

elephants drinking from the river, you can observe hyenas feeding or hippopotamuses swimming, just like when you find yourself just a few centimeters from the Small Five. If you are worried about safety, just remember that the guides are armed. But, in case of danger, all they have to do is shoot in the air.

Internet site www.zambiatourism.com/travel/nationalparks/luangval.htm

When to go *The dry season is from April to October, but the safari camps in South Luangwa are open until November-December, organizing itineraries in the green valley. Instead, in North Luangwa, access becomes impossible when the rains start.*

How long to stay *1 week to 10 days.*

Organization *The main international operators specialized in African safaris propose walking itineraries in the Luangwa Valley. Among these, we recommend those that have taken up Norman Carr's legacy and have their bases in South Luangwa and Robin Pope Safaris, which organizes safari wakale in North Luangwa too.*

Advice *In the Luangwa Valley malaria and typhoid are endemic, so before going start antimalarial treatments and get a typhoid vaccination.*

Curiosities

Son of a colonial administrator of a tobacco factory in North Rhodesia, Norman Carr (1912-1997) was very happy on his 18th birthday for having killed his 50th elephant. His following conversion to the conservation is narrated in his books, like Return to the Wild, where he tells of the reinsertion of two lion cubs, whose mother had been killed by poachers, back into the wild.

Near the riverbanks, the savannah is dominated by mopane trees, with their characteristic leaves shaped like butterflies that the "mopane worm" eats. This worm is actually a large centipede that is a delicacy in local gastronomy. These animals are dried, fried and served with tomatoes, chilies and peanuts. Try them.

In a wild place like this, you wouldn't expect to find one of the most exclusive spas on the planet. Yet there it is: the Mfuwe Lodge Bush Spa, where you can get treatments outdoors with indigenous plants like kigelia fruit, the sausage tree or baobab. Plus, the lodge reception gets daily visits from elephants.

| **46** *The Luangwa River is host to large populations of hippopotamuses.* | **47** *An elephant in South Luangwa National Park.*

TREKKING IN TIEN SHAN

From Lake Issyk Kul, walk across secret valleys, glaciers and the majestic peaks of the mountain range at the heart of Central Asia.

You've never heard of Jengiz Chokusu and Khan Tengri? If you are passionate about mountains, know that this is a serious omission because these two peaks, 7439 and 7010 meters respectively, are splendid summits in Kyrgyzstan and are two of the most majestic pyramids of the Tien Shan, the "celestial mountains" (as the Chinese call them) of the largest mountain range in Central Asia. Moreover, in terms of extension, they have nothing to be envious about in respect to the Himalayas. You could justify yourself by saying that it is rare to even hear about Kyrgyzstan, the most remote, mysterious and least populated of the central Asian ex-Soviet republics, and go search for these wonders on a map. You would find something blue, a sort of eye that breaks the Tien Shan in two. This is the Issyk Kul that, partially protected by a Biosphere Reserve and with

| 48 *Trekking through the mountains leads to the salty lake region of Issyk Kul.*

| 49 *In Mongolian, Khan Tengri means "Lord of Heaven."*

a 2400 kilometer surface, is the largest mountain lake on the planet after Titicaca and even the second saltiest lake, after the Caspian. Its name, in Kyrghyz, means "hot lake" because – at an altitude of 1600 meters and at this latitude, it never freezes over because of the intense geothermal activities in its abysses. And, situated only 450 kilometers from Bishkek, the capital of the Republic of Kyrgyzstan, Issyk Kul is also the starting (and ending) point for the most adventurous and least frequented trekking trails on the planet, where you can discover the largest glaciers found outside of the artic poles, a perfectly preserved mountain environment, phenomenal panoramas and camps of nomadic Kyrgyz. You need 10 days to walk the entire circuit that goes from the lake to the Khan Tengri basecamp at an altitude of 4050 meters. And take another couple of days to rest from the fatigue of the trek on the banks of the Issyk Kul. Just like the cosmonaut Juri Gagarin did after his trip to space.

Internet site www.kgembassy.org

When to go *From June to early September*

How long to stay *2 weeks.*

Organization *Among the local tour operators that organize trips and trekking itineraries in Kyrgyzstan, we recommend Asia Outdoor, located in Bishkek and also has experience in Spanish tourism, Central Asia Travel, Dostuck Trekking and Tien Shan Travel.*

Advice *When choosing an organized trek, privilege those that include a helicopter ride to the Khan Tengri basecamp in Karkara, one of the greenest gorges of the Kyrgyz Tien Shan: there you will have the possibility of sleeping in a Yurte camp, coming into contact with the nomadic traditions.*

NOT TO MISS

- THE JOURNEY THAT CROSSES **INYLCHEK GLACIER** MORAINE IS THE MOST THRILLING PART OF THE TREK. 60 KILOMETERS LONG AND DIVIDED INTO TWO PARTS, IT IS DOMINATED BY THE PEAKS OF JENGIZ CHOKUSU AND KHAN TENGRI: SLEEP A NIGHT AT THE SOUTH INYCHEK BASECAMP AND WAKE AT DAWN IN ORDER TO ADMIRE THE GIANTS TURNING RED.
- GO AROUND **LAKE MERTSBAKHER:** AT 3000 METERS, IT IS A MAGICAL MIRROR OF WATER COLORED BY THE SAPPHIRE HUE OF THE SURROUNDING MOUNTAINS AND, EVEN IN AUGUST, YOU CAN SEE LITTLE ICEBERGS FLOATING AROUND.
- STOP IN **KARAKOL,** THE 19TH CENTURY COSSACK SETTLEMENT THAT IS NOW THE CAPITAL OF THE ISSYK KUL REGION: MANY BUILDINGS ARE UNMISTAKABLY RUSSIAN, BUT THERE ARE STILL MORE EXOTIC JEWELS LIKE THE MOSQUE, ENTIRELY BUILT IN WOOD WITHOUT THE USE OF NAILS BY THE DUNGAN COMMUNITY, A CHINESE ETHNICITY WITH ISLAMIC BELIEFS THAT CAME HERE FROM THE HIGH PLAINS OF PAMIR.
- THE SOUTHERN BANKS OF THE LAKE IS THE MOST PICTURESQUE AND WILD (THERE ARE NO HORRID SOVIET ERA CONSTRUCTIONS): FROM HERE, HEAD TOWARD THE **KYZYL-BEL PASS,** WHERE THE **TASH RABAT GORGE** STARTS. FOLLOW ITS GREEN PASTURES AND THE REMAINS OF A 9TH CENTURY CARAVANSARY, AN ANCIENT STOP ON THE SILK ROAD.

PILGRIMAGE ON MT. KAILASH

Going all the way around the most sacred and mysterious mountain in the world pushes human limits. It is an incredible adventure for the spirit.

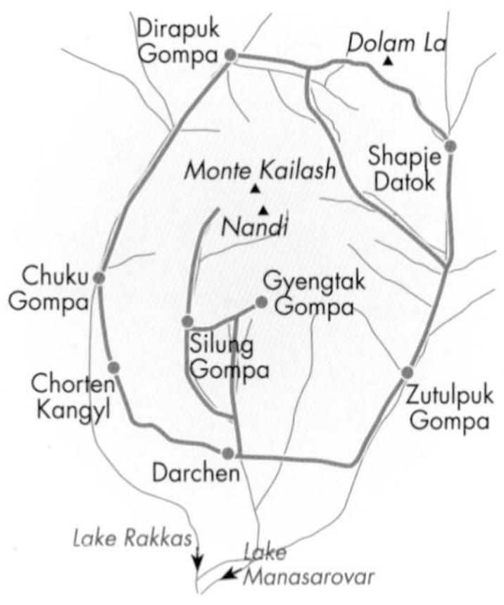

For a fifth of humanity, this is the most sacred place on earth. The Hindu identify it with Mt. Meru, the universal axis where Shiva and his consort Parvati are sitting in permanent meditation. For Jainists it is Astapada, the place where the first 24 Tirthamkara prophets were liberated. In the proto-Buddhist shamanic religion Bon it is Tise, inhabited by the goddess of the Heavens, while Buddhists call it Kang Rimpoche, "The Precious," home to Chakrasamvara, a benevolent tantric divinity with blue skin, 12 arms and4 heads, each with 3 eyes. Precisely because it is sacred, Kailash's peak, at 6638 meters, has never been reached. But, even if for Buddhists undertaking the kora, i.e. going clockwise around the entire 58 kilometer circumference at the mountain base, is the way to reach nirvana (to obtain its Hindu equivalent, moksha, all you have to do us see its divine light), Kailash is visted by just a few thousand pilgrims each year. The rea-

| **50** *Mt. Kailash is venerated by more than half a billion people in India, Tibet and Bhutan.*

| 51 *Mt. Kailash has never been climbed since it is a sacred mountain.*

son is its remote position in the west of Tibet, the bureaucratic obstacles posed by the Chinese government for visiting it and the difficulty of the trek through the thin Himalayan air, with spots at altitudes of over 5000 meters. All this makes for an exceptional trekking experience: the emotions of the majestic scenery of soaring mountains is added to that of witnessing manifestations of religious devotion that are incredible for the western mind. Like the sadhu Indians who come here barefoot, half-naked and with a ritual trident as their only luggage. Or the Tibetan pilgrims who undertake the circumnavigation of Mt. Kailash in an interminable series of prostrations, chanting hypnotic mantras.

Internet site www.xzta.gov.cn/yww

When to go *From May to September*

How long to stay *Depending on the path, the trek lasts from 13 to 25 days, including the journey from Kathmandu or Lhasa.*

Organization *Trekking in the Kailash area is only possible through an organized tour for bureaucratic and technical reasons. Many Nepalese companies with bases in Kathmandu propose foot tours starting in Simikot, Nepal, and also include an automobile tour to Lhasa. Among these, Karnali Excursions and Himalaya Kailash Travel&Tours have great experience in treks. In Tibet, we recommend Tibet Explorer Tours, located in Lhasa.*

Advice *For westerners, accessing Tibet is subject to sudden and unexpected changes in visa procedures (and the periodic closing of the entire province to foreigners) implemented by the Chinese government. Therefore, it is preferable to organize a trip with a Nepalese operator and, if things go wrong, have another Himalayan itinerary in reserve.*

NOT TO MISS

- THE TINY VILLAGE **DARCHEN** IS THE ONLY INHABITED CENTER AT THE FOOT OF KAILASH. PILGRIMS CAMP HERE, THERE IS A MARKET OF SACRED OBJECTS AND A CENTER FOR TRADITIONAL TIBETAN MEDICINE.
- THE CIRCUIT IS STUDDED WITH SMALL HINDU TEMPLES, CHORTEN (TIBETAN DALI LAMA TOMBS) AND MONASTERIES: SITTING HIGH UP ON A ROCK AT THE MOUTH OF AMITHABA VALLEY, **CHUKU GOMPA** IS HOME TO SOME OF THE OLDEST EXAMPLES OF BUDDHIST PAINTING.
- AT THE SOUTHERN FOOT OF KAILASH, AT 4590 METERS, **LAKE MANASAROVAR** IS THE HIGHEST SWEET WATER MIRROR ON THE PLANET. FOR THE HINDU, A SWIM IN THE ICY WATER CLEANS AWAY ALL SINS; THE BUDDHISTS WALK AROUND IT IN ORDER TO GAIN CREDIT FOR THEIR NEXT REINCARNATION.
- IF YOU ARE LUCKY, YOU'LL MEET THE MONKS WHO, MEDITATING AND PRACTICING A BREATHING TECHNIQUE CALLED LUNG-GOM, ARE ABLE TO WALK ALL THE WAY AROUND THE MOUNTAIN IN ONE DAY (WHILE THE MOST TRAINED TREKKERS DO IT IN THREE).

THE ANNAPURNA CIRCUIT

In the heart of the Himalayas, 180 kilometers on foot in the mystical reign of the ancient Salt Road between India and China.

| 52 *Annapurna is the 10th highest mountain in the world.*
| 53 *Thorong La Pass is situated at 5416 meters in central Nepal.*

NOT TO MISS

- LESS THAN AN HOUR'S WALK FROM MANANG, **BARGA** IS HOME TO THE OLDEST AND MOST SUGGESTIVE MONASTERY ON THE CIRCUIT. FOUNDED 500 YEARS AGO AND INHABITED FROM APRIL TO THE END OF OCTOBER BY A NUMEROUS COMMUNITY OF TIBETAN MONKS, IT HOUSES PRECIOUS FRESCOES AND RELIGIOUS ARTIFACTS.

- AT 3750 METERS, **MUKTINATH** IS A DESTINATION FOR HINDUS AND BUDDHISTS. IT HOSTS TIBETAN MONASTERIES AND ONE OF THE OLDEST TEMPLES DEDICATED TO THE GOD VISHNU, WITH AN ETERNAL FLAME SURROUNDED BY A FOUNTAIN WITH 108 SPRING WATER FOUNTAINS, CONSIDERED ABLE TO WASH NEGATIVE KARMA AWAY.

- IN THE LOW MUSTANG VALLEY, **MARPHA** IS A MARVELOUS VILLAGE WITH LIME MINERAL PAINTED HOUSES, FAMOUS FOR BEING NEPAL'S ORCHARD. DELICIOUS APPLES GROW IN ITS GARDENS THAT THE INHABITANTS USE TO MAKE JUICES AND SLIGHTLY ALCOHOLIC BEVERAGES.

- ON YOUR WAY BACK, STOP IN **TATOPANI:** IMMERSED IN THE THRIVING VEGETATION, THE VILLAGE SURROUNDS HOT SPRINGS; HERE A BATH AND A TRADITIONAL MASSAGE REPLENISH YOUR MUSCLES AND BONES.

On internet forums, veterans of the Himalayas complain that the Annapurna Circuit isn't like it used to be. Since 2011 a consistent part of Nepal's most popular trekking trail – 250 kilometers long, along an up-and-down ring that goes from an altitude of 8000 meters at the beginning (and end), near the little town Pokhara, to 5416 meters at Thorung La, the highest pass – has now become a road open to vehicles, although sometimes impracticable and full of surprises. Add to the fact that, every year, nearly 40,000 excursionists undertake it. And that some of the so-called *teahouses,* homes along the way prepared to receive travelers, now have a standard that is too "modern": hot showers powered by solar panels and global cuisine that includes strange versions of pizza and tacos served with the traditional *dhal bhat,* Nepal's national dish. Yet, there is no better thing than the Annapurna Circuit for a "sweet" initiation to the Himalayas, where the fatigue of the numerous, strenuous slopes are moderated, in the evening, by the comfort of familiar things, even if in a stark, mountain version. Besides, a few, rare passing jeep distracts little from a landscape that, crossing four regions – Lamjung, Manang, Basso Mustang and Myagd –, leads to rhododendron forests and cultivated fields in the presence of once of the most

| 54 *In Sanskrit, Annapurna means "Goddess of Abundance."*

spectacular massifs in the Himalayas, with the various summits of Annapurna (8091 meters), Dhaulagiri and Machapuchhare, the still virgin mountain with a peak in the shape of a fishtail.
Then, going from village to village, many of the Nepalese culture of the Himalayas can be experienced: from Hindus to Buddhists subdivided, little by little as you go up, into Gurung, heirs to the celebrated Gurka warriors, and Tibetans. Finally, Annapurna Circuit is just a small taste of the Great Himalaya Trail that crosses the entire length of Nepal (1700 kilometers, for a total of 150,000 meters of altitudinal difference), crossing passes at 6000 meters and in the presence of 14 more peaks over 8000 meters, her majesty Everest included. It takes 6 months to cross it, but it itself is only a section of the epic itinerary – still being planned – that will cross the entire Himalayan arc, from Pakistan to Bhutan.

Internet site http://thegreathimalayatrail.org

When to go *From September, October and March, April and May the climate is perfect, but you can walk the circuit all year: from November to February it is very cold and in the summer the lowest parts of the trail are in a monsoon zone.*

How long to stay *3 weeks.*

Organization *The Annapurna Circuit can be done independently, just get a trekking pass from the National Trust for Nature Conservation in Kathmandu. Most excursionists, however, prefer to go through one of the hundreds of agencies in Kathmandu and Pokhara that propose guided trekking with carriers along all or part of the circuit, taking the responsibility for all the bureaucratic formalities and providing housing and food included in the price.*

Advice *You can come to Nepal with an empty backpack and buy all the necessary equipment in Kathmandu or Pokhara, anything from clothes to sleeping bags, up to more technical accessories. The shops are well-stocked, the merchandise is of optimal quality and prices are significantly lower than in any other place in the world.*

TREKKING IN MUSTANG, THE LAST TIBET

In the heart of the Himalayas, 180 kilometers on foot in the mystical kingdom along the ancient Salt Road between India and China.

| 55 *A* chorten *in the Kali Gandaki valley, one of the main Nepalese rivers.*

NOT TO MISS

- IN MAY AND JUNE, MUSTANG HOSTS THE **TIJI FESTIVAL,** A CEREMONIAL RITE OF SOUNDS AND DANCES PERFORMED BY MONKS IN COSTUMES AND WEARING MASKS TO CELEBRATE THE ETERNAL STRUGGLE BETWEEN GOOD AND EVIL.
- BEYOND THE ENCHANTING MONASTERIES, VISIT THE **ROYAL PALACE MUSEUM** IN MANTHANG, IT HOLDS PRICELESS ANCIENT SACRED OBJECTS, INCLUDING STATUES OF BUDDHA AND TANGHKA.
- IF YOU PLAN TO STAY IN MANTHANG A FEW DAYS TO REST, YOU CAN WALK AN HOUR UP TO **NIPHU GOMPA,** A CLIFF MONASTERY JUST ONE HOUR FROM THE CHINESE BOARDER.
- THE TREK IS INTERRUPTED BY CHORTEN, SMALL DEVOTION CONSTRUCTIONS THAT, PAINED WHITE AND ORANGE-RED AND DECORATED WITH BAS RELIEFS, ARE **DALI LAMA BURIALS** AND, IT IS SAID, EMANATE GREAT ENERGY.

Internet site http://welcomenepal.com

Between the 14th and 15th centuries, salt was the white gold of the Himalayas. And the profound canyons that open from Kora La, the lowest of the Himalayan passes along the Kali Gandaki Valley, were the most accessible path for the flowering commerce between Tibet and India. So, for at least 300 years, the small kingdom of Mustang, sheltered north of the Annapurna massif, made its fortune with merchandise transportation. Here, centuries earlier, monks carrying the words of the Buddha passed here. The wealth took the form of palaces, forts and above all monasteries frescoed with lavish masterpieces of Tibetan art. From the 17th century, when commerce began to decline, the kingdom of Mustang was left practically isolated, becoming a part of Nepal in 1951, even if geographically it is an offshoot of the Tibetan plateau. Closed to tourism until 1992 (it was semi-independent until 2008) and crossed only by trails impracticable for cars, it has remained unaltered by time, with its 15,000 inhabitants spread out in minuscule villages that survive with agriculture and livestock. Sheep, but above all horses, a precious means of transportation for those who must endure more than 10 kilometers just to get to the nearest market. It is precisely for this magical atmosphere that Mustang has become, over the last few years, a destination for trekkers looking for a genuine experience, immersed in the wild beauty of dazzling gorges and arid plateaus, studded here and there by the green of the few inhabited centers. You need 5 to 7 days – depending on how much time you have and how good of shape you are in – to get to Manthang, the capital of Mustang, walking from Jomsom, modernity's last outpost at 2600 meters, where little planes from Pokhara will take you, landing on a strip just a couple of hundred of meters long and dug out of the extensive gravel on the riverbed. From there, once checked by the government offices in Kagbeni (access to Mustang is rigorously regulated and subject to a permit that costs $50 a day), the first section of the trek leads to Upper Mustang, the northern most part of the region. On the second section, that reaches Chuksang, a picturesque village with terraces of cultivated fields that look out over a steep sandstone cliff, you can walk on the riverbed, up until the height of the melting season, or along the newly constructed dirt road that guides define as the "Nepali flats": an endless up-and-down that isn't very steep.

Passing Kali Gandaki on the only bridge that crosses the river in this section of the trail, the hardest parts start. Heading toward Samar, Giling, Ghami and Tzarang – the intermediary stops for reaching Manthan – the dirt road becomes evermore impracticable, touching high points at Ghami La, at an altitude of over 4000 meters dominated from afar by the imposing Annapurna. Every day of walking, up and down, includes at least 1000 meters of slopes. However, one you get there, the reward will leave you breathless. Manthang has barely 1000 inhabitants and is seen settled in a green valley of cultivated fields, framed by the last peaks of the Himalayas, with the brick-red monastery walls enhancing the whiteness of the other buildings. There are 3 ancient temples in the city, Jampa Gompa, Thupchen Gompa and Chode Gompa, where about 30 local residents are restoring the temple's splendid frescoes to the glory of former times, guided by an Italian restorer, Luigi Fienni, the only foreigner who lives in Mustang, at least for 6 months each year. If you are lucky enough to meet him, he won't stop at showing you the results of his efforts. He will also take you up a rickety ladder to the top of Jampa, to let you see "the most beautiful office in the world."

When to go *From June to mid-October.*

How long to stay *2 weeks.*

Organization *There are around 900 Nepalese trekking agencies based in Kathmandu and many of them have guided itineraries with carriers that go to Mustang, including lodging in either tents or the so-called tea houses (that, although quite simple, show you the traditional way of life in Tibetan villages). On the Trekking Agencies' Association of Nepal's official site, there is a directory of agencies and all the information on trekking permits and relative costs. The operators with a good selection of tailor made itineraries in Mustang, we recommend Nepal Environmental Treks & Expeditions and Unique Path.*

Advice *When you book your return trip, it is useful to take a couple extra days before the international flight to Kathmandu. Often the route between Jomson and Pokhara is closed due to precarious weather conditions and can put your travel plans behind schedule.*

Curiosities

- *Mustang's vertical walls are dotted with thousands of caves that are nearly inaccessible that were dug out over the centuries by the regions inhabitants. Many of them were made thousands of years ago, when they were used as mortuary chambers, although they were later inhabited at least until the mid-1900s. Some were sacred grounds and still hold treasures of Buddhist art.*
- *Even if he no longer has any administrative functions, and lives between Kathmandu and India most of the time, it isn't rare to meet Jigme Dorje Palbar Bista, the last King of Mustang, here especially during the Tiji Festival.*
- *Kali Gandaki, the river whose course outlines the region, is a tributary to the Ganges and in the lower parts of Mustang it creates the deepest gorge in the world.*

| 56 *An ancient Buddhist temple in Upper Mustang.* | 57 *The peak of Mt. Dhaulagiri (8167 meters).*

TAKTSANG MONASTERY

To get there, you have to go up 3000 winding stairs on a mountain wall. But this, plus a trek, is a journey to happiness.

Until 1961, there wasn't a single road open to vehicles. Television arrived in 1989 and internet in 1999. It is the only country in the world where inhabitants, by law, must wear traditional clothing, a gho for men and a kira for women. It is the only nation where smoking is prohibited anywhere within national boarders. And, above all, it is the only place where wealth isn't measured in GDP but in GDH (gross domestic happiness). In the end, it doesn't seem like part of our world: with a surface area of 47,000 km2 distributed between 2000 and 7000 meters and mostly covered by forests in one of the most remote corners of the Himalayas, it has just 600,000 peaceful inhabitants and is the real transposition of the literary myth of Shangri-La. The most sacred and picturesque place in Bhutan is the Taktsang Monastery, also known as the Tiger's Den because, as legend would have it, the guru Rimpoche came here from Tibet, cradle of Mahayana Buddhism, on a winged tiger. He defeated an evil dragon and then meditated in a cave for 3 months. When he came out, purified, he founded the first Buddhist nation on earth.

Internet site www.tourism.gov.bt

| 58 *There are 3000 stairs to get to the Taktsang Monastery's front door.*

NOT TO MISS

- MAKE THE EFFORT TO GO UP TO **TAKTSANG AT NIGHT,** SO YOU CAN WATCH THE PRAYER WHEEL CEREMONY AT 4 A.M. IN THE UGAY TSEMO TEMPLE, PRESIDED OVER BY THE OLDEST MONK IN THE COMMUNITY.
- TAKE TIME TO EXPLORE ALL THE BUILDINGS TO ADMIRE THE FRESCOES, THE ***TANGKA*** AND THE ORNATE SCULPTURES OF PRECIOUS STONES, ACCOMPANIED BY A MONK WHO WILL EXPLAIN THEIR MEANINGS.
- SPEND AT LEAST 2 DAYS IN THE LITTLE TOWN **PARO,** VISITING THE TEMPLES AND FARMS THAT DOT THE REGION: YOU WILL BE GREETED EVERYWHERE WITH ALARMING HOSPITALITY (EVEN IF YOU WILL BE CONSTANTLY BEGGED TO DRINK TRADITIONALLY PREPARED TEA WITH A TOUCH OF RANCID SALT BUTTER).

| **59** *On a vertical rock face, the Taktsang Monastery is made up of about 10 buildings.*

Situated about 10 kilometers from the little town Paro, at an altitude of 3120 meters on a nearly vertical mountain wall that dominates the residence, the Taktsang Monastery – which, in the morning, before the first rays of sun disperse them, looks like it is floating on clouds – can be reached by an arduous trail with 3000 steps along the mountain ridge, always in the company of crowds of monks and pilgrims who leave prayer flags and offerings at each little temple along the way. We can't assure you that once you reach the monastery doors (and you still have another 700 steps to go from here to get to the top of the complex that has at least 10 buildings rich with priceless frescoes and other artwork that is constantly surrounded by incense), you will obtain bliss, instituted by decree of His Majesty Druk Gyalpo Jigme Dorji Wangchuck III, Bhutan's beloved king. But, by itself, the serene beauty of this place is worth a trip to this country made from dreams.

When to go *From September to November and from March to May.*

How long to stay *You need at least 2-3 hours to reach the monastery, but spend 7-10 days in Bhutan.*

Organization *In order to preserve its environment and traditions, Bhutan has choses to limit tourism to extremely motivated visitors: every foreigner has to pay $200 per day – that drop to $165 in January, June and July, the least climatically favorable months – if you are part of a group of at least 3 people, while there is a $40 supplement if you are alone and $30 if in a couple. This sum includes entrance, lodging, food, transportation and an official guide at your total disposition. All international tour operators must refer to local agencies approved by the government. Among those specialized in trekking, we recommend Adorable Brothers Adventure, Happy Bhutan Adventures and Shangri-La Bhutan Tours & Treks.*

Advice *Plan your vacation in Bhutan during the most important and scenographic Buddhist festival, Tsechu, that is held in Paro at the beginning of the spring. The dates follow the lunar calendar and vary year by year, so check the official tourism website or contact tour operators.*

AT THE SPRING OF THE GANGES

Internet site www.uttaranchaltourism.in

Walking with the swarms of Shiva's devotees, follow the sacred river's Himalayan route in a fascinating purification ritual.

In the remote Indian state of Uttarkhand, Gangotri is the last stop for the colored and rickety buses that unload hundreds of pilgrims each day: families from the south guided by florid matrons in saris, schoolchildren in colonial uniforms and young couples with the elaborate symbols from their recent marriage still showing on their skin. And, above all, a crowd of *sadhu,* saintly men with extremely long hair, dressed in yellow and ochre with unmistakable beaded *rudraksha,* all creating a confusing and contradictory scene that reveals the true face of India. Since Gangotri is the gate to the High Ganges Valley, or the Gang-Ma, the water mother of this formidable country. From here, the river falls in a spectacular waterfall, dispersing into a thousand little streams, that according to tradition is Shiva's hair, and is the beginning of a trek that has the charm of an initiation to the roots of Hinduism. Always crowded, the path winds along the river Bhagirathi, which

| **60** *The name Shivling is derived from sacred references to Shiva's lingam.*

| **61** *A* sadhu *doing meditation exercises near the source of the Ganges.*

showers down rom the Himalayas and whose banks are full of flowers and little offering plates smoking with incense, until arriving at the greenish blue Gaumukh, the great cavern of the Gangotri glacier at an altitude of 3800 meters, where the Ganges waters spring from a glacial fault, the symbol of Shiva. Most pilgrims stop here, in ecstatic meditation, but the actual source of the river is higher up, in the unexplored heart of Kailash, the sacred Tibetan mountain. And the sacred aura stays with you across the glacier and up the long slopes of the Himalayan valleys flowering with rhododendrons all the way up to the pastures of Topoban. Here, in the presence of the bright, imposing Shivling column, with its phallic form, you enter into the realm of great mountaineering challenges, in front of the spectacle of mountains as high as 7000 meters that mark the Himalayan boarder between India and Tibet.

When to go *In May-June and from mid-August to October.*

How long to stay *1 week, 2 for a more strenuous trek.*

Organization *Taking a bus from Dehradun, you reach the capital Uttarkhand (itself connected to New Delhi with daily flights), Gangotri is home to many agencies for pony rental, carriers and guides. If you prefer an organized trek, we recommend Peak Adventure and Snow Leopard Adventures.*

Advice *Since it is a sacred place, it is impossible to find non-vegetarian food and alcoholic beverages in Gangotri.* Dhaba, *traditional restaurants for pilgrims, serve rice and lentils almost exclusively: bring energy bars, chocolate and other comfort foods to get through the fatigue of the trek.*

NOT TO MISS

- DON'T EXPECT ANYTHING TOO COMFORTABLE, BUT YOU HAVE TO STAY IN AN ***ASHRAM*** IN GANGOTRI, A HINDU SPIRITUAL CENTER. WE RECOMMEND DANDI SWAM, ISHAVASYAM (THAT ORGANIZES YOGA COURSES) AND TAPOVAN, WHOSE GURU IS A PHOTOGRAPHY LOVER.
- FROM FANFOTRI, TAKE 2 DAYS FOR A TREK TO **KEDAR TAL,** THE GLACIER LAKE AT 4750 METERS IDENTIFIED AS ONE OF THE GANGES' SOURCES. 17 KILOMETERS LONG, THE TOUGH WALK WINDS THROUGH HIMALAYAN BIRCH FORESTS, WHOSE WOOD WAS USED FOR THE ANCIENT SACRED TEXTS WRITTEN IN SANSKRIT.
- YOU NEED A BIT OF COURAGE, BUT PARTICIPATING IN A ICE-WATER PURIFICATION RITUAL IN THE **GAUMUKH CAVERN** TOGETHER WITH HINDU PILGRIMS IS A FORMIDABLE EXPERIENCE.

ON THE JAPANESE ALPS

Mountaineering among the 100 majestic peaks of Chubu-Sangaku National Park owes its birth to an English missionary.

| 62 *Chubu-Sangaku National Park was created in 1934.*

Monkeys, as we all know, are the animals closest to us. You could say we are their big brothers. And, as with all brothers, the little ones like to copy the big ones. This happened in a striking way when, in Japan in 1963, observing a young couple reveling in the hot water of an *onsen,* the natural hot springs that stud the mountains, a red-faced female Macaque (*Macaca fuscata:* evolved on the Japanese islands, this species is the northernmost primate in the world) thought that the experience might be pleasurable and decided to imitate them. Since then, monkeys bathing in a pool especially dedicated to them, in the snowy landscape of the Jigokudani Yaen-Koen Park, is the most photographed attraction in the Nagano Prefecture. Having been home to an edition of the winter Olympics, Nagano is the heart of the Japanese Alps, thus baptized by the English missionary Walter Weston who, in 1896, explored them, teaching the Japanese people to the joys of mountaineering: on the first Sunday of June there is a festival dedicated to him, officially kicking off the trekking and climbing season that goes until November. The entire Prefecture has been traced with hundreds of routes of varying difficulty, and the most spectacular are found near Kamikochi, at 1500 meters of altitude, surrounded by the 100 peaks (many over 3000 meters high), the glacial cirques and the narrow valleys of Chubu-Sangaku National Park.

NOT TO MISS

- IN LINE WITH JAPANESE AESTHETIC, TREKKING IS BEST BETWEEN JUNE AND MID-JULY, WHEN YOU WILL SEE WHAT LOCAL TRADITION CALLS THE **"MAGIC GREEN FOG,"** RISING IN THE FORESTS AND OVER THE LAKES, REFLECTING THE COLOR OF THE YOUNG BIRCH LEAVES. IN THE AUTUMN, YOU CAN ADMIRE THE FLEETING, TRANSCENDENTAL POETRY OF THE LEAVING CHANGING COLORS BEFORE THEY DIE.

- BESIDES THE BATHING MONKEYS OF JIGOKUDANI YAEN-KOEN PARK, THE RESORT CITY NAGANO IS A PERFECT BASE FOR REACHING **TOKAGUSHI,** VILLAGE HOME TO AN 800-YEAR-OLD NINJA SCHOOL THAT INCLUDES A MUSEUM DEDICATED TO THEIR WEAPONS.

- BETWEEN NAGANO AND KAMIKOCHI, THE ***MATSUMOTO*** AREA IS RICH WITH HOT SPRINGS WITH TRADITIONAL ONSEN IMMERSED IN MAGICAL AND REMOTE MOUNTAIN LANDSCAPES. AMONG THESE, YOU WILL FIND THE SHIRAHONE ONSEN AND THE NORIKURA KOGEN *ONSEN:* BOTH ARE CONNECTED BY TRAILS THAT HAVE ***RYOKAN*** ON THEM, ANCIENT INNS WHERE YOU CAN SLEEP.

- IN THE NORTHERN PART OF THE JAPANESE ALPS, **IYAMA** IS NOTED FOR THE CURATIVE EFFECTS OF ITS FOREST. BELIEVE IT OR NOT, *GREEN THERAPY* IS DONE BY WALKING THE FORESTS PATHS AND PARTICIPATING IN THE MANY HOLISTIC ACTIVITIES THAT ARE ORGANIZED IN SUMMER MONTHS.

| **63** *Red-faced macaques bathing in an* onsen *in Jigokudani Yaen-Koen Park.*

Don't miss the Yarigatake trek (40 kilometers at 3180 meters) in an itinerary that first follows the Azusa river through bamboo forests to then rise along slopes covered in birch trees and crisscrossed by waterfalls, finally arriving in the Yarisava valley. Here the strenuous walk up 1000 meters to the peak in a suggestive mountain landscape. During the route, it is easy to spot Japanese Macaques and, on your way back to Kamikochi, you can reward yourself with a bath in the hot waters of an *onsen*.

Internet site www.go-nagano.net and www.kamikochi.or.jp/english

When to go *From June to October for trekking; in the winter, Nagano Prefecture offers a vast array of skiing options (and the possibility to see the bathing monkeys in a snowy panorama).*

How long to stay *1 week.*

Organization *All the mountain trails can be trekked independently, and the tourism offices and Japanese Alpine Clubs offer perfect advice for choosing the right itinerary. And English-managed and Japanese-based tour operator, Quest Japan is specialized in walking tours throughout the country.*

Advice *The hardest part about trekking is that all the signs (including the danger signs) are written in Japanese. So, it is fundamental that you get a good guide that gives detailed information about the trails and that has a translated glossary of ideograms.*

PILGRIMAGE TO KOYASAN

| 64 *Gravestones in the Koyasan region, an important destination for Japanese pilgrims.*

In the ancient and remote Kumano Kudo region, live monastic traditions and travel the paths of mysticism in untamed nature.

"Greet travelers with an open smile and a friendly heart": this is one of the (many, often incomprehensible for those unfamiliar with exasperated Japanese formality) indications contained in the section dedicated to manners in the tourist brochures you will find in Koyasan. Besides, here everything follows precise ceremonial rituals: situated in a striking green valley at an altitude of 900 meters and permanently inhabited by 4000 monks, this village was founded in 804 by the monk and calligrapher Kobo Daishi, Japan's spiritual father and Shingon master, an esoteric current of Buddhism. Even if it is just a 2 hour train ride from Osaka, this is a astonishing place with 117 splendid temples, 53 of which have *shukubo,* monastic guesthouses that host travelers. Although just the experience of being here is extraordinary in itself, you should also add a pilgrimage through the year-round suggestive landscape (flowering in May with cherry blossoms, in July with rhododendrons, in the autumn when leaves turn fire-red and mid-November under the snow), along the Choishi Michi trail: 24 breathtaking kilometers studded with temples, votive tabernacles and gates that open to the even more remote and mystical monastic center of Danjo Garan, peacefully resting high atop Mt. Koya. Finally, Koyasan is connected by a demanding trail (it takes up to 4 days to travel) to other monastic Buddhist, Shintoist and Zen communities in Kumano Kodo, the wild region in the southwest of the Kii peninsula where over 2000 kilometers of ancient pilgrimage routes are in the "loving heart" of all Japanese. And they are even protected by UNESCO's World Heritage Sites.

NOT TO MISS

- THE MOST IMPORTANT TEMPLE IS **KONGOBUJI** THAT HAS A LONG SERIES OF ROOMS PROTECTED BY *FUSUMA*, SLIDING DOORS MADE OF GOLD PAINTED PAPER. HERE, YOU CAN ALSO ADMIRE **BANRYUTEI,** THE LARGEST AND MOST SUGGESTIVE ROCK GARDEN IN JAPAN.

- SHORTER, BUT JUST AS SCENOGRAPHIC, IS THE **KOYA SANZAN** TRAIL THAT CONNECTS KOYASAN WITH AN ITINERARY SHAPED LIKE A LOTUS. ORIGINALLY, IT WAS RESERVED FOR WOMEN, WHO COULDN'T GO TO SACRED SITES SO THEY COULD ADMIRE THEM FROM AFAR.

- TRY ***SHOJIN RYORI,*** THE MONK'S DEVOTIONAL VEGETARIAN CUISINE: SPECIALTIES INCLUDE *KOYADOFU* (ICE-DRIED TOFU), *GOMADOFU* (SESAME TOFU) AND *SHIRATAKI,* GELATINOUS NOODLES MADE FROM KONYAKU POTATOES, RICH IN MINERALS AND PROTEINS BUT LOW IN CALORIES.

- KOBO DAISHI, FOUNDER OF KOYASAN, IS ALSO NOTED FOR HAVING INVENTED *KANA,* THE PHONETIC SYLLABLES STILL USED IN JAPAN TODAY. IN HIS HONOR, YOU CAN PARTICIPATE IN THE **CALLIGRAPHY SESSIONS** AND COPY SACRED TEXTS, A PRACTICE AKIN TO MEDITATION.

When to go *All year.*

How long to stay *From 3 days to 1 week.*

Organization *Pilgrim trails are well marked and can be walked independently. Koyasan's tourism office has free detailed maps in English. The Japan Tourism Board (JTB) organizes 2/3-day tours in the area.*

Advice *You should know that in Shukubo lodgings (that cost around 9000 yen, or $100 dollars, meals included) mean sleeping on futons, using communal, Japanese-style baths and respecting a precise timetable: you must arrive before 5 p.m., dinner is served at 6 p.m. and breakfast at 7 a.m., while visitors are encouraged to participate in the morning prayer at 6 a.m.*

Internet site http://eng.shukubo.net

| **65** *Kongobuji Temple, Shingon Buddhists' main place of worship.*

AMONG THE PAPUA NATIVES

The last frontier of exploration, through uncontaminated rainforests and a myriad of ethnic groups.

Three official languages - English, Tok Pisin and Hiri Motu - may seem like a lot, but that's only the beginning. With hundreds of sparse ethnic groups across the heart of the rainforest, Papua New Guinea is the most linguistically diverse country in the world: there are around 850 different languages, nearly 10% of those spoken on the planet. This gives you an idea of the isolation that many Papua populations still live in. And although English is spoken by a small minority of inhabitants, for some time Tok Pisin has assumed the role of *lingua franca* in this country.

Between an infernal equatorial climate, primordial nature and the wealth of human groups, there is plenty to do in Papua, one of the last frontiers of adventure. Even more overwhelmingly so if you chose to go into the forests on foot, also because the roads connect only the most populated centers.

Internet site
www.papuanewguinea.travel

| **66** *Huli men with their faces painted and their characteristically decorated wigs.*

| **67** *Falls near the Ora Resurgence Cave on the island of New Britain.*

There are many possibilities for moving without vehicles, starting with the most fascinating Kokoda Trail, a weeklong trek through the mountains, that connects the northern coast to the west cost on a path forged by Japanese soldiers during WWII. Or the 4-day excursion to Mount Wilhelm that, with an elevation of 4509 meters, is the highest mountain in the country. The possibilities are endless. But what is certain is that during a Papua trek you can't miss the occasion to participate in a sing-sing. These are the periodic gatherings where different ethnic groups meet to share food, customs, dances and traditions. This is really the only way to taste the priceless cultural heritage of Papua New Guinea.

When to go *The dry season lasts from May to October and is when there are the most celebrations and festivities.*

How long to stay *You should take at least 2 weeks to explore Papua, during which you can organize treks varying in length from 1 day to 1 week.*

Organization *Numerous local tour operators offer trekking itineraries. Among the many options, Trek Papua has the widest selection of possibilities and has the advantage of being managed by a team of Papua guides.*

Advice *Whatever type of trip you intend to take, we strongly advise you not to drive. Roads are in horrible conditions, usually very narrow, while the rare asphalted sections can actually be the most dangerous since they are littered with holes.*

NOT TO MISS

- THE **GOROKA SHOW** IS PAPUA'S MAIN SING-SING THAT HAS BEEN HELD IN THE CITY OF THE SAME NAME, THE CAPITAL OF THE EASTERN HIGHLANDS PROVINCE, ON SEPTEMBER 16TH EVER SINCE THE 1950S. HUNDREDS OF DIFFERENT ETHNIC GROUPS PARTICIPATE. A GOOD ALTERNATIVE IS THE **MOUNT HAGEN SING-SING,** HELD ON THE THIRD WEEKEND IN AUGUST.
- IN THE NORTH, VISIT **NEW BRITAIN PROVINCE,** A VOLCANIC ISLAND AND EX-COLONY, IT IS PREDOMINANTLY INHABITED BY THE TOLAI, WHERE MASKS, SPIRITS AND SHELLS USED AS MONEY STILL HAVE NOTABLY CULTURAL VALUE.
- AT THE NORTHWESTERN END OF THE COUNTRY, THE **SEPIK RIVER** FOLLOWS THE BORDER OF THE INDONESIAN PROVINCE IRIAN JAYA, IMMERSED IN THE JUNGLE. MOSTLY OF ITS 1126 KILOMETERS ARE NAVIGABLE, LEADING YOU TO THE MOST REMOTE COMMUNITIES OF PAPUA.

THE GREAT OCEAN WALK

Eight days of walking to experience the nature of the wild coasts of Victoria. Two steps (more or less) from Melbourne.

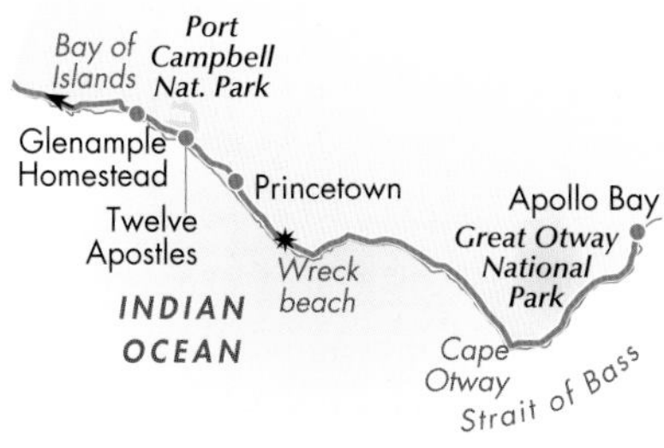

| 68 *The Twelve Apostles, one of the postcard perfect scenes along the Great Ocean Walk.*
| 69 *Cape Otway's lighthouse.*

For hundreds of thousands of European emigrants, Cape Otway's lighthouse was the first thing they saw in Australia after months of navigation. A place of great charm, this lighthouse was build in 1848 on the cliffs facing the Bass Strait and is not only the country's oldest functioning one, but also a monumental opera realized by man on the wildest ocean cliffs in Victoria, only 3 hours from Melbourne by car. With dizzying cliffs, deserted beaches and rainforests inhabited by koalas, wallabies, echidnas and various kangaroo species – and even paleontological remains – this coastline (where you probably won't see another living soul) connects the picturesque fishing village of Apollo Bay and Glenample Homestead, another remote outpost of civilization, crossing due protected areas – the Great Otway and Port Campbell National Park – and postcard marine scenes. Like the Twelve Apostles, the 12 limestone pinnacles forged from ocean waves breaking against the shore in all their primordial beauty.

Internet site www.visitvictoria.com/greatoceanwalk

NOT TO MISS

- YOU HAVE TO GO DOWN (AND BACK UP) 350 STEPS CARVED INTO THE CLIFFS TO REACH THE MAGNIFICENT (AND SINISTER) **WRECK BEACH.** HERE, GIGANTIC ANCHORS FROM THE MARIE GABRIELLE AND THE FIJI, TWO SHIPS THAT NEVER MADE IT, REST IN THE SAND.
- GO UP TO THE **GABLES VIEWPOINT,** ON THE TOP OF MOONLIGHT HEAD CLIFF, 50 METERS ABOVE THE OCEAN: TAKE BINOCULARS WITH YOU TO ADMIRE THE MARINE BIRDS AND - FROM JUNE TO SEPTEMBER - WATCH WHALES IN LOVE JUST OFF THE COAST.
- IN **GREAT OTWAY NATIONAL PARK,** TAKE THE OTWAY FLY TREETOP WALK, A NETWORK OF CATWALKS BUILT IN THE TREES ABOUT 50 METERS UP: A SPECTACULAR EXPERIENCE.
- AFTER TREKKING, TAKE A HELICOPTER RIDE TO ADMIRE THE COAST - WITH THE **TWELVE APOSTLES** AND THE **BAY OF ISLANDS** - FROM AN EXCITING AERIAL PERSPECTIVE.

When to go *The trail is open all year round, but the best time is between September and December, before it gets too hot.*

How long to stay *You will need 8 days to walk the entire trail.*

Organization *Well marked, the Great Ocean Walk can be done alone: the map is available at Apollo Bay's visitor center; since there are limited places, you need to get a permit from Parks Victoria to stay in the well-equipped camps along the way. Among the tour operators that organize custom guided itineraries, we recommend Great Ocean Walk Holidays and Walk 91.*

Advice *Be very careful along the steep passages on top of the cliffs and along the beaches, inaccessible at high tide. Always wear high socks because venomous snakes populate the cliffs and the forests.*

IN FIORDLAND

A journey through forests, mountains and fiords in New Zealand's most extreme national park, the fantastic setting of "Lord of the Rings."

Facing the Tasmanian Sea, Fiordland National Park covers over 200,000 hectares on the southern tip of South Island. By itself, it has 3 of the 9 Great Walks of the World – Kelper Track, Milford Track and Routeburn Track – that, maybe with a forgivable excess of parochialism, are all in New Zealand. In any case, Fiordland's natural settings are more beautiful that you can imagine: they include immense, dense, virgin forests, 14 deep fiords, a myriad of glacial lakes, innumerable waterfalls and peaks that reach as high as 2700 meters. The Maori baptized them Ata Whenua, or "The Land of Shadows," because rarely does the sun manage to penetrate the blanket of clouds that cover its narrow valleys. It goes without saying, this is one of the places with the most rainfall on the planet, up to 10,000 millimeters each year: it would be easier to measure in meters! So, it rains here at least 200 days a year, so much that botanists consider it a natural colossal hydroponic farm, while geologists, usually less accustomed to romantic expressions, consider the erosive powers of the waters (and before them, the glaciers) "a marvelous geological voyage of the Pacific, 80 million years long."

NOT TO MISS

- IN THE SMALL TOWN OF TE ANAU, **FIORDLAND CINEMA** SHOWS A FILM EVERYDAY - DIRECTED AS WELL AS ANY HOLLYWOOD MASTER COULD - THAT TELLS ABOUT THE PARK'S MARVELOUS NATURE OVER THE SEASONS. INCLUDED IN THE PRICE OF THE TICKET, YOU GET A GLASS OF REMARKABLE MALBOROUGH SAUVIGNON BLANC TO SIP DURING THE SHOW.

- **MILFORD SOUND,** 114 KILOMETERS FROM TE ANAU, IS ACCESSIBLE BY CAR ON THE ONLY, PANORAMIC ASPHALT ROAD THROUGH THE PARK. HERE YOU CAN TAKE A **BOAT TOUR** TO ADMIRE THE MANY WATERFALLS OVER 100 METERS HIGH THAT SURGE INTO THE FIORD'S WATERS AND SEE SEA LIONS LAYING AROUND ON THE ROCKS: FIORDLAND IS HOME TO THE MOST NEW ZEALAND'S DENSEST POPULATION OF THEM, ESTIMATED AT 50,000 MEMBERS.

- **MILFORD DEEP** IS AN OBSERVATORY BUILT IN MILFORD SOUND AND ALLOWS YOU TO OBSERVE THE PARTICULAR MARINE ECOSYSTEM: HERE, THE SUPERSTAR IS THE **ULTRA-RARE BLACK CORAL** (THAT IS ACTUALLY WHITE, DESPITE ITS NAME) THAT "FLOWERS" INTO BRANCHES UP TO 4 METERS TALL.

- TREAT YOURSELF TO A **HELICOPTER TOUR** TO ADMIRE THE MOUNTAINS AND FIORDS FROM AN ORIGINAL AERIAL PERSPECTIVE.

| 70 *Trekking in the wild landscapes of Fiordland National Park.*

| 71 *Its uncontaminated nature and majestic scenery are Fiordland's secrets.*

If you're not afraid of rain, and if 80 million years in 4 or 5 days doesn't seem like too much to take in, know that each of the 3 Great Walks leaving from Te Anau, the splendid "border town" that gives access to the park, are incredible sights. Dominated by red beeches that are, in terms of majesty, on par with the American redwoods, these low-level forests include various species of conifers – like the *miro, rimu, totara* and *kahikatea* – and have the same mystical atmosphere you find in great gothic cathedrals; the underbrush is an endless carpet of gigantic ferns and moss that cover tree trunks and any flat terrain. Little by little, as you move up, this landscape gives way to a mountain prairie with bunches of grass blowing in the wind, rocks covered with lichens and, finally at the summit, mountain snows and a view of the fiords and the parks 365 islands. Under the sunlight, they look like shiny green confetti thrown into dark blue waters. Dusky and Doubtful Sound, the largest fiords wedged at least 50 kilometers into U-shaped valleys dug out from glacial erosion, are one of the few places in the world where it isn't an exaggeration to use the word "uncontaminated." Yet, the Maori have known this paradise since time immemorial, coming here with their canoes to extract *pounamu* from the rocks, a green mineral similar to jade that they used to create arms and ornaments. On his first trip to discover the Pacific, in 1770, James Cook came to the entrances of the two fiords but decided not to enter with his *Endeavor* because it was already sunset (the islands that dot it would have been dangerous obstacles), but didn't forget to give them a name: Dusky Sound.

However, destiny has a sense of humor: in 1785 the fiord became home of the first and most populated settlement in

New Zealand, made up of 244 shipwrecked sailors from William Bompton's vessel, who took refuge here for a couple of years, enough time to rebuild the ship. A paradise, if you think about the fact that the entire Fiordland is completely uninhabited. It was again Cook who named the wide and just as magnificent Doubtful Sound: he pondered for a long time at its mouth about whether or not to sail into a land that he thought populated by monstrous beings. In the end, he decided to explore it but after him – and many floods – it seems that no one else came through. So, borrowing the title of a famous Simon & Garfunkel song, it is nicknamed *The Sound of Silence.*

Internet site www.fiordland.org.nz

| 72 *A waterfall cascading in the Milford Sound.* | 72-73 *Snowy peaks reflecting in the waters of Milford Sound.*

When to go *From October to April.*

How long to stay *The treks take from 3 to 5 days, but stay at least 1 week to enjoy the park's beauties.*

Organization *Although you can go it alone, the Great Walks inside Fiordland are accessible to a limited number of visitors (40 per day, the number of places in the refuges along the way). If you prefer a guided tour, contact Ultimate Hikes, Trips & Tramps and Fiordland Nature Observations.*

Advice *The refuges have kitchens, but you have to bring your own food and cook it. Before leaving, get goods at supermarkets in Te Anau. You will also need water bottles: the rivers and spring waters are potable. Regarding clothing, plan for hot forest days and cold elevated heights. And, naturally, bring rainproof clothes.*

Curiosities

- *Like many places in New Zealand, Fiordland was the setting for the* Lord of the Rings *trilogy.*

- *Due to isolation, Fiordland is home to very particular fauna. Like the kea, the only mountain parrot on the planet, and the* tahake, *a goose with iridescent plumage first seen in 1948, years after it had been declared extinct.*

- *However, you could go without the sand flies that infest the forest and the costal zones. When they sting, the wound can last for months. A Maori legend tells that they were created by* Hinenui-te-po, *the goddess of hell, to sting lazy humans who admire the great beauty of Fiordland too long.*

AMBRYM, THE BLACK ISLAND

Internet site http://vanuatu.travel

Two of the planet's most active volcanoes and a culture based magic for an exceptional adventure, but be careful.

The Rom dance costumes – part of the initiation ceremony that is one of the most extraordinary examples of Vanuatu culture – are made up of a cone-shaped mask in banana fiber and a long dress that reaches the ground, hiding the person wearing it and made of dried banana leaves. Only a handful of people in the community know the art of making them: laying eyes on an unfinished costume means breaking one of he most sacred taboos, so much so that anyone guilty must sacrifice a pig and is subjected to a series of whippings, given by the village leader. In order to not find yourself in an unpleasant situation, you should get familiar with local customs before venturing into Ambrym, a remote and sinister island, even for the inhabitants of the archipelago. The Vanuatu call it the "black island," and if this little nickname seems quite obvious observing the geography – it is dominated by Marum and Benbow, two of the world's most active volcanoes whose enormous craters are surrounded by a desert of ashes – you should know that the attrib-

| 74 *Benbow is one of the two main craters of Ambrym's characteristic volcano.*

| 75 *A Rom dance during the Back to the Roots Festival.*

ute referred to is that the indigenous are considered capable of dangerous magic. Whatever you think about that, you should believe in the unexplainable to live in a place where violent eruptions, lava flows and clouds of ashes and lapillus are daily occurrences. More than a south-pacific paradise, Ambrym looks like the devil's playground. And, we all know, "bad things" are often the most interesting: beyond the trek from the forested coasts to the volcanic caldera, people come to this island to visit its villages and get close (with caution) to the culture – better yet, to the multiple local cultures since here, in this small territory, there are at least 10 different languages – and the art of totems and *tamtam,* gigantic wood and volcanic stone drums that decorate each village, as well as the ones designed in the ashes, just as elaborate as ephemeral, that the Ambrym people use to represent their world. A world full of the understanding of being the fleeting guests of a powerful nature. That is anything but benevolent.

When to go *From May to October.*

How long to stay *From 3 days to 1 week.*

Organization *Ambrym can be reached by plane with Air Vanuatu from Port Vila and Espiritu Santo, the archipelago's main tourist destinations. There are no modern tourist structures on the island so you sleep in simple bungalows in the local villages. Specialized in ecotourism, the local operator Wrecks to Rainforest organizes walking tours through Ambrym villages and treks up to the volcanic craters.*

Advice *Before leaving, so you are not unpleasantly surprised, check the volcanic and seismic activities on the island.*

NOT TO MISS

- IN AUGUST, THE **BACK TO THE ROOTS FESTIVAL** IS HELD ON THE NORTH OF THE ISLAND: A VILLAGE LEADER WITH A KNACK FOR MARKETING INVENTED IT, BUT THE ROM DANCE AND THE OTHER CEREMONIES PERFORMED HERE ARE REAL AND TRULY FELT BY THOSE WHO PARTICIPATE.
- THE **CRATERS OF MARUM** AND **BENBOW** ARE ACCESSIBLE BY 4 PATHS: LASTING 2 DAYS, THE MOST SPECTACULAR TREK ACROSS THE ISLAND, TO RANVETLAM IN THE NORTH AND ENDU IN THE SOUTHEAST, WILL ALLOW YOU TO CAMP IN THE ASH DESERT AND OBSERVE THE RARE MOSSES THAT GROW AROUND IT.
- FROM THE VILLAGES OF LALINDA AND PORT VATO, RENT A BOAT TO OBSERVE THE **DUGONG** THAT POPULATE AMBRYM'S SOUTHERN BAY.
- BORN JUST A FEW YEARS AGO FOLLOWING AN ERUPTION, **LAKE FANTENG** IS A NATURAL RESERVE WHERE OVER 30 BIRD SPECIES NEST.

ON THE LAVA OF KILAUEA

Walking on Hawaii's most explosive volcano, home to Pele, the "earth-eating" goddess, according the island peoples.

| 76 *A river of lava flows down Kilauea toward the ocean.*
| 77 *In Poynesian, Kilauea means "Rising cloud of smoke."*

In August 1959, geologists at the Hawaiian Volcano Observatory started to see powerful seismic activity on the Big Island. The phenomenon exponentially intensified over the next few months until, at 8:08 on November 14th, a rift opened on the southern face of the Kilauea volcano, spurting lava that, in the following days, reached over 80 meters high. That eruption – that pushed out 71 million cubic meters of lava at 1217°C – formed a new volcanic cone, the Pu'u Pua'i. Today, Pu'u Pua'I is the main attraction on the Kilauea Iki Trail that, along its 6.4 kilometers, is the most spectacular paths across the Hawaii Volcanoes National Park. Even if it isn't the highest volcano of the archipelago's islands, Kilauea is in the top ten most active volcanoes on the planet and is almost entirely covered by enough lava that has flowed out over the last 1000 years that it could pave a road around the equator three times. Crossing the lush forest at the volcano's base, the path leads to the edge of the crater and even takes you down inside where, surrounded by smoke steaming from the lava, you can almost feel the earth's heartbeat.

Internet site www.nps.gov/havo

NOT TO MISS

- RECONSTRUCTED IN 2005 AFTER BEING DESTROYED BY A LAVA FLOW, THE **KILAUEA VISITOR CENTER** IS FOUND AT THE PARK ENTRANCE AND HOSTS AN EXPOSITION ON THE GEOLOGY, ERUPTIONS, ECOSYSTEMS AND *MO'OLELO*, THE INDIGENOUS LEGENDS.

- STOP ON THE CRATER'S EDGE TO SEE THE PROFILE OF **MANUA LOA,** HAWAII'S MOST IMPOSING VOLCANO: IT SOARS OVER THE OCEAN AT 4100 METERS, BUT IT MUCH HIGHER THAN EVEREST IF YOU CONSIDER THE SUBMERSED PART.

- PAY ATTENTION TO THE **WILDLIFE IN THE CRATER FOREST,** FROM SPLENDID TROPICAL BIRD TO PLANTS LIKE KAHILI, WITH ITS FRAGRANT YELLOW FLOWERS THAT BLOOM AT THE END OF AUGUST, AND OHI'A LEHUA, A BUSH WITH RED FLOWERS THAT IS THE FIRST SPECIES THAT ROOTS IN LAVA.

When to go *The park is open year round, although some parts are closed without notice if volcanic activity causes sulfur oxide to steam out. The Big Island's climate is unpredictable, but the dry season is (generally) from March to October.*

How long to stay *The trek lasts 2-3 hours.*

Organization *Like all protected areas in the United States, Hawaii Volcanoes National Park is well-organized for receiving visitors and offers an ample choice of activities, including individual treks, guided walks, lodging in bungalows, camps and much more.*

Advice *Although short and well-marked, the Kilauea Iki Trail is difficult and can become dangerous. Seismic shocks cause falling rocks and the summit climate abruptly changes. Bring a hat and sunscreen, at least 2 liters of water each, rainproof jackets and a flashlight: the walk is quite suggestive at sundown but it isn't fun finding yourself in the pitch-black night.*

THE JOHN MUIR TRAIL

In the Sierra Nevada Mountains – from Yosemite to Sequoia National Park – this legendary trail honors the prophet of the wilderness.

NOT TO MISS

- THE **GRANITE HALF DOME** IS YOSEMITE'S ICON (ALSO FOUND IN THE SIERRA CLUB'S LOGO). ALTHOUGH IT WAS DECLARED "PERFECTLY INACCESSIBLE" AT THE END OF THE 1800S, TODAY AROUND 800 EXCURSIONISTS REACH THE TOP EACH DAY, AIDED BY A SYSTEM OF STEEL CABLES ALONG THE LAST 400 METERS OF THE STEEP ASCENT.

- THE ARCHITECT HENRY H. GUTTERSON WAS INSPIRED BY THE TRULLI CONSTRUCTION IS PUGLIA (ITALY) TO DESIGN HIS **MUIR MEMORIAL HUT** IN 1931. THIS SHELTER IS FOUND ON MUIR PASS AT AN ELEVATION OF 3644 METERS IN KING'S CANYON NATIONAL PARK. ON EACH SIDE, YOU CAN ADMIRE **LAKE WANDA AND HELEN,** THUS BAPTIZED IN HONOR OF JOHN MUIR'S DAUGHTERS.

- **DEVIL'S POSTPILE NATIONAL MONUMENT** PROTECTS THIS GEOLOGICAL FORMATION. IT IS A WALL OF HEXAGONAL BASALT COLUMNS 60 METERS HIGH THAT, TOGETHER, PRESENT AN UNUSUAL SYMMETRY. CLOSE BY, ADMIRE THE SPECTACULAR RAINBOW FALLS.

- SOME OF THE MOST MAGICAL HIGH MOUNTAIN PASSES ON THE TRAIL ARE IN **SEQUOIA NATIONAL PARK.** HOWEVER, DUE TO THE ALTITUDE, YOU WON'T SEE ANY OF THE MONUMENTAL SEQUOIAS THE PARK IS FAMOUS FOR.

Sito internet www.johnmuirtrail.org

| 78 *Half Dome at sundown.* | 79 *The trail's minimum elevation is 2400 meters.*

"Everyone needs beauty as well as bread, places to play in, places to pray in, where nature may heal and give strength to body and soul." This is only one of the thousand thoughts that John Muir, during the long winters is the high Sierra Nevada Mountains in California, feverishly jotted down in his notebooks. Today conserved in the Sierra Club library, these shabby little books all have an apparently infantile header: "John Muir, Planet Earth, Universe." He has been called the most illustrious person in Californian history, the prophet of the wilderness and the father of national parks. However, born in Scotland in 1839 and adolescent emigrant to the United States, John Muir preferred to be remembered as a simple citizen of the universe. In a period when industrialization took great strides forward and nature was seen as a resource to exploit, his non-anthropocentric vision of it was revolutionary: he considered human beings part of a whole and was convinced that losing part of that whole meant losing part of ourselves. In his heroic life, John Muir scaled the peaks of the Sierra, crossed glaciers in Alaska, was a great botanist (discovering, among other things, a new species of orchid, Calypso borealis, of which he said: "I never before saw a plant so full of life, so perfectly spiritual, it seemed pure enough for the throne of its Creator") and lived years of solitude in the wild. He was, above all, the pioneer of environmental conservation, founding the Sierra Club – today the most important

| **80-81** *Mount Whitney reaches an altitude of 4421 meters.* | **81** *Rainbow Falls at Devil's Postpile National Monument.*

American NGO working to protect the wilderness – and convinced President Theodore Roosevelt to institute what was the first national park in history: Yosemite, resting high up in the Sierra Range. At his death, members of the Sierra Club decided to honor his memory by forging a high altitude trail through the places he loved so much. Inaugurated in 1939, 100 years after his birth, the John Muir Trail, you can rightly call heavenly. 340 kilometers long (actually 356, since it unexplainably ends near the summit of Mount Whitney and there are another 16 kilometers of rough going before returning to "the human world"), it stars in Yosemite Park, going through the Inyo and Sierra National Forests, both included in the area protected by the John Muir and Ansel Adams Wildreness, the Devil's Postpile National Monument and King's Canyon National Park, ending in Sequoia National Park. It winds along a path with a minimum elevation of 2400 meters and crosses 6 passes, the highest of which reaches an elevation of 4009 meters. The trail traces just over 65% of the epic Pacific Crest Trail (4286 kilometers, from British Colombia in Canada to the U.S./Mexico border) that itself can be divided into a series of parts inside each protected area, right for those who don't have the time or training to trek the whole thing. Along with its inherent difficulty, the John Muir Trail adds others, like the presence of bears – you need special devices when camping – and a scarcity of supply stations along the way. Among these, an honorable mention goes to the scenographic Vermillion Resort, on the banks of Lake Edison, that give all travelers the first night and first beer free. Right along the lines of the spirit of solidarity between man and nature found in John Muir's writings.

When to go *From mid-June to mid-September.*

How long to stay *3 weeks.*

Organization *On the official website, all the information for obtaining permits, advice for preparing the trip (including directions on how to send goods to the resupplying points by mail) and information of the different parts and difficulties of the walk, including instructions on how to behave if you meet a brown bear. In addition, it is fundamental to get a detailed map of the trail. Use internet to find traveling companions by signing up in any of the many forums dedicated to excursions along the JMT every summer.*

Advice *The most important thing to have is the bear box, an airtight container for anything that could attract a bear. Cook and consume food at least 100 meters from your campsite and, at night, don't take any foodstuffs into your tent, not even toothpaste: curiously, brown bears love it!*

Curiosities

John Muir's heroic life is celebrated in the names of many places, from Muir Clacier in Alaska to Muir Memorial Park in Wisconsin, all the way to Muir Nature Trail, a green path through a park in the Bronx, in New York. In Dunbar, Scotland, we find Muir Country Park and his house is now a museum. On April 21st, California celebrates John Muir Day.

Yosemite Park is also tied to another immortal character: Ansel Adams, the father of landscape photography. Managed by his heirs, his studio is found near the Visitors' Center and sells, among other things, his original photos that are worth between 8,000 and 50,000 dollars on the international market.

The sight of the mountains in summer, at dawn and sunset, changing red is a phenomenon called alpenglow. It is due to the chemical composition of the rocky walls that contain calcium carbonate and magnesium. You can see this phenomenon especially either in the Sierras or in the Dolomites.

ATOP CORDILLERA BLANCA

Walking along the impervious and extreme elevation trails in the Parque Nacionál Huscarán, in the presence of Alpamayo, the most desired Andean peak.

"Aceso dificil pero no imposible" says a sign that – in an improbable compromise between mountain efficiency and Latin American approximation – marks the entrance to the Pastoruri trail, one of the rare glaciers still in the Andes' tropical latitudes. At an elevation of 5250 meters, it is found in the southern part of the Cordillera Blanca, that with 22 peaks at over 6000 meters, is the mountain range second only to the Himalayas in extension, altitude and opalescent landscapes. The tiring climb to Pastoruri represents the shortest of the treks that wind through the Parque Nacionál Huscarán and also incudes the peak of the same name at 6788 meters (the second highest in the Americas) and the lower but more celebrated Alpamayo peak, a perfectly pyramid-shaped mountain that is both the dream and nightmare of every mountaineer. However, you don't have to be armed with an ice ax and crampons in order to enjoy the spell of these two white giants: the two massifs stand out on the path along the entire itinerary of the most popular

| 82 *Laguna Jancarurish at the foot of Alpamayo.*

| 83 *An Andean family in traditional clothing.*

trek (even if not everyone can do it), Santa Cruz, long 50 kilometers that extends through bristling passes and spectacular gorges, glacial lakes and high plateaus characterized by an abundance of curious plant species. Like the queñua, a strange tree with red bark, similar to cork, and the Puya raimondii, the planet's largest bromeliad that only grows between 3700 and 4200 meters on the most sunny sides: it can reach a height of 10 meters and, before dying at around 40, shows the best of itself by producing, all at once, 8000 white flowers and a few million seeds.

Internet site www.visitperu.com

When to go *From May to September.*

How long to stay *The treks last 1, 4 or 7 days, but plan for at least another 2 days to explore the Andean villages.*

Organization *In Huaraz, the capital of the Ancash region and home of Andean mountaineering, you can find an authorized guide and rent ponies to transport equipment to Casa de Guias. For some of the most challenging itineraries, like the circuit to the Alpamayo basecamp, you should consult a specialized operator: we recommend Andean Kingdom in Huaraz and Pony's Expeditions, near Caraz.*

Advice "Chocolate, coramina, coca!" *shout the indios boys along the trail, selling excursionists the most used local remedies for altitude sickness. Which, it goes without saying, is something you have to deal with here. Before trekking, you should spend a few days in and around Huaraz to get used to it and – like the indigenous – chew coca leaves or drink* mate: *the leaves keep salivation going, soothing your stomach, regulating your cardiac rhythm and blood pressure. And they are nothing like their illegal derivative, cocaine.*

NOT TO MISS

- FROM HUARAZ TO THE PARQUE NACIONÁL HUASCARÁN, TAKE THE **PORTACHUELO LLANGANUCO,** THE MOST PANORAMIC ROAD OF THE ANDES, BUILT BY THE INCA PEOPLE.
- TRY THE EXPERIENCE OF "ANDEAN LIFE" WITH THE QUECHUA NATIVES IN CASHAPAMPA, THE STARTING POINT FOR THE **SANTA CRUZ TREK:** THE PICTURESQUE VILLAGE IS SURROUNDED BY A MOSAIC OF CORN, POTATO AND QUINOA FIELDS, THE LATTER A LEAFY PLANT THAT IS THE MAIN SOURCE OF PROTEIN FOR ANDEAN POPULATIONS.
- RELAX ON THE BANKS OF **LAGUNA LLANGANUCO** AND **LAGUNA DE SIETE COLORES,** THE MARVELOUS HIGH ALTITUDE LAKES AT AN ALTITUDE OF OVER 3500 METERS, NOTABLE FOR THE INCREDIBLE COLORS OF THEIR WATERS, THAT RANGE FROM MIDNIGHT BLUE TO TURQUOISE.
- 30 MINUTES FROM HUARAZ, IN THE CORDILLERA NEGRA, **HATUN MACHAY** ("GREAT CAVE" IN QUECHUA) IS A MAJESTIC CATHEDRAL OF GRANITE, THE PERFECT GYM FOR ROCK CLIMBING. SOME OF ITS CAVES ARE HOME TO ANCIENT ROCK CARVINGS.

TREKKING IN PARQUE NACIONÁL LOS GLACIARES

At the foot of the slopes of Cerro Torre and Fitz Roy, among the great lakes and Campo de Hielo Patagónico, see the largest continental glacier on earth.

| **84 and 85** *Perito Moreno is a glacier in continuous movment and from its face, that advances about 2 meters a day, enormous spires of ice break off.*

NOT TO MISS

- A HUNDRED KILOMETERS NORTH OF EL CALAFATE - A 1 DAY EXCURSION - YOU WILL FIND THE **LA LEONA PETRIFIED FOREST,** AN INCREDIBLE NATURAL LANDSCAPE DOMINATED BY TRUNKS TRANSFORMED INTO ROCK AND GREAT DINOSAUR BONES.

- PATAGONIA IS THE LAND OF THE GUACHOS AND, EVEN IF TREKKING IS THE MOST NATURAL SPORT IN THIS REGION, YOU CAN'T LEAVE WITHOUT GOING ON AT LEAST ONE **HORSEBACK EXCURSION.** IT ISN'T DIFFICULT TO GET ONE, TOGETHER WITH A GUIDE, AT THE MANY ESTANCIAS THAT ARE FOUND AROUND CALAFATE.

- IF THE YOU AREN'T AFRAID OF THE WATER TEMPERATURE, DECIDEDLY COLD EVEN IN SUMMER, NUMEROUS LOCAL OPERATORS OFFER **RAFTING ON THE RIO SANTA CRUZ,** IN EL CALAFATE, OR ON THE **RIO DE LAS VUELTAS,** IN THE ZONE NEAR EL CHATÉN. IF IN DOUBT, ITS BETTER TO TAKE A HOT AIR BALLOON FLIGHT OVER THE INCREDIBLE PANORAMA OF THE ANDEAN GLACIERS.

After the failure of legends Cesare Maestri and Walter Bonatti, in 1974 the "Spiders of Lecco" – Daniele Chiappa, Mario Conti, Casimiro Ferrari and Pino Negri – were the first to make a documented climb to the summit of Cerro Torre, one of the most inaccessible mountains in the world, despite being just over 3000 meters high. Up there, at the end of an interminable climb along a 900 meter vertical wall of granite, the few mountaineers who are able to reach the summit find themselves face to face with the ice "mushroom" that protects one of the Parque Nacionál Los Glaviares' symbols, the natural sanctuary of the Argentinian province Santa Cruz.

A few kilometers east, Cerro Fitz Roy stars, or Cerro Chaltén that, with its 3405 meters is another of the highest peaks – and most difficult climbs – of the Cordillera Patagonia, that tower over Campo de Hielo Patagónico, the largest continental glacier on earth, with a nearly 17,000 square meters of surface. At its feet, many glacial valleys grind down to the region's 2 great lakes, Lake Viedma and Lake Argentino, the most celebrated of which are Upsala Glacier, Viedma Glacier and, the superstar, Perito Moreno.

Francisco Pascasio Moreno, awarded the title of "expert" at the beginning of the 1900s, was 25 when, in 1877, he was the first to explore these lands, discovering the widest body of sweet water in the country and the tongue of ice nearly 5 kilometers wide that periodically reaches the Magallanes Peninsula, on the other side of Lake Argentina, forming a natural dike that completely separates the two arms of the lake. Many years later, the Argentinean government would name what is one of the most impressive natural spectacles in the world.
Although the summits of Cerro Torre and Fitz Roy are destinations only for experienced mountaineers, without even mentioning the practically unreachable heart of Campo de Hielo Patagónico, the nearly 4500 square meters of the Parque Nacionál Los Glaciares offer opportunities to less equipped visitors. Start with navigating Lake Argentino, leaving from the region's main center, El Calafate, thanks to which it is possible to come within a few hundred meters of Perito Moreno, that reaches 80 meters high, to admire the gigantic imposing ice face that ranges from candid white to intense turquoise. Boats land on the opposite side of the lake where, putting on indispensable ice crampons, you can venture on the first offshoots of the glacier on a half-day trek.
More difficult, although more unusual, are the walks that leave from El Chaltén, a village with 900 souls at 200 kilometers from El Calafate founded at the feet of Fitz Roy in 1985 and thus boasting the title of the "youngest village in Argentina." The fact is that since its birth, El Chaltén has become a destination for travellers passionate about trekking. From here, you can take the trail that leads to the Poincenot basecamp in 5 hours, at the feet of Cerro Fitz Roy and the Laguna de los Tres, a small glacial lake with cobalt blue waters in the presence of an ancient moraine. Just as suggestive, and more or less at the same distance, is the trek that leads to the De Agostini basecamp, named after Alberto Maria De Agostini, a Salsian missionary and Biella explorer who spent more than 30 years in Patagonia. The viewing site to admire the immaculate spires of Cerro Torre is a 15-minute walk from the lake, a water mirror where small icebergs that have broken off the Grande glacier gather. Shorter walks take you to Piedras Blancas glacier and to the Rio Eléctrico Valley, 2 more spectacular observation points close to Fitz Roy.

| 86 *Trekking on the glaciers of Perito Moreno.*

| 87 *La Laguna de los Tres and a view of Cerro Fitz Roy.*

In the ancient times, Fitz Roy was called Chaltén "the smoking mountain" by the indigenous – in the Teheulche language – because of the cloud that, with frustrating regularity, hides the peak, when Moreno De Agostini came through these parts. But the moderate impact of humans in these lands has left nature uncontaminated, dominated by glaciers and the majestic flight of condors, where a trek of just a few hours is enough to take a journey through millenniums.

Internet site www.losglaciares.com.

When to go *From December to February.*

How long to stay *1 week.*

Organization *There are around 50 local tour operators that organize treks and excursions in the area, all based in El Calafate. The main one, the official concessionary of the Parque Nacionál Los Glaciares, is Hielo y Aventura, which manages navigation on Lake Argentino and expeditions to Perito Moreno. Among the companies that offer excursion packages, we recommend Morresi Viajes and Mil Outdoor Adventure. Less equipped is the El Chaltén zone, where you can still find lodging in private houses and modest hotels.*

Advice *During a trip to Patagonia, you should always stay a few nights in an estancia, where you can enjoy the life (and cuisine) of these large farms that mostly raise sheep. It isn"t difficult to find lodging during the 300-kilometer trip from Rios Gallegos to El Calafate, along the coast, the capital of Santa Cruz Province.*

Curiosities

- *Perito Moreno is one of the few glaciers actually advancing and that is why it is the object of discussion regarding global warming. An Argentinean researcher, Jorge Rabasa, in the summer of 2007, revealed that the glacier had lost 14 meters of thickness at the edges over the last 2 years, thus supporting the hypothesis that this glacier is too subject to global warming.*
- *Cesare Maestri's 1958 expedition to Corre Torre caused quite a storm. Maestri and the Austrian Toni Egger attempted the climb but, after a week, Maestri was found in a confused state and said that he and Egger had reached the summit but that during the descent Egger fell and the camera, along with their proof, was lost.*
- *The park's treasures include the Spegazzini Glacier, named after Carlo Luigi Spegazzini, one of the many Italo-Argentinians. Botanist and mycologist, he conducted important studies on the local mushrooms and succulent plants, earning him a series of plants and mushrooms named after him.*

ON THE ROAD

IT DOESN'T TAKE MUCH: JUST BUY A TRAIN OR BUS TICKET TO EXPERIENCE A GRAND ADVENTURE.

Jules Verne took us around the world in 80 days in his novel and then lead us to its core, saying that the most important roads take us to destiny rather than to a destination. You discover it riding a 4x4, a train or on public transportation in any one of the itineraries suggested in this section. Depending on your choice, you will find out if your destiny will be falling in love in the silence of the Sahara's great empty, or in the cacophony of one of the planets "fullest" destinations, the Indian subcontinent. Or you won't be able to help but being moved by the great fauna, during the wildebeest migrations in the African Serengeti or finding yourself in the presence of polar bears in northern Canada. Or, again, if you will aspire to meet people with lives that are much different than your own, whether they be the indigenous peoples of the Omo river valley, in the cradle of humanity, or those that live in the Ambrym, one of the Pacific islands where human settlement is still "young." In every case, you will discover that every road is a life teacher. And that every true traveler is an excellent student.

ETHNOGRAPHIC JOURNEY
WILDLIFE WATCHING
CAVING
TREKKING
SNOWMOBILE
AUTOMOBILE
OFF-ROAD

BUS
TRAIN
ICE-BREAKING SHIP
MOTORBOAT
KAYAK
WHALE WATCHING
HOT AIR BALLOON
HORSEBACK

OR INVENT YOUR VERY OWN ROAD, ABOARD A 4X4, TRACING YOUR LANE IN A DESERT OF SAND, SNOW OR SALT.

ON THE ROAD

CHOOSING THE RIGHT EMOTION

JOURNEY	PG	TIME ZONE	WHEN TO GO	NOT TO MISS
Egypt - From Cairo to Gil Kebir	94	GMT+2	October-April	*Wadi Sura Cliffs*
Ethiopia - In the Omo Valley	98	GMT+3	June-September	*Dimeka Market*
Tanzania, Kenya - The Great Wildebeest Migration	102	GMT+3	All year	*Grumeti River*
Madagascar - On the Fianarantsoa-Côte Est Railway	104	GMT+3	April-November	*Sahambavy*
Pakistan, China - Along the Karakorum Highway	106	GMT+4/+8	May-October	*Hunza Valley*
Pakistan, India, Bangladesh - On the Grand Trunk Road	109	GMT+4/+5:30/+6	November-April	*Taj Mahal*
Laos - Among the Ethnicities of Luang Nam Tha	112	GMT+7	November-April	*Luang Nam Tha National Park*
Mongolia - In the Land of Genghis Khan	114	GMT+7/+8	May-September	*Erdene Zuu Monastery*
China - In the Kingdom of the Lugu Hu Women	116	GMT+8	March-November	*Tiger Leaping Gorge*
Japan - Wild Hokkaido	118	GMT+9	All year	*Kotan village*
Russia - Chukotka, the Last Frontier	120	GMT+12	July-September	*Ergav Festival*
United States - On Kodiak Island	122	GMT+9	May-September	*St. Paul Harbor*
Canada - In Churchill, with Polar Bears	124	GMT+6	October-November	*Wapusk National Park*
Mexico - A Rrain Ride through the Barrancas del Cobre	126	GMT+7	Feb-Apr/Oct-Dec	*Batopilas*
Bolivia - In the Salar de Uyuni	128	GMT+4	Apr-May/Sep-Nov	*Laguna Colorada*

| 92-93 *Crossing the Egyptian desert is like following the tracks of past explorers.*

DON'T FORGET	A CLASSIC BOOK FOR EVERY JOURNEY
Tent	*Michael Ondaatje*, The English Patient
Antimalarial Pills	*Hans Silvester*, Ethiopia: Peoples of the Omo Valley
Camera	*Karen Blixen*, Out of Africa
Antimalarial Pills	*Ian Malcolm*, Madagascar
Sleeping bag	*Rudyard Kipling*, The Man Who Would Be King
Earplugs	*William Dalrymple*, Nine lives
Camera	*Christopher Kremmer*, Bamboo Palace
Sleeping bag	*John Man*, Genghis Khan: Life, Death, and Resurrection
Camera	*Mathieu - Erche*, Leaving Mother Lake
Train pass	*Will Ferguson*, Hitchhiking Rides with Buddha
Colored beads	*Dolitsky - Rust - Semenova*, Living Wisdom of the Far North
Tent	*Mykle Hansen*, HELP! A Bear is Eating Me!
Mosquito repellent	*Achim Zahren*, The Last Polar Bear
Camera	*Antonin Artaud*, Las Tarahumaras
Sunscreen and sunglasses	*R. Santos - J. Sanjines*, The Fat Man from La Paz

FROM CAIRO TO GIL KEBIR

A 4x4 adventure in the Egyptian Sahara that, in a magical setting, leads to the pharaohs of prehistory, from Alexander the Great to *The English Patient.*

Dancers, musicians, hunters and characters reflecting in the waters... Scenes of daily life created with a passion for details, lifting the veil from the habits and customs of a world disappeared, revealing an exceptionally interesting glimpse, and an unusual quantity of prints from hands, feet, gazelle and giraffe hoofs and feline paws, all done using ochre ink and with extraordinary elegance. Not by chance, the large cave carved out of the Wadi Sura cliffs, a part of the extraordinary and exhilarating limestone and sand plateau called Gilf Kebir, in the so-called Libyan desert on the border between Egypt, Libya and Sudan, has been defined the "Sistine Chapel of the Sahara." It was discovered in 2002 by Massimo Foggini, an Italian businessman, who having retired, dedicated himself, body and soul, to his passion for travel and archeology. On that occasion, he was exploring Gilf Kebir with his son, Jacopo, on an evocative adventure following the Hungarian Count László Almásy who, in turn, many decades before, had discovered the Cave of Swimmers on the banks of the now dried out lake, and after his death became well-known to a wide audience as the main character of the book The English Patient, Michael Ondaatije's best seller. So, by pure chance, the "amateur" Foggini found himself in the presence of this marvel that testifies to a Neolithic civilization that lived between 12,000 and 7000 years ago.

| **94** *A rock painting in Gilf Kebir.* | **95** *The ghost town Shali in Siwa.*

NOT TO MISS

- THE FIRST PAVED ROAD WAS OPENED IN 1986 AND NOW THERE IS EVEN AN AIRPORT. BUT **SIWA'S** CHARM IS TIED TO ITS IMMUNITY TO PASSING TIME. WITH 25,000 INHABITANTS SUBDIVIDED INTO ABOUT 10 VILLAGES SCATTERED AROUND A VAST AREA OF OLIVE AND PALM TREES, IT HOSTS **GEBEL AL MAWTA** ("MOUNTAIN OF THE DEAD"), A HILL THAT IS A COLLECTION OF PHARAOH TOMBS DECORATED WITH REFINED PAINTINGS.
- THE SMALL **FARAFRA OASIS** IS A JEWEL: ITS HOUSES ARE PAINTED BRIGHT BLUE (ACCORDING TO TRADITION, THIS COLOR PROTECTS YOU FROM THE EVIL EYE!) AND YOU CAN HAVE THE LUXURY OF SWIMMING IN AN ANCIENT POOL STILL USED TODAY BY THE INHABITANTS, ALL OF BEDOUIN ORIGIN.
- AT THE EDGE OF GILF KEBIR, **ABU BALLAS** IS NOTED AS "JAR PLACE," AND WAS POSSIBLY A SUPPLY STATION ALONG AN ANCIENT CARAVAN ROUTE: HERE YOU CAN ADMIRE STRANGE CLAY FORMATIONS CALLED "MUD LIONS" BECAUSE THEY LOOK LIKE SEA LIONS TRAPPED IN THE DESERT FOR ETERNITY.
- ON YOUR WAY BACK, STOP AT **BAHARIYA OASIS:** SURROUNDED BY FRUIT GROVES AND DATE PALMS, THE MAIN VILLAGE, BAWITI, HAS A PICTURESQUE MARKET TO SHOP IN. AND DON'T FORGET TO VISIT THE EXCELLENT LOCAL **MUSEUM** THAT, IN THE **GOLDEN MUMMY** ROOM, HAS SOME OF THE FAMOUS GREEK-ROMAN MUMMIES FOUND IN THE AREA IN 199, DECORATED WITH MASKS AND JEWELS AND HELD IN SARCOPHAGUSES PAINTED IN GOLD.

| **96** *The White Desert, near Farafra, gets its name from these rocky limestone formations.*

This splendid place, which the state of Egypt has officially named Foggini Cave, is at the root of the civilization of the pharaohs. This is because, as the desert slowly advanced, these were the original populations that would then colonize the Nile valley - the entire Egyptian stretch of the Sahara is, in open contradiction with the term "deserted," a place that is exceptionally full of archeological riches and strikingly suggestive historical citations. In the great Siwa Oasis, a kind of magical and unexpectedly thriving human capital in the Great Sand Sea, you will have the royal honor of finding what tradition holds as the beneficial spring that creates a magical pool that Cleopatra herself loved to swim in. However, again mixing historical fact with powerful mythologies, you will find the imposing remains of the famous oracle Ammon who, in 331 B.C., Alexander the Great consulted with to confirm that he really was the son of Zeus destined for greatness. And every part of a duly long and tiring trip into the Egyptian Sahara will give you dreams of abundant oases, ancient *ksour* built with raw earth for defensive purposes or to welcome caravans, as well as the traces of explorers' camps like Almásy, Hassanein Bey, Kemal el Din, Bagnold and Clayton, fathers of an epic that is the inspiring soul of the Long Range Desert Group's activities, the legendary British "desert brigades" during WWII. Added to all this, the off-road adventure in an Egypt far from the "usual," although grandiose, tourist destinations along the Nile, will also inevitably seduce you with its natural landscapes, which are just as exceptional as they are bizarre, that suddently appear like magic on the horizon beyond the mobile cordilleras of the sif, the long lines of winding sand dunes. Among these, there is the fabled White Desert infinitely extending beyond the palms of Bahariya Oasis and where, in the hot golden sand, a jungle of blindingly bright towers, hills and protrusions of white rise to the sky that, at sunrise and sundown, change to red, yellow, blue and pale violet. The singularity of these formations that look like casts, but that instead are limestone and kieselguhr, make this land an absolutely unbeatable place for deep philosophical contemplation. A short distance from here, an expanse of geodes as big as tennis balls announce "Crystal Mountain," a cave with stalactites and stalagmites opened up following the movement of the earth's crust and now showing extraordinary crystalline formations. And then you will find the Black Desert, a stretch of volcanic cones of iron pyrite that rise majestically like natural pyramids. Instead, in Gilf Kebir, we find the Glass Desert, a shining expanse of crystallized silicon formed after the impact of an enormous meteorite when the earth was young. Finally, on your way back, you can go into the Qattara depression that in the quaternary period was a seafloor where crumbling limestone, due to erosion, suddenly reveals fossils of shells, shark teeth, sea urchins and coral: don't miss this gran finale before you get back onto the paved road that will take you, blazing through the desert, straight to Cairo.

Internet site www.egypt.travel

When to go *From October to April.*

How long to stay *2-3 weeks.*

Organization *The main international tour operators specialized in 4x4s in the Sahara propose various itineraries here. Among them, we recommend Badawiya Expedition Travel and Zarzora Expedition. The latter helped Massimo Foggini when he discovered "his" cave.*

Advice *Sleeping in a tent (or, even better, weather permitting) on the dunes is one of the most magical desert experiences. But treat yourself to spending a night in Adrère Amellal, a fabulous ecolodge at the gates of Siwa: built using traditional materials, it looks like a rocky monastery and a giant sand castle at the same time.*

Curiosities

- *Mentioned in a few 15th century manuscripts, Zerzura is a legendary city in the Libyan desert described as "white as a dove" and rich with precious treasures. The search for this lost oasis has been (and still is) an obsession for explorers and archeologists all over the world (László Almásy even tried). But, up until now, every attempt has been in vain.*

- *Equipped with an irrigation system made of canals called* foggaret, *the Siwa oasis also hosts the ghost city Shali. Built with* karshif *(a mud and dry grass paste gathered along the banks of the nearby salt lake) in the 13th century, it was inhabited until 1926, when a series of torrential downpours literally melted it: what is left today is truly poetic beauty.*

- *According to historian Erodoto, Cambyses II, son of the Persian king Cyrus the Great, sent 50,000 soldiers from Thebes to Siwa to destroy the oracle at the Temple of Ammon. But this enormous army was buried by a sand storm and the mystery of the missing Cambyses army has impassioned generations of archeologists: in 2009, an Italian mission discovered the remains of shields and spears near Wadi Abdel Melik.*

97 *The black desert near Bahariya.*

IN THE OMO VALLEY

From Mursi to Karo, all the way to Hamar: travel among the many peoples of Ethiopia's "human museum" and discover the origins of our civilization.

| 98 *A Mursi woman with labial plate.* | 99 *The village Korcho, on the Omo river.*

In 1980, UNESCO declared the Lower Omo Valley a World Heritage Site with the motivation that no other place on this planet hosts such a large number and variety of genetically and linguistically diverse people in such a small area. There are 8 ethnicities here – in turn divided into just as many subgroups, for a total of 200,000 individuals – that live on pasturing, hunting and sustenance farming based on the cultivation of sorghum and corn on lands made fertile by the receding waters of the river during the dry season. They follow ancestral rituals and adorn themselves to express their social status and their tribal membership: they style their hair with a paste made of animal fat and clay, practice scarification on their chests, loins and faces, wearing ornaments of glass beads and bone and color their bodies by covering them with tar, limestone, red and ochre clay and their only modern convenience are the plastic jars used to gather water. Paleontologists found the oldest human skeleton similar to our own (dated at around 195,000 years ago) and the DNA analysis of the peoples from the Omo Valley suggest that we are all their direct descendants. If there were still any need for evidence – after finding, in Ethiopia, the skeleton of the celebrated Lucy, the Australopithecus that assumed a biped position 3 million years ago – this is even more proof of the fact that the Horn of Africa is the cradle of humanity.

NOT TO MISS

- PAY CLOSE ATTENTION TO THE NATURAL SURROUNDINGS THAT, PROTECTED BY THE **OMO AND MAGO NATIONAL PARKS,** HOSTS DIVERSE ECOSYSTEMS, FROM THE SAVANNAH STUDDED WITH EVERYTHING FROM ACACIA TO FLOODPLAINS, FROM VOLCANIC HILLS TO THE LAST STRETCH OF RIPARIAN FOREST IN THE CONTINENT'S SEMIARID LATITUDES. THE CREATION OF THE TWO PROTECTED AREAS AND THE CONSEQUENT BAN ON HUNTING HAS INCREASED SICKNESSES DUE TO MALNUTRITION.
- **DIMEKA** IS A VILLAGE THAT, ON SATURDAYS, HOSTS THE BIGGEST MARKET IN THE VALLEY. AN EXCELLENT OCCASION TO ADMIRE THE HAMER WOMEN, WHO EXHIBIT ELABORATE HAIRSTYLES AND HEAVY BONE, METAL AND BEADED JEWELRY. INSTEAD, AN THE **CHENCHA MARKET,** ON THE BANKS OF DORZE LAKE, YOU CAN BUY SHAMA, TRADITIONAL COTTON FABRICS COLORED WITH CLAY DIES.
- THERE IS AN ELECTRICAL GENERATOR, A WI-FI CONNECTION AND RUNNING WATER IN **LUMALE,** THE MOST MODERN AND CONFORTABLE TENT CAMP IN THE VALLEY. AT A RIVER BEND, IT IS A PERFECT BASE FOR EXPLORING THE SURROUNDING TERRITORIES.
- NEAR **AWASSA,** ALMOST AT THE BORDER WITH THE KENYAN REGION OF TURKANA LAKE, YOU CAN WATCH THE CURIOUS RITUAL OF THE **"SINGING WELLS":** BORANA MEN GATHER WATER FROM DEEP HOLES, PASSING ALONG BUCKETS AND SINGING A HYPNOTIC MELODY.

From here in the Omo Valley, between 120,000 and 60,000 years ago, groups migrated toward Arabia and would then populate the planet, while those that remained subdivided themselves into the 14 genetic groups that all Africans descend from. At the beginning of Italian colonization – that, however, never reached the southern extremes of Ethiopia – the anthropologist and linguist Carlo Conti Rosselli described the Lower Omo Valley as "a human museum." Although this definition is still valid and widely used by tourism operators, today it should pose moral concern, because a trip here is a safari where humans are observed in the same way wild animals are observed elsewhere. You should always remember this, and make sure your adventure in this exceptional place is organized responsibly. Besides, those who find the fact that the tribe members ask for money to be photographed should remember that we are the ones responsible for this "bad habit." And then, a few birr (the weak Ethiopian currency) are a modest price to pay for the privilege of taking a glimpse in, and maybe understanding, how we were at the dawn of our human civilization. On their part, the first to understand that whites could become a source of economic sustenance - and those most aggressive in taking a fee for being seen - are the Mursi, noted for their woman's habit of putting a flat wooden or terracotta disk in their lower lip. Seen as the supreme example of an "uncontaminated" primitive condition, in reality, this practice has become much more common over the last few decades, i.e. when western tourists started considering it interesting. In the same way, the Karo – who, with 1,000 individuals, are the smallest tribe on the continent – practice the bull jump, the traditional test of courage among the males of the community, has become a performance especially done for eager visitors. This doesn't mean it is less true: simply that contact with western civilizations has made it so they changed they way this ritual is performed. Besides, the whole of these small and large changes are not anything but the what we call "progress" and that, starting from the hunter-gatherers that inhabited the Horn of Africa 100,000 years ago, made us into who we are today. And today, there are those who realize – like the NGO Survival International – that maybe "progress" isn't all it's cracked up to be: they are doing everything they can to stop Ethiopia from building the largest damn on the continent across the gorgeous Omo River.

| **101** *The Karo paint their bodies and faces with white clay, iron dust and ashes.*

Although the Ethiopian government has assured that, once completed, it will release water in such a was as to recreate the right environment for traditional agriculture, it is quite probable that the "human museum" disappears forever, in the name of progress. This is how the entire population of Ethiopia, one of the porest countries in the world, will have electricity and won't have to depend on the rains to cultivate the food necessary for its survival.

Internet site www.tourismethiopia.gov.et

When to go *The dry season, between June and September, is when the roads are in the best condition and it is easiest to reach remote villages. January and February, after the seasonal harvest, are the months when most traditional ceremonies are held: prepare yourself for mud and a torrid climate.*

How long to stay *Between 1 and 2 weeks.*

Organization *The best international tour operators specialized in African adventures propose trips in the Lower Omo Valley. Among these, a particular mention goes to Origins Safaris, located in Nairobi, which distinguishes itself for the anthropological education of their guides and for their profound knowledge of the territory. Among the local operators, we recommend EthioGuzo Tour and Travel that has indigenous personnel from the valley.*

Advice *You should know that this is a very tiring trip: expect long and unexpected off-road trips and sleeping in tents or guesthouses with bone-minimum comidites. Antimalarial treatments are advised.*

Curiosities

At the age of 15, Mursi women cut their lower lip where they insert little plates that, little by little over time, they increase in size (up to 12 centimeters). Called dhebi a tugoin, *the labial plate is the expression of reaching the age of reproduction.*

Among the Karo, children born outside of marriage, twins and babies who grow a top tooth before a bottom tooth are called mingi. Considered bad luck for the entire community, they are killed by the eldest in ritual ceremonies or are left to die of hunger. To prevent this infanticide, the Ethiopian government has instituted a register of pregnancies at the clinic in Dus.

The first European to meet the peoples of the Lower Omo Valley was, in 1895, the Italian explorer Vittorio Bottego as he went up river from Turkana Lake.

THE GREAT WILDEBEEST MIGRATION

From Serengeti to Maasai Mara, the cyclical voyage of the wildebeest in the search for green pastures is the animal kingdom's most thrilling "mass event."

According to a Maasai legend, God created the wildebeest using parts left over from the other animals. Called the "clown of the savannah" for their awkward appearance and swaying gait, this bovid is the protagonist of one of the biggest natural spectables, the cyclical voyage in search of green pastures in the enormous Serengeti ecosystem, that includes the National Park, in Tanzania, and the plains of Maasai Mara, in Kenya. There are around 1.5 million wildebeests, together with 250,000 zebras and just about the same number of gazelles that partake in the great migration that follows the annual schedule of the rains clockwise around triangular pattern of 2500 kilometers, starting from the Ngorongoro crater in the south all the way to the banks of Lake Victoria in the north and back. Their trip is full of danger: there are a great number of predators waiting along the way (from lions to enormous crocodiles, from hyenas to the vultures that complete the job), so much that the great migration is, above all, a macroscopic representation of the epic struggle for survival. This is even more evident when considering the obstacles they must overcome: with crocodiles waiting to ambush them from the waters and the great felines stationed not far away, crossing the Grumeti River, between June and July, is the animal kingdom's most thrilling and cruel "mass event."

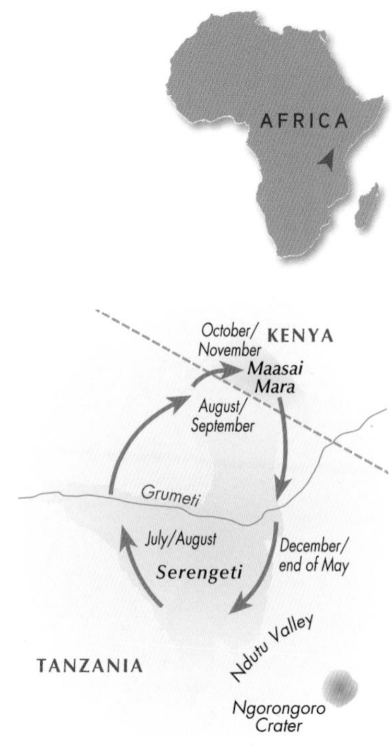

Internet site www.serengeti.org

NOT TO MISS

- BETWEEN THE NGORONGORO CRATER AND THE SERENGETI, **NDUTU VALLEY** IS, IN A CERTAIN SENSE, THE WILDEBEESTS' "HOME." THEY SPEND 3 MONTHS HERE, FROM JANUARY TO MARCH, FINALLY FULL, AND IT IS HERE THAT THEY GIVE BIRTH TO CUBS. EVERY YEAR AROUND 250,000 ARE BORN, ALL IN THE ARC OF 3 WEEKS.
- FEEL THE EMOTIONS OF WATCHING THE GREAT MIGRATION FROM THE SKY, ABOARD A **HOT AIR BALLOON:** SERENGETI BALOON SAFARIS HAS 6 OF THEM IN THE CENTRAL AND WESTERN PARTS, AND SEASONALLY IN THE SOUTH OF THE PARK. THEY ORGANIZE EXCURSIONS THAT LEAVE AT DAWN, ENDING AT 9:30 WITH A SAVANNAH BREAKFAST JUST LIKE IN *OUT OF AFRICA*.

| **102** *A herd of zebra drink from a watering hole during the migration in the Serengeti.*

| 103 *Around 1.5 million wildebeests annually migrate across the Mara River.*

Precisely due to their "walking lifestyle," wildebeests are the main tile in the complex mosaic of the Savannah ecosystem. They are an abundant source of food for predators and, eating the grass (around 4000 tons a day!), they clean the ground that, fertilized by their excrement (420 tons a day), will be ready to grow more. Scholars have still not been able to understand how this great migration happens following an unchanged route since the beginning of time. Maybe it is instinct, since no one believes that the wildebeests are able to smell the rain from hundreds of kilometers away? Maybe it is "acquired knowledge," since the little ones are taken on a "guided visit" by their mothers in their first year of life? Or maybe it is their utilitarian alliance with zebras – a species that belongs to another family – that have an extraordinarily developed sense of sight? And then, why haven't their predators acquired the ability to follow their migration along the entire route? All these questions remain unanswered, for now. But maybe this is precisely what, in our eyes, makes this perpetual voyage of the circle of life and death even more magical.

Organization *The best destinations for observing the great migration are Grumeti Camp, in June-July, near the river of the same name in the Serengeti National Park, and Governers' Camp, in September-October, near the Mara Rivier, inside the Maasai Mara Reserve. Both propose off-road safaris and other activities in nature. All international tour operators specialized in African safaris organize trips to the Serengeti and in Maasai Mara coinciding with the great migration.*

When to go *The great migration never stops, and it is up to you to decide where to go based on the "when" listed on the map. In the Serengeti, the rainy season is between March and April and between October and November (while, although unpredictable, in the Maasai Mara rains are much less strong), but even the experience of a violent downpour in the Savannah – and the rainbow that follows – merits a visit.*

How long to stay *1 or 2 weeks.*

ON THE FIANARANTSOA-CÔTE EST RAILWAY

It is only 163 kilometers long, but with 67 bridges and 48 tunnels, the formidable landscapes and unexpected surprises make it one of the most spectacular railways in the world.

On the map, the train ride from Fianarantsoa, the Malagasy wine capital at an altitude of 1200 meters, on the eastern coast, lasts 8-10 hours. But in Africa, we all know, time is crazy variable in every equation. Here the unexpected is the norm, whether it be engine failure, a herd of cattle or a family of lemurs stopped on the tracks. On the other hand, these stops let you process the adrenaline caused by a ride like that of a rollercoaster, that in 163 kilometers has 67 bridges and 48 tunnels, one of which is a kilometer long. The tracks were laid between 1926 and 1936 by the French, using materials discarded from an Alsatian railway.

From the window, the landscape is enchanting and goes from forests to cliffs and waterfalls, from banana cultivations and rice paddies to the expanses of *ravinala,* a plant called the "travelers' tree." And life aboard is just as interesting. The train has 3 cars, one first class and two second, with only 1 toilet. You should bring some water and a heavy coat because the windows don't have any glass. As far as food is concerned, every station offers a gourmet experience: in Ampitabe, the ambulant sellers have spiced grilled chicken, in Ranomena they have fried shrimp, in Tolongonia fried bananas, and so on.

| **104** *The Fianarantsoa-Côte Est railway was built by the French between 1926 and 1936.*

NOT TO MISS

- FIANARANTSOA IS SURROUNDED BY VINEYARDS. TO TASTE (DECENT) REDS, WHITES AND ROSÉS, GO TO THE **MAROMBY TRAPPIST MONASTERY.**
- FOR THE FIRST 20 KM, UNTIL **SAHAMBAVY,** TAKE THE "MICHELINE," A KIND OF MOTORIZED CAR ON THE TRACKS BUILD IN THE '30S BY MICHELIN FOR THE FIANARANTSOA-CÔTE EST.
- A 1-2 DAY STOPOVER IN SAHAMBAVY ALLOWS YOU TO SEE THE ONLY TEA PLANTATION IN THE COUNTRY AND STAY AT THE DELICIOUS **LAC HOTEL.**
- MANAKARA IS THE STARTING POINT FOR A TOUR ALONG THE WATERWAYS OF THE **CANAL DES PANGALANES** THAT EXTENDS PARALLEL TO THE CÔTE EST THROUGH VANILLA PLANTATIONS.

| **105** *Fianarantsoa's lands are characterized by interesting agricultural products.*

Although it is a passenger train, locals use it to take their products to the coast to buy rice, which is the base of their diets. Every year, over 3000 tons of coffee and 6000 of fruit are transported and, it goes without saying, it takes a whole lot of time to load and unload all of those goods!

In 2000, violent rains caused over 280 mass landslides along the railway, completely interrupting railway service. International studies had shown that the sustenance of over 100,000 people depend on the trade of foodstuffs with the coast and that, without this precious lifeline, there would have soon been wide deforestation for growing rice in the area. They had therefore retained the restoration of the railway crucial to the local economy and environmental protection. So, it was brought back up and working almost immediately thanks to generous financing from the United States and Swiss Railways, while Thailand sent a team of agronomists who, on the slopes on the side of the tracks, started vast cultivations of vetiver, a useful and efficient plant for preventing soil erosion.

When to go *The austral winter, between April and November, corresponds to the dry season, with pleasurable temperatures.*

Timetable *The train leaves Fianarantsoa Tuesday, Thursday and Saturday at 7 in the morning. A first class ticket costs 25,000 Ariay (9 Euro), while second class costs 13,000 Ariary (4.80 Euro).*

Organization *The "do-it-yourself" trip is easy, but most local tour operators propose this railway itinerary.*

Advice *The best places for admiring the landscape are on the left side of the car.*

Internet site www.madagascar-tourisme.com

ALONG THE KARAKORUM HIGHWAY

You have to admit it: its a little dangerous. But the "vertical road" that goes through Khunjerab Pass to arrive to Kashgar is a mythical trip.

Founded in 1853 by Major James Abbot, Abbottabad was the English district capital of Hazara of the Raj. Once the epoch of the immense and glorious colonial empire passed, it would remain an anonymous, dusty little town, until May 2011 when an American special forces unit flushed out and killed the most wanted man on the planet there, Osama Bin Laden. Based on what was leaked in the international press, he was living undisturbed in Wahaziri Haveli, a luxurious compound hidden behind high walls of raw earth, probably protected by the complicity, or simply the silence, of the local population. Abbottabad is also the place where, technically, the Karakorum Highway begins, the highway (even if this term should be taken with a grain of salt because, often, it is a single-lane strip of asphalt, when its not interrupted by landslides) created in 1980 that holds the record as the highest road that corsses and international border: the one a short distance from Khunjerab Pass, at an elevation of 4693 meters, between Pakistan and China. The road reaches the border after having run most of its 1250 kilometers through Pakistani Kashmir, the tribal zone Northwest Frontier, "with no roof nor law" (confining with Afghanistan) and then the most turbulent Chinese province, Xinjiang, where the majority of the population is Muslim and is often subject to violent requests for autonomy.

| 106 *A stretch of the Karakorum Highway on the Pamir plateau, in China.*

NOT TO MISS

● PERSIAN IN ORIGIN, AND MUCH APPRECIATED BY THE BRITISH, POLO IS A POPULAR SPORT IN PAKISTAN. IN **GILGIT** THERE ARE VARIOUS POLO FIELDS AND THE ONE IN **SHANDUR,** AT 3700 METERS, IS THE HIGHEST IN THE WORLD. IN GILGIT THERE ARE MATCHES NEARLY EVERY DAY AND, ON THE FIRST WEEK OF JULY, SHANDUR IS THE MARVELOUS SETTING FOR THE TRADITIONAL SHANDUR POLO FESTIVAL.

● GILGIT IS ALSO THE STARTING POINT FOR MOUNTAIN TREKKING AND OFF-ROAD ADVENTURES IN THE REMOTE **CHITRAL VALLEY,** POPULATED BY THE KALASH ETHNIC GROUP THAT, IN MUSLIM TERRITORY, HAS MAINTAINED THEIR PAGAN AND POLYTHEISTIC BELIEFS. THEY EVEN PRODUCE WINE.

● SPEND A COUPLE OF DAYS IN **HUNZA VALLEY,** CONSIDERED THE MOST EXOTIC DESTINATION IN PAKISTAN: IN THE CAPITAL, **KARIMABAD,** YOU SHOULD SEE THE SPLENDIDLY RESTORED BALTIT FORT, AND THE MARKET (KNOWN FOR ITS EMBROIDERED FABRICS).

● ON THE BANKS OF LAKE **KARAKUL,** AT THE FEET OF THE MUZTAGH ATA, YOU CAN STAY IN THE NOMADIC KIRGHIZI'S YURTS. HOSPITALITY IN THIS EXTRAORDINARY MOBILE FELT ARCHITECTURE IS WARM AND IT IS WORTH THE EFFORT TO SPEAK WITH A FAMILY PATRIARCH TO ORGANIZE A WALK OR HORSE RIDE THROUGH PAMIR, REACHING THEIR SUMMER CAMPS WHERE THEY GO TO PASTURE THEIR FLOCKS.

| **107** *A view of the Hunza Valley, famous for its inhabitants, among the most long-lived on the planet.*

If you add to that the fact that, since September 11th, 2001, Pakistan is at the top of the list of the most dangerous countries in the world, you might think that an on the road adventure along the Karakorum Highway should be put off for a bit, at least until the threat of Islamic extremism is replaced by an era of peace and harmony. Or, more likely, by another bogeyman. Instead, the aura of danger, more ideal than real, adds charm to a journey that traces one of the main itineraries of the ancient Silk Road and has been the main theater of The Great Game, term coined by writer and adventurer Rudyard Kipling in his novel *Kim* to describe the intense activity of exploration and intrigue that, for the whole of the second half of the 1800s, sent the secret services of the British Raj and the Russian Empire to these lands with the intention of dominating Central Asia.

From Rawalpindi, the city adjacent to the Pakistani capital Islamabad that is the most obvious starting point for a trip, the landscape wildly climbs straight up following the turbulent course of the Indo and then turns around Karakorum, the mountain range (itself a part of the Himalayas) that boasts an unparalleled concentration of the highest mountains in the world. So, along the way, you will find yourself in the presence of the legendary K2, Nanga Parbat, Gasherbrum and the nearly incongruous flat walls of the apparently sweet Muztagh Ata that, actually in Chinese territory, dominates the Pamir plateau. And if the natural environment here is exceptional, the inhabited centers are no less so, whether they are small villages or ancient centers of culture and tradition, like Gilgit, that before becoming the home of one of the richest Khanates in this part of the Silk Road, it was one of the cradles of Buddhism, or Karimabad, home of the Ismaili Muslim sect whose leader is Prince Aga Khan and located in the middle of the splendid Hunza Valley, famous for its apricot orchards. Also, crossing the border con China, you will find yourself in front of the imposing and magical earthen fortress Tashkorgan before descending from Pamir to reach the merited finish line, Kashgar. Inhabited by Islamic peoples of the Uyrghur ethnic group, every Sunday since time immemorial it hosts the largest and most fascinating caravan market in all Central Asia. Here goats, snow leopard skins, magnificent silks and Turkmen rugs are sold. Right next to the newfangled products *made in China.*

When to go *From May to the beginning of October.*

How long to stay *The whole trip takes about 30 hours, but plan on at least 1 week to make the trip stopping along the way.*

Organization *Even if many international tour operators propose itineraries in small groups along the Karakorum Highway aboard tourist buses, we think that the "protected environment" of an organized trip takes most of the charm out of this adventure, without however diminishing the risks. Its better to use public transportation like the locals: from Pakistan to China go to the Rawalpindi bus station (vice versa, go to Kashgar) where various public and private transportation companies make 4 or 5 trips each day to Gilgit (about a 20 hour trip); from there to Sust, where crossing the border (on foot), more buses go to Kashgar, via Tashkorgan. For each of the lengths, you can buy tickets, at ridiculous prices for a westerner, just before departure and this will give you the freedom to stop at the various intermediary points for as long as necessary to visit them and to take excursions into the mountains.*

Advice *Pack light (you will have to put your luggage onto the bus roof yourself) but bring a sleeping bag and clothing suitable for the frigid nights of a high altitude climate. Avoid military style clothing or clothing with American flags on it.*

Internet site www.tourism.gov.pk

Curiosities

- *Discovered in 1931 by a sheep herder, the Gilgit Buddhist manuscripts date back to the 5th century. Written in Sanskrit on birch wood, they contain the celebrated Lotus Sutra, believed to be the original transcription of the speech given by Buddha just before his death.*

- *Anthropologists have identified the inhabitants of Hunza Valley as descendants of Macedonian soldiers who arrived here with Alexander the Great: so they are a kind of classical Greek "shipwreck" in Central Asia, testified to also by Gandharan art that, developed here between the 1st century B.C. and the 4th century A.C., is syncretic between Buddhist iconography and themes from Greek mythology.*

- *The Hunza Valley population is one of the longest-lived of the planet. Some scholars believe (although no definitive conclusion has been reached) that this is due to the vitamins and minerals contained in the apricots that grow here. Whatever it is, the apricots are exquisite, either just harvested or dried in the sun.*

| **108** *A Kirghiz nomad near the banks of Lake Karakul, at the feet of the Muztagh Ata.*

ON THE GRAND TRUNK ROAD

Traveling on the great artery between Peshawar and Calcutta, ready to let the stories and chaos of a "moving subcontinent" lead the way.

| 109 *The Golden Temple in Amritsar.*

"Look! Brahmins and chumars, bankers and tinkers, barbers and bunnias, pilgrims and potters - all the world going and coming. It is to me as a river from which I am withdrawn like a log after a flood." Thus wrote the masterful author Rudyard Kipling in his acclaimed novel *Kim*. This picturesque masterpiece was written in the last year of the 19th century, but his description of the largest thoroughfare on the Indian subcontinent is still perfectly accurate today. If anything, the constantly flowing river of people and things is even more impetuous that the one this writer noted over a hundred years ago – although he did forget to mention the cows – and added to this spectacle today we find a procession of employees of the successfully emerging hi-tech and automobile industries and, above all, the multi-colored trucks that, next to lucky religious effigies, have "Horn Please" written in fluttering letters on the back, as if it were necessary to further incite the drivers, all with a easy horn trigger. Moreover, most of it now has four lanes with a concrete divider in the middle, even if it does seems more like a decorative accessory, just like the rest of the traffic signs do. The Grand Trunk Road is 2000 kilometers long, from the caravan city (and Taliban outpost) of Peshawar, along the explosive border between Pakistan and Afghanistan, all the way to Calcutta, the "new city" that was the capital of the British Raj in Indian Bengal.

NOT TO MISS

- IN **PESHAWAR,** LOSE YOURSELF IN THE MARKET HAGGLING FOR JEWELRY AND FABRICS FROM AFGHANISTAN AND VISIT THE PESHAWAR MUSEUM: INAUGURATED IN 1907 AND DEDICATED TO QUEEN VICTORIA, IT HOLDS THE VASTEST AND MOST PRECIOUS COLLECTION OF GANDHARA ART IN THE WORLD, IN A FASCINATING DECADENT-COLONIAL SETTING.
- A TRIP ALONG THE GRAND TRUNK ROAD IS ALSO AN ADVENTURE IN THE SUBCONTINENT'S **REGIONAL GASTRONOMY,** FROM BALTI (IN PAKISTAN) CUISINE'S LAMB SPECIALTIES, TO PANJAB'S TANDOOR OVER TREATS, ALL THE WAY TO VARANASI'S DESSERTS MADE OF MILK AND COVERED IN GOLDEN LEAVES. DON'T BE AFRAID, TRY THEM IN THE LITTLE SHOPS ALONG THE ROAD.
- IT GOES WITHOUT SAYING YOU SHOULD STOP IN LAHORE, AMRITSAR, DELHI, AGRA AND CALCUTTA. AMONG THE LESS FAMOUS CITIES (AT LEAST FROM A TOURISTIC POINT OF VIEW), DON'T MISS OUT ON THE INCREDIBLE **LUDHIANA,** IN PUNJAB (THEY MAKE EVERY INDIAN BICYCLE HERE) AND **LUCKNOW,** THE CAPITAL OF UTTAR PRADESH THAT IS AN ABSOLUTE JEWEL OF ISLAMIC ARCHITECTURE.
- FROM THE HUMAN RIVER OF THE GRAND TRUNK ROAD TO THE RIVER OF INDIA: STOP IN **ALLAHABAD,** WHERE THE GANGES AND THE YAMUNA JOIN AND WHERE, EVERY 12 YEARS, THE **KUMBH MELA** IS HELD, THE LARGEST RELIGIOUS FESTIVAL IN THE WORLD. THEN LET YOURSELF BE TAKEN AWAY BY THE ATMOSPHERE OF THE GHAT, THE STEPS ON THE GANGES IN THE SACRED CITY OF **BENARES** (VARANASI).

However, more than geography, it's history that marks this journey. Although its current name was given to it by the English, Alexander the Great's troops came down over this road, bringing to the Indo plains those echoes of Greek civilization recognizable in the Gandhara Buddhist masterpieces, viewable in Taxila. Then, Maurya soldiers marched down it to found the greatest and most powerful political empire of ancient India. Still again, many centuries later, the Mongols stormed down it from Central Asia and governed over much of what is today Pakistan and along the whole Ganges plains, building their own great architectonic works along the road, from the fort and gardens of Shalimar in Lahore to the palaces and minarets of their capital, Delhi, to the most grandiose monument ever built for love, the Taj Mahal, in Agra. And if it was the Mongols – under the Emporer Sher Shah Suri, at the end of the 15th century – who first mapped the road and delimited it with little minarets as markers, the subcontinent entered into the modern era when the Grand Trunk Road became a Highway under British colonial rule. And today it connects 2 nations – and nuclear powers – opposed and yet very similar. This road can be interpreted as a thread that connects the subcontinent's great religions: from the many places sacred to Islam to the destinations of Hindu pilgrims (of the many, there is Varanasi, sacred to Shiva, the god that creates and destroys), from the Sikh's Golden Temple in Amritsar, all the way to Bodhgaya, the capital of the extremely poor Indian state Bihar, where Buddha was illuminated. Or, more prosaically (because, despite its aura of spirituality, the subcontinent is very material), you should pay attention to the economic activities, from the large ones that make this area of the world one of the most dynamic and aggressive, to the tiny ones of the traveling salesmen along the streets and the ubiquitous *chaiwhalla* stands where this dense and spiced Indian tea is prepared

| 110 *The Taj Mahal.* | 110-111 *The Ghat in Varanasi that lead to the Ganges.*

and served. In the end, however, the Grand Trunk Road should be experienced, immerging yourself in the river of people, sounds, colors (and odors) without the worry of arriving some place, ready to accept and second the unexpected adventures and open to casual encounters that often become extraordinary. The only rule is Kipling's rule: let yourself be swept away like a log in a flood.

Internet site www.tourism.gov.pk and www.incredibleindia.org

When to go *From November to April, during the dry season.*

How long to stay *A lifetime wouldn't be enough!*

Organization *A trip along the Grand Trunk Road (or part of it) should be done using public transportation: in Pakistan and India it passes often, is quite cheap and allows for maximum flexibility. So, organization isn't being organized per se. Besides, India is the most unorganized and chaotic country in the world and yet - inexplicably - everything works great in the end!*

Advice *Pack light. If you travel at night, you'll need earplugs: bus drivers blast Bollywood film music at high volume 24/7.*

Curiosities

The Grand Trunk Road owes its name to the large banyan trees that, during the Raj, delimited its route. Today there are not many of those secular giants left, but along many parts of the road there are lines of eucalyptus and acacia trees.

India is the second producer of automobiles in the world, after China. However, according to estimates, thanks to companies like Tata and Mahindra, they will pass China in the next ten years. It is predicted that by 2050 over 611 million automobiles will travel on Indian roads.

At the end, in Calcutta, the Grand Trunk Road crosses the Howrah Bridge that, build with 26,000 tons of steel and inaugurated in 1942, was dedicated to the Nobel Prize winning writer Rabindranath Tagore in 1965. Everyday over 100,000 vehicles and 200,000 pedestrians cross here, making it the most trafficked bridge in the world.

AMONG THE ETHNICITIES OF LUANG NAM THA

Internet site www.tourismlaos.org

From the Hmong to the Akha, from the Tai Dai to the Yao: northern Laos has the province with the highest number of ethnic minorities in Southeast Asia.

Saying "tell me how you dress and I'll tell you who you are" could be a snobby thing that a fashion nut would say. But that's not how it is in northern Laos, delimited by the Mekong River and its borders with Myanmar and the Chinese province Yunnan: only the Luang Nam Tha province has 145,000 inhabitants that belong to 39 different ethnicities (without counting the many subgroups), and each one of them loves to show their uniqueness, starting with their clothing. Among the Hmong – who are the largest group – children learn at a very young age the art of Paj Ntaub, i.e. the embroidery they use to reproduce in bright colors the elaborate motifs associated with every subgroup and even with every family: the Hmoob Txaij women – literally "white Hmong" – wear candid clothes with black stitching (but the list could go on and on), while all the Hmong ornate their headdresses and jackets with silver and pearl coins as a symbol of wealth.

| **112** *Hmong women harvesting tobacco leaves.*

| 113 *A Hmong woman in traditional dress at the market.*

Among the other ethnicities, the Lanten are also called Indago, because they wear clothes dyed with it and even their skin assumes a blue hue, while the Tai Dam wear black and are noted for their ability to weave silk. But a trip to this area is not only an excursus into ethnic fashion: every group – and they all live in such close proximity that from the little town Luang Nam Tha, in just one day, you can visit at least 7 villages, each with strongly characteristic architecture – has different habits, customs and religious practices, combining Buddhism and even Taoism with ancestral shamanic rites. All this takes place in an environment of idyllic landscapes that alternate between little rice paddies, sandstone hills and the lush Luang Nam Tha National Park, one of the most extensive areas of protected virgin forest in Southeast Asia.

NOT TO MISS

- STOP AT LEAST A COUPLE OF DAYS IN **LUANG NAM THA:** TO GET AN IDEA OF THE MELTING POT, GO TO THE EVENING MARKET WHERE THE VARIOUS ETHNIC GROUPS PREPARE THE EXOTIC SPECIALTIES OF THEIR CUISINE. THERE IS NO BETTER PLACE THAN THIS FOR ETHNO-SHOPPING, WHERE YOU FIND FABRICS, SILVER AND MUCH MORE. AND YOU HAVE TO HAGGLE.
- IT TAKES 3 HOURS IN A CAR (OR A BIT MORE IN PUBLIC TRANSPORTATION) TO GO FROM LUANG NAM THA TO **MUANG SING,** THE LARGE VILLAGE NEAR THE CHINESE BORDER. IN THE AREA, VISIT THE VARIOUS HMONG, YAO, TAI DAM, AKHA AND LANTEN COMMUNITIES.
- TREK THROUGH THE **LUANG NAM THA NATIONAL PARK:** ACCOMPANIED BY A GUIDE, YOU WILL SEE ELEPHANTS, VARIOUS SPECIES OF MACAQUES, GAURS (A RARE ASIAN BOVINE) AND, IF YOU'RE REALLY LUCKY, EVEN SPOTTED LEOPARDS AND TIGERS. FOR A GUIDED TREK, SEE ECOTOURISM LAOS.

When to go *From November to April*

How long to stay *1 or 2 weeks.*

Organization *Northern Laos is a perfect destination for a do-it-yourself adventure, even if it is better to have a "cultural mediator" when you visit the villages. The tourism office in Laung Nam Tha and Nam Ha Ecoguides offer affordable guides. If you prefer an organized vacation, we recommend Lao Youth Travel, Exotissimo and Tiger Trail Laos.*

Advice *Northern Laos is an extremely tranquil place with hospitable people and relaxing landscapes, so you might want to consider a prolonged stay. After having explored the Luang Nam Tha province, continue toward the adjacent Bokeo that is just as rich from a cultural point of view and even wilder from a natural point of view. Here, Bokeo Nature Reserve, one of the last habitats of the crested gibbon, is only accessible through Gibbon Experience, managed by an indigenous community that offers forest treks and extremely charming vacations in wooden cabins built in the treetops.*

IN THE LAND OF GENGHIS KHAN

From Ulaanbaatar to Gobi, from Kharkhorin to the Khentii region, travel off-road in the footsteps of the legendary leader. And his heratige.

When you go into a ger, you have to follow the etiquette of the nomad herders: a wrong move could irritate the evil spirits and have catastrophic consequences. So, when you go into the great felt tents where the Mongols live, make sure you don't step on the threshold and don't brush up against the poles that support the structure and, when leaving, move clockwise around the stove at the center of the ger. The main rule, however, is to never refuse anything that you are offered, even if it's difficult to get used to the flavor of airag, fermented mare milk, or aaruul, curd left to dry until it becomes as hard as a rock. Besides, these modest requests are part of the extraordinary experience of Mongol life. Stopping every night in ger camp, you travel on barely visible paths over an immense territory, starting from the alienating "cement camp" that is the capital Ulaanbaatar to discover, in the south, the Gobi (an extremely varied desert, where just 5% is made up of sand dunes) or, in the steppes at the heart of the country, the Khustain Nuuru National Reserve, instituted to protect the takhi, the legendary Mongolian horses that were the a fundamental part of the conquests of the even more legendary leader, Genghis Khan.

| **114** *Camels are thought to be originally from the Gobi Desert.*

NOT TO MISS

- A SHORT DISTANCE FROM KHARKHORIN, THE SMALL CITY NEAR GENGHIS KHAN'S ANCIENT CAPITAL, YOU WILL FIND **ERDENE ZUU,** THE MOST IMPORTANT BUDDHIST MONASTERY IN MONGOLIA, FOUNDED IN 1568 AND RICH IN PRECIOUS ARTWORK. TODAY, THE COUNTRY IS GOING THROUGH A BUDDHIST RENAISSANCE AND 30 MONKS INHABIT THE MONASTERY.

- GENGHIS KHAN'S FACE APPEARS ON ALL THE CURRENCY IN MONGOLIA, AND THE ULAANBAATAR AIRPORT AS WELL AS MANY PUBLIC BUILDINGS ARE DEDICATED TO THE "WOLF OF THE STEPPES." **ERDENE,** SITUATED ALONG THE ROAD THAT GOES FROM THE CAPITAL TO THE GOBI, DESERVES A STOP IN ORDER TO SEE THE **HORSE STATUE** OF THE LEADER ERECTED IN 2006 TO CELEBRATE HIS 800TH BIRTHDAY: IT WEIGHS 250 TONS AND IS 40 METERS HIGH.

- AT THE EDGE OF THE GOBI, THE SÜKHBAATAR PROVINCE IS A LUNAR LANDSCAPE LITTERED WITH 180 EXTINCT VOLCANOES: TREK NORTH TO THE **EDGE OF THE SHILIN BOGD CRATER,** CONSIDERED SACRED, AND THEN HEAD TOWARD GANGA NUUR, A LAKE SURROUNDED BY EXTREMELY HIGH SAND DUNES.

- A "MUST-BUY" IS A CASHMERE HAT: THE MOST SOUGHT-AFTER WOOL IS MADE FROM THE TENS OF MILLIONS OF SHEEP THAT GRAZE IN THE MONGOLIAN STEPPES. THE MAIN COMPANY THAT WORKS THIS WOOL IS **GOBI CASHMERE,** WHICH HAS AN OUTLET AT THE DOORS OF THE CAPITAL.

| **115** *The Gobi Desert is mostly steppes and dry flats, the sand limited to a few areas: the main one is in Alashan.*

Considered a Mongolian hero and the glue of national identity, the leader still lives in the few, but fascinating, ruins of the ancient Kharkhorin, the capital of the Mongolian Empire established in 1235 by his third son, in the eastern Khentii area, where it is said that Genghis Khan was buried in what is today the Gurvan Nuur National Reserve: it is believed that the 1000 warriors sacrificed after his funeral in order to guarantee the secrecy of his tomb are buried here on the banks of the Kheren River. If the search for the scarce historical evidence that testifies to Genghis Khan is a perfect excuse to travel through untouched Mongolian nature, his heritage is clear in the Naadam, the "Mongolian Olympics" that are held every year between the 12th and 14th of July in a field not far from the capital. Between horse races, wrestling and archery contests, the "arms" that lead to the construction of the vastest empire in history, from the Black Sea to China, are celebrated.

When to go *From May to September*

How long to stay *3 weeks.*

Organization *Of the tour operators that propose motorized vacations, we recommend Open Tour Around Mongolia and Steppe Nomad Travel & Tours.*

Advice *Want to start your trip in Mongolia with an adventure? Instead of flying, you can reach Ulaanbaatar by train from Beijing, along the mind-blowing Transmongolian Line that follows the old tea caravan route, active between the 18th and 19th centuries. The trip lasts (around) 30 hours and can be booked through the Chinese tourist agency CITS.*

Internet site www.mongoliatourism.gov.mn

IN THE KINGDOM OF THE LUGU HU WOMEN

A journey to the banks of a lake hidden in the Yunnan Mountians to experience the feminine side of the Mosuo people.

In the Mosuo's language, there are no words to express the concepts of "father," "husband" or "war." It is this ethnicity that lives on the banks of the Lugu River (or Lugu Hu, In Chinese), at an altitude of 2685 meters on the border between Yunnan and Sichuan provinces, where the last matriarchal society on earth survives. Women don't hold exclusive power but they transmit family lineage since the Mosuo have never had any institution similar to marriage: they prefer the status of "permanent lover," called Zou hun, or a "walking marriage," according to which women are free to have sexual relations, welcoming men into their homes, but only for one night. To cover the distance between this female arcadia and Lijiang, a pearl of tourism in Yunnan, it takes 6-8 bus hours along a narrow road that crosses mountains covered in conifers, rhododendrons, deep canyons cut by silver waters, and prairies of grazing yaks. Although arriving in Luoshui, the main village of Lugu Hu, can be disappointing – it's a collection of neo-classical buildings, karaoke and guesthouses for Chinese tourists hoping to get lucky – all you have to do is go to the lakefront to be enchanted by the scene of the Himalayan peaks reflecting in the water and by the interesting Mosuo customs. Quite hospitable, they invite visitors to ride in the *zhucaochuan,* their traditional canoes, to take them to the "kingdom of women" and discover the green islands that dot the turquoise lake.

| **116** *Mosuo women on the banks of Lugu, situated on the border with Sichuan province.*
| **117** *A pagoda in the Deyue pavilion in Lijiang.*

NOT TO MISS

- THE STARTING POINT OF THE ADVENTURE IS **LIJIANG,** A ROMANTIC CITY WITH FAIRYTALE PAGODA ARCHITECTURE, AN IMPORTANT STOP ALONG THE ANCIENT "TEA ROAD." IT IS PROTECTED BY UNESCO AS A WORLD HERITAGE SITE.
- ALONG THE ROAD BETWEEN LIJIANG AND THE LAKE, STOP TO TREK AT **TIGER LEAPING GORGE,** ONE OF THE DEEPEST AND MOST SPECTACULAR CANYONS IN THE WORLD. IT IS THE HIGHER PART OF THE YANGTZE RIVER WITH A SERIES OF VERTICAL DROPS AND WATERFALLS.
- THE MOSUO PRACTICE DABA, A RELIGION THAT MIXES BUDDHISM AND SHAMANISM: DON'T MISS THE LAMA'S **TEMPLE** ON **LIWUBI ISLAND.**
- YOU JUST HAVE TO PHOTOGRAPH THE MOSUO WOMEN WHEN, ABOARD CANOES, THEY PROTECT THEMSELVES FROM THE SUN WITH THEIR TYPICAL HATS LIKE ABAT-JOURS WHILE GATHERING FLOWERS FORM THE FLOATING PLANTS.

When to go *Lugu Hu has an eternal spring climate. However, in the winter, the road can be blocked by snow on the 3 mountain passes.*

How long to stay *1 week.*

Organization *From Lijiang it is easy to organize an independent trip. Destination reached, Mosuo villages offer hospitality, even to male foreigners. The tour operator Yunnan Adventure proposes an ethnographic tour that combines off-road trips with brief treks and boat rides.*

Advice *Go soon, before the lake changes forever: the Chinese government plans to build an airport in Luoshui.*

Internet site www.mosuoproject.org

WILD HOKKAIDO

Light years from Tokyo's skyscrapers, the northeastern part of the island is the reign of an incredible natural environment. And the mysterious Ainu people.

They live off fishing but they have a particular fondness for bear meat, they have squat bodies and light skin. The men always sport thick, long beards and the women tattoo the corners of their mouths and palms of their hands as a sign of beauty. They wear clothes woven from a fiber obtained from the bark of a elm tree and sewn with fish skin. Their origins are a mystery and recent DNA studies tie them to Southeast Asia and Tibet. They are the Ainu and, according to official estimates, number around 25,000, even if only a small part of them have not been assimilated into Japanese modernity yet: now, there are only 100 people who can still speak their ancestral language and even fewer still follow the traditional shamanic religion. Their enclave is the peninsula on the northeast of the big island Hokkaido: facing the Okhotsk Sea, this is a vast area with a formidable natural beauty, light years away from the futuristic Japan in our collective imagination. Here mountains, forests and nearly arctic tundra host rich fauna and a series of water-

Internet site http://en.visit-hokkaido.jp

| **118** *Manchurian cranes dance on the ice plains of Hokkaido Island.*

| **119** *The Okhotsk Sea reaches a depth of 3521 meters.*

falls and lakes, including Akan Lake, which is the habitat of a phenomenal vegetal curiosity, the marimo (or torasanpe, "lake phantom," in Ainu), a floating algae the shape and size of a tennis ball. After all, however, even the wildest destinations in Hokkaido are shaped by the proverbial Japanese determination. So much that every angle, even the most remote, is easily reachable with a rental car or even on high-speed trains. And, in a week's stay, it is possible to cross the Shiretoko National Park, following the mountain path of one of the most panoramic drivable roads in the country, reach the Ainu settlements and spend a couple of days in Abashiri, a small city on the Okhotsk Sea where you can experience a tour on an icebreaker.

When to go *The northeaster part of Hokkaido is splendid in every season. If you're not afraid of the cold, go in the winter.*

How long to stay *1 or 2 weeks.*

Organization *Apart from linguistic difficulties, a trip to these parts is doable independently. If you chose the train, you should buy the convenient Japan Rail Pass before leaving, valid for 7, 14 or 21 days. Alternatively, once you arrive on the island, the Hokkaido Rail Pass, valid 3, 4, 5 or 7 days: both allow an unlimited number of trips while valid. If you prefer an organized tour, the Japanese operator BFH Tours is specialized in custom vacations on the island, with rental car.*

Advice *Over the course of a year, there is only one period when it is absolutely no recommended to visit Hokkaido (and all of Japan): it is the so-called Golden Week, in March - the dates vary year to year - when everyone, absolutely all Japanese, are on vacation. The prices of receiving structures, already high, double and it is difficult to find places on the train and hotel rooms.*

NOT TO MISS

- NOT FAR FROM ABASHIRI, THE PORT OF MONBETSU HOSTS THE **SEA ICE OBSERVATION TOWER OKHOTSK,** THE ONLY UNDERWATER OBSERVATORY ON THE PLANET WHERE IT IS POSSIBLE TO TAKE A PEAK UNDER THE ICE. IT IS BRIMMING WITH LIFE: ADMIRE, AMONG OTHER THINGS, THE SO-CALLED "SEA ANGELS," SMALL, MYSTERIOUS TRANSPARENT GASTROPODS.

- ON LAKE AKAN, THE **AINU KOTAN** VILLAGE IS THE PAR EXCELLENCE DESTINATION FOR EXPERIENCING AINU TRADITIONS, VISITING THE ETHNOGRAPHIC MUSEUM, TASTING THEIR CUISINE AND WATCHING THEIR DANCES IN THE YUKAR THEATER, HONORED AS JAPANESE CULTURAL HERITAGE SITE.

- OBSERVING THE MANCHURIAN CRANE'S COURTING DANCE (THE RED-HEADED BIRD THAT IS THE SYMBOL OF JAPAN) ON **LAKE KUSHIRO**, IN THE KUSHIRO SHITSUGEN NATIONAL PARK IS AN EXPERIENCE THAT WILL ENTHRALL BIRDWATCHERS AND PHOTOGRAPHERS ALIKE.

- IN THE SPRING, FROM ABASHIRI GO TO **TAKINOUE** (ASAHIKAWA PREFECTURE), IN THE EXACT CENTER OF HOKKAIDO, WHEN ITS VALLEYS BECOME A FANTASTIC PINK CARPET OF SHIBA ZAKURA FLOWERS. IN JULY AND AUGUST, A SPECTACULAR BLOOM OF PURPLE IRISES COLORS THE OKHOTSK SEA'S COASTAL PLAINS.

CHUKOTKA, THE LAST FRONTIER

Internet site www.visitchukotka.com/eng

Russia's most northeastern edge provides an extreme nature adventure in the Arctic and encounters with the most isolated populations on the planet.

It is 6400 kilometers as the crow flies from Moscow. You can only get there by plane because the roads aren't worthy of that name. We'd bet that, at least if you don't work in the oil industry (here, the oilfields are rich and mostly untapped), you've never even heard of Chukotka, Russia's most northeastern province and the only one that partially sits in the western hemisphere. Its capital, Anadyr, is a village with 14,000 residents and its vast territory facing the Bering Strait is inhabited by the Chukchi, Evenki and Yukagir peoples – and also a handful of Eskimo tribes – also subdivided between nomadic reindeer shepherds and marine mammal fishers. Having said that, if you asked yourself Bruce Chatwin's question "What am I doing here?," know that a trip to the end of the world is the adventure of a lifetime: off-road, on caterpillar trucks, on foot, riding boats and snowmobiles, here the extreme nature of due oceans (the Pacific and the Arctic),

| **120-121** *Permafrost on Wrangel Island*
| **121** *It is estimated that the ancient Chukchi population has about 1500 members.*

4 spectacular mountain ranges and 40 rivers: and you can even go always to the mind-blowing intersection between the Arctic Circle and the 180° parallel, the international date line, meeting polar bears and whales and enjoying the hospitality of people that still dress in skins and practice shamanic rites.

When to go *During the brief summer, between July and early September, the temperature oscillates between 10° and 5° C. In the winter, it drops down between -45° and -15° C and snowstorms can last for an entire week. If you're up to it, you can visit Chukotcha via snowmobile in March and April.*

How long to stay *1 week or 10 days.*

Organization *In order to obtain a visa, you need a special permit available through a tour operator. On the Autonomous Province of Chukotka's official tourism site you will find the links to tour operators that propose trips in the area, specialized on either nature or ethnography, of varying length and difficulty.*

Advice *Before leaving, buy flashlights, Swiss army knives, fishing line, needles for sewing leather or, incredible to believe, colored beads: these are the gifts most appreciated by the Chukotka populations.*

NOT TO MISS

- SPEND AT LEAST A DAY IN THE **EVENKI** TUNDRA CAMPS, FOLLOWING THE SHEPHERDS TO WORK WITH THEIR IMMENSE HERDS OF REINDEER.
- TAKE A BOAT CRUISE IN THE BERING STRAIT: YOU TRAVEL FROM ASIA TO NORTH AMERICA AND VISIT THE **WRANGEL ISLAND NATURAL RESERVE,** A LIVING MUSEUM OF ARCTIC FLORA AND FAUNA.
- TRANSLATABLE AS "COMPETITIVE SPIRIT," **ERGAV** IS THE MAXIMUM EXPRESSION OF CHUKCHI TRADITION: IN EARLY SEPTEMBER, TRIBES GATHER IN **ANADYR** FOR A COLORFUL FESTIVAL WITH DANCE, MUSIC AND ABILITY CONTESTS.
- THE REMAINS OF AN ANCIENT HUMAN SETTLEMENT WERE FOUND IN **CAPE DEZHNEV:** ARCHEOLOGISTS CALLED THEM THE "ESKIMO WHORE," AN EXCEPTIONAL TESTIMONY TO A CULTURE ADAPTED TO LIVING IN AN EXTREME CLIMATE.

ON KODIAK ISLAND

Just off the Alaskan coast, an astonishing "Emerald Isle" is the place to go for close encounters with brown bears. Even more majestic than grizzlies!

Cousins of the grizzly bear, the Kodiak Island bears – the main island of the archipelago just off the coast of Alaska, the United State's second archipelago after Hawaii – are the more majestic subspecies of the brown bear. Adult males that can weigh up to 600 kilograms share the honor of being the biggest living carnivores with polar bears. Actually, that's only partially true: they are omnivores. They much appreciate salmon (preferring the skin, head and eggs, the most nutrient parts) but spend more time feeding on berries and grass. Besides, they don't have too much time to hunt, because during the summer they are "subjected to" a massively fattening diet that allows them to survive the seven months they spend hibernating. In summer months, observing the bears is the main reason for a trip to Kodiak Island: there are around 3500 of them, they are quite healthy and their population is continually growing.

Internet site www.kodiak.org

| **122** *The Kodiak bear, omnivorous, is a skilled fisher.*

| 123 *Adult males can weigh up to 600 kilograms.*

Even if they are timid by nature, you can encounter them during a trek (better if guided) in the primordial forests covered in moss or the flowering prairies on what is called the "Emerald Isle," along the rivers as they hunt salmon. And they could even appear in front of your car as you drive the 150 kilometers of super panoramic and winding coastal roads. But Kodiak Island as much more to offer: salmon fishing, whale watching, kayaking the bays, visiting fishing villages that can only be reached by sea or with small seaplanes, going down the trails blazed by the Alutiiq tribe, the island's first inhabitants. And discover that the small town St. Paul Harbor was, at the end of the 1700s, a kind of Russian capital in America, with an orthodox church with its characteristic dome. It was on Kodiak that a large community of the Zar's subjects settled and prospered, thanks to sealskins.

When to go *From May to September (when the bears are active).*

How long to stay *1 week.*

Organization *Kodiak Island is connected to Anchorage, Alaska's capital, by flights with Era Aviation and Alaska Airlines. To organize a bear sighting tour or other activities on the island, contact Kodiak Adventures and Kodiak Wild Side.*

Advice *Before wandering into the island wilderness (or even just take a walk around the populated centers) or pitch your tent, carefully read the rules to follow in case of an anything but rare close encounter with a bear on the Alaska Department of Fish and Game's website.*

NOT TO MISS

- OF THE (FEW) PAVED ROADS, THE **CHINIAK HIGHWAY** IS THE LONGEST AND MOST SPECTACULAR, TRAVELING AROUND HIGH CLIFFS, FORESTS AND LAKES: STOP IN THE TOWN OF PASAGSHAK, AT FOSSIL BEACH, WHERE YOU CAN ADMIRE **SHELL FOSSILS.**
- ON THE 4TH OF JULY THE ISLAND CELEBRATES INDEPENDENCE DAY WITH THE **KODIAK CRAB FESTIVAL.** BESIDES, RIGHT HERE IN THE WATERS OF THE ARCHIPELAGO YOU CAN FISH FOR THE FAMOUS (AND SUPER DELICIOUS) ALASKAN CRABS, PROTAGONISTS IN THE *DEADLIEST CATCH,* A REALITY-DOCUMENTARY SERIES THAT BECAME A DISCOVERY CHANNEL CLASSIC.
- IN KODIAK, THE **ALUTIIQ MUSEUM** TELLS THE HISTORY OF THE NATIVE AMERICANS WHO LIVED ON THE ISLAND STARTING 7000 YEARS AGO WITH A COLLECTION OF ARCHEOLOGICAL AND ETHNOGRAPHICAL REMAINS AS WELL AS PHOTOGRAPHS THAT DOCUMENT THEIR FIRST CONTACT WITH EUROPEAN COLONISTS.
- KODIAK IS WILD, BUT ITS ARCHIPELAGO ALSO INCLUDES THE LITTLE **RASPBERRY ISLAND** THAT IS EVEN WILDER. BOOK A STAY AT REMOTE LODGE AND SPEND A FEW DAYS FISHING PACIFIC SALMON AND HALIBUT. THE OWNERS ALSO ORGANIZE BEAR-SIGHTING TOURS.

IN CHURCHILL, WITH POLAR BEARS

In the north of the province of Manitoba, an adventure aboard a vehicle with tank-tracks to have close encounters with the pachyderms of the Arctic.

● SOUTHEAST OF CHURCHILL, **WAPUSK NATIONAL PARK** IS THE ONLY PLACE IN THE WORLD WHERE, IN THE WINTER, YOU CAN SEE POLAR BEAR CUBS, BORN BETWEEN NOVEMBER AND DECEMBER. DURING THE SUMMER, THERE ARE SPECTACULAR LANDSCAPES OF ARCTIC VEGETATION POPULATED BY MANY RARE BIRD SPECIES. YOU CAN ONLY GET THERE BY HELICOPTER AND TUNDRA TREKS ARE ORGANIZED THERE.

● BETWEEN JULY AND AUGUST, WHEN THE ICE FREES THE ESTUARY OF THE CHURCHILL RIVER, AROUND 3000 **BELUGA,** OR WHITE WHALES, COME HERE. THEY ARE THE MOST COMMUNICATIVE AND FRIENDLY OF THE GREAT CETACEANS AND YOU CAN EVEN SNORKEL WITH THEM. WITH A THERMIC WETSUIT, OF COURSE.

● THE PHENOMENA OF THE NORTHERN LIGHTS AND THE **AURORA BOREALIS** ARE ESPECIALLY VISIBLE HERE: NATURE'S OWN LIGHTS SHOW!

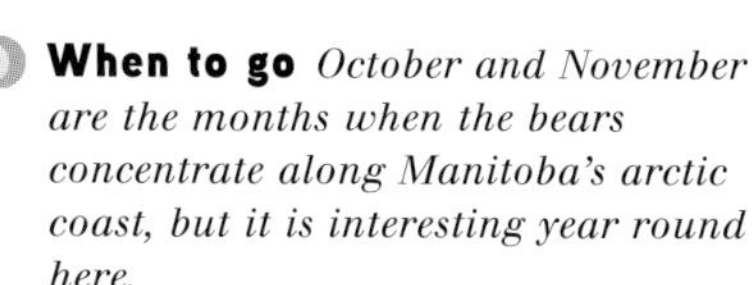

When to go *October and November are the months when the bears concentrate along Manitoba's arctic coast, but it is interesting year round here.*

How long to stay *1 week.*

Organization *From Winnipeg, Manitoba's capital, you can reach Churchill on a 2 hour flight with Calm Air and Kivalliq Air, or take a 2 day train ride through the tundra. For operators who organize polar bear tours that last from 1 week to 9 days, we recommend Churchill Wild and The Tundra Buggy Adventure.*

Advice *Like in all arctic zones, in the hottest months, Churchill and its bay are literally infested by terrible simulidae, known as buffalo mosquitoes. Once you are in Canada, we advise you to buy a specific repellant or, better yet, specially treated windbreakers and hats with a net to protect your face.*

| **124 and 125** *Churchill is the polar bear world capital. The largest land carnivore can weigh up to 600 kilograms.*

Churchill residents take so good care of polar bears that they build a "prison" especially for them. If someone sees one close to a city, they call a special toll number and a "police" squad immediately gets on the case to capture it (not before first putting it to sleep) and put it into what looks like a little hanger for small planes. The bear stays there, imprisoned, just until helicopter transportation can be arranged to take it, hanging in a sling, to the ice, their favored habitat. Watching this operation, for anyone passionate about wildlife photography, is an exceptionally lucky opportunity. But, if you come to Churchill in the right season, you are guaranteed to see many of them in their natural habitat. Besides, this little town in Manitoba – the remotest populated place in Hudson Bay that doesn't even care if it has not stoplights or an international hotel chain – is the undisputed polar bear world capital. Surprise, they aren't even white: they have black skin and translucent fur and the white is the result of the light refracting from these clear hairs. You will discover this, and much more, during an exciting tour aboard automobiles with crawlers that, leaving from Churchill, explore the bay's wild arctic coast. It is here that these majestic animals meet to wait for the sea to freeze – it is fascinating to learn that these pachyderms have developed the ability to jump on ice blocks to test how strong they are – and thus start the seal-hunting season.

Internet site www.churchill.ca and www.polarbearsinternational.org

A TRAIN RIDE THROUGH THE BARRANCAS DEL COBRE

NORTH AMERICA

From Chihuahua to Los Mochis for an exciting itinerary in the Sierra Tarahumara canyons and the ancient, revolutionary heart of Mexico.

| **126** *The El Chepe train goes through one of the canyons that line the mountain region of Chihuahua.*

The departure station is Chihuahua, the city - in the state of the same name, the largest in Mexico - synonymous with the legend of the revolutionary Pancho Villa. Arrival is in the modern (and not very pleasant, to tell the truth) Los Mochis, facing the Cortés Sea in the state of Sinaloa. Separating them are 645 kilometers of Ferrocarril Chihuahua-Pacífico, Mexico's most spectacular railway, studded by 37 bridges and 86 tunnels in a dizzying and panoramic rollercoaster ride that touches 2400 meters at Creel and Divisadero stations in the Tarahumara Sierras. If the trip aboard the train El Chepe, as it is usually called around here, is already an experience in itself thanks to exceptionally different landscapes – you see the powerful collision between deserts thick with cacti, dry tropical forests and mountain conifer woodlands – its dutiful stops make it unforgettable. Because El Chepe, beyond its geography, also travels through time. Even to the beginning of creation: for the Tarahumara, the population of Azteca origins noted for their shamanistic practices that involve peyote, for their crazy parties (even by Mexican standards) and for their colorful clothes woven by their women, their land is as old as the earth itself. It's not hard to believe, in the presence of the Barrancas del Cobre, a labyrinth of canyons that more than 1000 meters deep and extend over 60,000 square kilometers in the heart of the Sierras.

NOT TO MISS

- 65 KILOMETERS FROM CHIHUAHUA, GET OFF AT **CUAHTÉMOC** STATION: IT WILL BE LIKE STEPPING INTO A SCENE FROM LITTLE HOUSE ON THE PRAIRIE. AROUND 50,000 MENNONITES LIVE HERE, ARRIVED IN THE 20TH CENTURY FROM CANADA (WHERE THEY HAD MIGRATED TO FROM HOLLAND IN THE 16TH CENTURY). SIMILAR TO THE AMISH, THEY ARE IMPERMEABLE TO MODERNITY: THEY LIVE ON AGRICULTURE AND HERDING AND FOLLOW STRICT RELIGIOUS PRINCIPLES.
- DIVISADERO IS THE STATION THAT LEADS TO THE **BARRANCA DE URIQUE** THAT, AT 1879 METERS, IS THE DEEPEST CANYON IN MEXICO. TAKE THE TIME HERE FOR AN EXCURSION INTO THE **BARRANCA DE SINFOROSA,** THE MOST SPECTACULAR IN THE SIERRAS: AMONG ITS MARVELS THERE ARE ROSALINDA AND SAN IGNACIO FALLS AND THE VILLAGE OF **GUACHOCHI,** WHICH HAS A CHARACTERISTIC ARTESIAN TARAHUMARA MARKETPLACE.
- TO EXPERIENCE THE BARRANCAS DEL COBRE FOLLOWING THE TARAHUMARA TRADITIONS, STAY (AND PARTICIPATE IN THE ACTIVITIES LIKE TREKKING AND HORSEBACK RIDING) IN THE STUNNING **COPPER CANYON SIERRA LODGE,** 20 KILOMETERS FROM CREEL, AND **RIVERSIDE LODGE,** IN BATOPILAS.
- IN THE STATE OF SINALOA, YOU SHOULD STOP IN **EL FUERTE,** A SMALL CITY IN MEXICO'S PUEBLOS MÁGICOS CIRCUIT FOR ITS SPLENDID COLONIAL ARCHITECTURE AND CULTURAL WEALTH. HERE, BOOK A ROOM IN THE HISTORICAL POSADA DEL HIDALGO: IT IS SAID THAT IT WAS THE HOME OF DON DIEGO DE LA VEGA, BETTER KNOWN AS ZORRO.

| 127 *Basaseachi Falls are 246 meters high and can be admired aboard El Chepe.*

After having admired them from the window, you should experience them on foot, going down the steep rock walls that turn red, orange and pink in the vivid sunlight, to discover natural paradises with waterfalls, hot springs and remote indigenous communities. Like the Batopilas, the burg hidden in the mouth of the river of the same name that, surrounded by cornfields and orchards populated by thousands of butterflies, that has stayed in the 16th century, when the Spanish conquistadores started exploiting a rich silver mine here. Its very hospitable inhabitants are all of Tarahumara ethnicity. And they have remained so true and candid that their "cousins" in the village where the train passes, way up there on top of the canyon, call them *cimmarones,* "wild ones."

Internet site www.chepe.com.mx

When to go *From February to April and from October to December.*

How long to stay *The train ride takes about 14 hours, but divide it into at least 3 parts, with 3-4 day rests in between.*

Organization *You can organize a trip yourself along the El Chepe railway, nooking tickets on the site listed here. The comfortable Primera Express (equipped with air conditioning and restaurant) leaves daily, while the Económica leaves Chihuahua Monday, Thursday and Saturday. In first class, the ticket from Chihuahua to Los Mochis costs 130 Euro, less than half that in second class. Among the tour operators that organize itineraries in the Barrancas del Cobre, we recommend Tarahumara Tours and Viajes Dorados de Chihuahua.*

Advice *The trip aboard El Chepe is very popular and should be booked well in advance: every Primera Express train only has 2 or 3 cars with 64 places each.*

IN THE SALAR DE UYUNI

| 128 *25,000 tons of salt are extracted from the Salar de Uyuni every year.*

An off-road trip through earth and sky to discover the surreal landscape of the largest salt flat on the planet, in the heart of the Andes.

Ten million tons of salt: that's how much the Salar de Uyuni, the largest mass of salt on the earth, extending over 10,500 square kilometers at an elevation of 3700 meters in the southwest of Bolivia. Yet, it isn't merely salt: it has precious deposits of magnesium, boron, potassium and, above all, about 50% of the planet's lithium, the base element for producing modern batteries. Isn't it ironic that here, in this exaggeratedly photogenic surreal landscape, it is nearly impossible to find a plug in to recharge your camera. Except for July and August, when you need to be prepared to face temperatures that drop below 20° C and possible snow (crating an alienating "white on white" effect), Salar de Uyuni is a formidable off-road adventure for every season: during the dry season the surface breaks into an infinite series of perfectly hexagonal "bricks," while in the rainy season (nearly) everything is covered by a thin later of water, creating an extraordinarily suggestive mirror effect that makes the earth and the sky indistinguishable so that when you walk on it, you feel as if you were suspended in emptiness. Surprisingly, then, you discover that this sea of salt is host to curious and unexpected life forms: in the exact center of the Salar, Isla Incahuasi – the remains of a volcano submersed 40,000 years ago when the entire area hosted an immense prehistoric lake – is made of rocks that are corral and algae fossils where cacti up to 12 meters high and *paja brava* plants, similar to porcupines, grow. Meanwhile, on the edges of salt flats, strong colors dominate Laguna Verde, not far from the Chilean border, reflecting the powerful Licambur volcano, that soars nearly 6000 meters up, and the Laguna Colorada, that owes its red color to algae. Between September and November, this is the home of tens of thousands of flamingos.

Internet site www.boliviatravelsite.com

NOT TO MISS

- ITS NAME ALREADY SAYS IT ALL: YOU MUST GO TO THE **SOLAR DE MAÑANA,** A "COLLECTION" OF GEYSERS AND BOILING MUD POOLS AT AN ELEVATION OF 4850 METERS ON THE SOUTHERN EDGE OF THE SALAR, TO ENJOY THE SUNRISE. THE **ARBOL DE PIEDRA,** A SENSATIONAL ROCK SHAPED BY THE WIND IS BEST SEEN AT SUNSET.
- 80 KILOMETERS FORM UYUNI, **COLCHANI** HAS 600 RESIDENTS THAT ALL LIVE OF THE SALT HARVEST. DON'T MISS A PHOTO-OP OF THE **CHOLITAS,** THE WOMEN WORKING IN TRADITIONAL ANDEAN DRESS, AND PICK UP A SOUVENIR: MADE OF SALT, NATURALLY.
- LAGUNA COLORADA IS THE ACCESS POINT TO THE **RESERVA NACIÓNAL DE FAUNA ANDINA EDUARDO AVAROA.** WITH INTENSE GEOTHERMIC ACTIVITY, THIS IS THE BOLIVIAN YELLOWSTONE AND IS HOME TO PUMAS AND A GREAT NUMBER OF VICUÑA (OR VICUGNA), A PROTECTED SPECIES OF ANDEAN CAMEL.
- SPEND A NIGHT AT **PALACIO DEL SAL,** A HOTEL CONSTRUCTED ENTIRELY WITH BLOCKS OF SALT, FURNITURE INCLUDED. IT IS ON THE NORTHERN EDGE OF THE SALAR AND ALSO HAS A SPA AND A 9-HOLE (SALT) GOLF COURSE: YOU PLAY WITH COLORED BALLS!

When to go *From April, May and from September to November. During the rainy season, between November and March, you get the "mirror effect" (with exceptional photographic opportunities) but the trip can become dangerous.*

How long to stay *From 3 days to 1 week.*

Organization *The main point to access the Salar is the city of Uyuni. Literally swarms of tourist agencies propose jeep adventures varying form 2 days to 1 week, with food and lodging included in the price. Before booking a tour, make sure that the vehicle is in good working order. The most trusted tour operators in the country that organize adventure vacations throughout the country are Tupiza Tours, in La Paz, and Ruta Verde, based in Santa Cruz. The latter organizes a trip to Salar de Uyuni with lodging in the characteristic Tayka hotels, managed by a community of indigenous and attentive to environmental sustainability.*

Advice *To avoid altitude sickness, it is better to gradually acclimatize yourself to the elevation by coming to Uyuni after a few days in lower Bolivian destinations. Don't forget a strong sunscreen and a good pair of sunglasses: the reflections off the salt and the burning sun are unforgiving.*

129 *The Salar de Uyuni covers 10,500 square kilometers and is the largest salt flat in the world.*

BY SEA

IT'S NO CHANCE THAT THE OCEANS COVER ABOUT TWO-THIRDS OF THE EARTH DESTINED TO MAN, WHO DOESN'T EVEN HAVE GILLS...

"The sea has never been friendly to man. At most it has been the accomplice of human restlessness," wrote Joseph Conrad. Even he, above all an adventurer, knew the feeling that animates those who experience traveling as a necessity. Needless to say, some of the most epic and exciting journeys we suggest in this section forge through extreme seas, often turbulent, like the one that separates the Moskenesøya Islands in the Norwegian Lofoten, with its Maelström, the most violent ocean current imaginable. Or like the one at the end of the world, Drake Passage, up to the eternal ices of the Arctic Peninsula.
Never fear, though, because you can also chose those sea journeys – calmer but nonetheless rewarding – that are trips between dream islands, from the Whitsundays in the Australian Great Barrier Reef to the infernal paradise in the Galápagos, following in the footsteps of Charles Darwin. And we'll take you to visit the whales or to immerge yourself in the most spectacular abysses in the world. Or, finally, to paddle a kayak along the costs of the Hebrides or Madagascar. And take a cruise on a postal ship in the most remote archipelago of the South Seas.

ETHNOGRAPHIC JOURNEY
WILDLIFE SPOTTING
TREKKING
OFF-ROAD
SHIP
SAILING
MOTORBOAT
KAYAK
DIVING
FISHING
WHALE WATCHING

...BECAUSE THERE IS NOTHING LIKE THE SEA - WITH ITS ENDLESS LANDSCAPES AND ITS MARVELOUS DEPTHS - TO GIVE US A SENSE OF ABSOLUTE FREEDOM.

BY SEA

CHOSE THE RIGHT EMOTION

JOURNEY	PG	TIME ZONE	WHEN TO GO	NOT TO MISS
Greenland (Denmark) - In the Ilulissat Icefjord	136	GMT-4	All year	*Eqi Moraine*
Norway - Cruising to Spitsbergen	138	GMT+0	June-September	*Longyear Breen Glacier*
Norway - Fishing in Lofoten	140	GMT+1	July-August	*Lofotr Vikingmuseet*
United Kingdom - Kayaking the Outer Hebrides	142	GMT+1	May-September	*Barra*
Sudan - Diving Cruise in Port Sudan	144	GMT+3	October-June	*Sha'ab Suedi*
Madagascar - Kayaking Masoala	146	GMT+3	Apr.-May/Sep.-Nov.	*Nosy Behento*
Myanmar - In the Mergui Archipelago	147	GMT+6:30	April-December	*Cavern Island*
Indonesia - Komodo, the Island of Dragons	148	GMT+9	April-December	*Pantai Merah Beach*
Indonesia - Diving safari in Raja Ampat	152	GMT+9	October-May	*Pesar Remu Market*
Russia - On the Ring of Fire	154	GMT+12	May-July	*Komandorsky Natural Reserve*
United States - The Humpback Whale of Frederick Sound	156	GMT-9	June-September	*Tongass National Forest*
Canada - Along the Coasts of Baffin Island	158	GMT-6	April-September	*Sirmilik National Park*
Mexico - Whale Watching in El Vizcaíno	162	GMT-7	January-March	*Los Cabos*
Belize - Diving the Great Blue Hole	164	GMT-6	March-May	*Ambergris Caye*
Ecuador - Galápagos Cruise	166	GMT-6	December-May	*Española*
French Polynesia - Cargo Boating the Marquesas Islands	170	GMT -10/-9:30	March-October	*Hiva Oa Jeep Safari*
Australia - Sailing the Whitsunday Islands	172	GMT+10	All year	*Whitehaven Beach*
Palau - Diving Cruise through Rock Islands	174	GMT+9	All year	*Ongeim'l Tketau*
Argentina, ATS - Cruising Antarctica	176	GMT+13	November-March	*Grytviken, South Georgia*

| **134-135** *The rock islands of the Palau archipelago offer exceptional seabeds for scuba diving.*

DON'T FORGET	A CLASSIC BOOK FOR EVERY JOURNEY
Binoculars	*Johannes V. Jensen,* The Fall of the King
Soccer ball	*Georgina Harding,* The solitude of Thomas Cave
Fishing equipment	*Jules Verne, 20,000* Leagues Under the Sea
Waterproof clothing	*Peter May,* The Blackhouse
Underwater Photographic Equipment	*Tayeb Salih,* The Wedding of Zein
Binoculars	*Gerald Durrell,* The Aye-Aye and I
Underwater camera	*George Orwell,* Burmese Days
Hat and sunscreen	*R. Lutz - M. Lutz,* Komodo: The Living Dragon
Antimalarial treatments	*Alfred Russell Wallace,* The Malay Archipelago
Camera	*Aleksandr Solzhenitsyn,* The Gulag Archipelago
Binoculars	*Jack London,* Call of the Wild
Arctic clothing	*A. Troubetzkoy,* Arctic Obsession
Waterproof clothing	*Jon Steinbeck,* The Log from the Sea of Cortez
Scuba diving license	*J-Y. Cousteau,* Galapagos, Titicaca, the Blue Holes
Camera	*Kurt Vonnegut,* Galápagos
Sunscreen	*Robert Louis Stevenson,* South Sea Tales
Boating license	*David Colfelt,* 100 Magic Miles of the Great Barrier Reef
Logbook for diving	*Paul W. Dale,* The Discovery of the Palau Islands
Telescope	*E. Shackleton,* Heart of the Antarctic & South

IN THE ILULISSAT ICEFJORD

Really experience the ice age on a trip through icebergs as high as skyscrapers that break from the fastest glacier in the world.

NORTH AMERICA

It is known that Greenland is the biggest island in the world. But not everyone knows that you can find Jakobshavn Isbræ (or Sermeq Kujalleq as it is called in Greenlandic), the fastest glacier on the planet. It moves at a rate of 40 meters every 24 hours and every year 46 kilometers cubed of ice break, with a deafening roar, from it: enough water for the annual consumption of entire population of the United States, to give you an idea of these unconceivable dimensions in concrete terms. You also have to use a an imaginable comparison to describe the icebergs made from this glacier: the largest have a base equivalent to 30 football fields under the sea covered with a volume of ice as high as Everest. They are so immense that they would have to float down to the south of Great Britain in order to melt but, since they weigh so much, most of the time they stay "parked" in the Ilulissat Icefjord for years, itself a part of the ample Discko Bay, creating phantasmagoric white architecture and breaking up every so often. Jakobshavn Isbræ is, for scientists, a formidable hotspot for studying climate change (above all over the last decade that has brought on an acceleration of the glacier), while the exceptional arctic landscape of Ilulissat Icefjord – experienced on an exciting boat ride – was listed as a World Heritage Site by UNESCO in 2004. The motivation lies in the fact that it is, in the northern hemisphere, the only destination where you can experience the Ice Age.

Internet site www.ilulissaticefjord.com

NOT TO MISS

- FACING THE FJORD AND 250 KILOMETERS NORTH OF THE ARCTIC CIRCLE, **ILULISSAT** HAS JUST UNDER 5000 INHABITANTS (AND 6000 HUSKIES) AND IS THE THIRD MOST POPULATED PLACE ON THE ISLAND. IT IS A WONDERFUL BUNCH OF BRIGHTLY PAINTED HOUSES WITH A PICTURESQUE FISHING PORT. FROM HERE, A TRAIL LEADS TO AVANGNARDLIT HILL FROM WHICH YOU CAN ENJOY A FANTASTIC PANORAMA OF THE FJORD.

- MOST INHABITANTS OF THIS PLANET EXPERIENCE CLIMATE CHANGE AS A FAR OFF, INTANGIBLE RISK. THAT ISN'T HOW IT IS IN GREENLAND, WHERE IT HAS HAD SIGNIFICANT EFFECTS ON THE ENVIRONMENT, ECONOMY AND SOCIETY. AN INTERESTING INTERACTIVE EXPOSITION AT THE **KUND RASMUSSEN MUSEUM** IN ILULISSAT, ENTITLED "BREAKING ICE," EXPLAINS THE HOW AND WHY.

- THE BEST DESTINATION FOR WATCHING ICEBERGS BREAKING OFF IS **MORENA DI EQI,** ON THE SOUTHERN SIDE OF THE FJORD WHILE, AT THE END OF DISKO BAY, THE HUNDE EJLAND ISLANDS HAVE REMAINS OF ANCIENT INUIT SETTLEMENTS.

- IN THE SUMMER, WHALES COME INTO THE FJORD: GO SEE THEM DURING A BOAT EXCURSION IN **OQAATSUT,** AN ANCIENT SETTLEMENT OF DANISH WHALERS SITUATED 15 KILOMETERS NORTH OF ILULISSAT.

| 136-137 *An enormous iceberg floating in Ilulissat.*

When to go *You can do the adventure year round, but remember that you can see the aurora borealis in the winter and that the sun never sets between May 21st and July 24th.*

How long to stay *1 day for a boat ride, at least 1 week for a Greenlandic adventure.*

Organization *The local operators World of Greenland and Ilulissat Tourist Nature organize 1-day boat trips as well as helicopter rides over the glacier and fjord. The Danish tour operator Arctic Adventure proposes lodging and activities in Ilulissat all year round, while the British company Aqua-Firma has a cruise along the west coast of Greenland board a schooner that takes 13 days with departures in September and October.*

Advice *Don't be intimidated by Ilulissat Icefjord's climate: despite the minimums (-20° C in February) and maximums (8° C in July), the air is dry and the perceived temperature is much more pleasurable, so much that during the summer it feels like 20° C. So pack a few light jackets too.*

CRUISING TO SPITSBERGEN

In the Isfjord, at Svalbard, observing arctic fauna in wild landscapes and discovering lively, unsuspected hi-tech communities.

Internet site www.svalbard.net

From outside it is nearly invisible, only a large reinforced concrete door looking out over the sea. But the Svalbard Global Seed Vault is an imposing structure, with a long access tunnel and three refuges dug into a sandstone massif, itself protected by permafrost, that hosts a bank of millions of seeds of the vegetal species on this planet. Inaugurated in 2008, it is a hibernating garden of Eden as well as an insurance for the future of biodiversity. Choosing Svalbard – and precisely Spitsbergen, the main island – was due to the fact that the archipelago is protected by ice, yes, but it is also a part of Norway, a calm and advanced country. In addition, it is easily accessible, a characteristic that also makes it the "easiest" Arctic destination. Every summer, Isfjord, Spitsbergen's great bay, is the destination for cruises that, along with uncontaminated white landscapes, let you observe arctic fauna, from polar bears (around 3000 live here)

| 138 *Enormous ice expanses characterize Svalbard, accessible in winter aboard an icebreaker.*

| **139** *Spitsbergen is populated by around 3000 polar bears.*

to walruses, from arctic foxes to muskoxen, all the way to the great herds of reindeer, a endemic subspecies of caribou and the crowded colonies of puffin birds. Every stop along the way offers passengers the possibility of exploring the coasts during excursions in rubber dinghies or adventuring into the island on a trek. Or even visiting the island's inhabited centers like Barentsburg, homet o a Russian mining community, Ny Alesund, where an international Arctic research center is located, and Longyearbyen, the archipelago's capital. Despite its mere 2000 inhabitants, this typical mining town has become very modern, very quickly: it even has a rich theater season and a soccer championship!

When to go *From June to mid-September. You can witness the aurora borealis between late-September and March.*

How long to stay *1 week.*

Organization *Founded in 1893, the Norwegian navigation company, Hurtigruten, proposes summer cruises into Spitsbergen's fjord with departures every Tuesday and Friday that last 6 days. They can be booked on the company's site or through local and international tour operators. Among these, we recommend Spitsbergen Travel, useful for the variety of archipelago vacations offered.*

Advice *To meet Longyearbyen's residents, participate in the barbeque organized every week in the hunters' cabins. Instead, live jazz is offered every night in the ultramodern Svalbad.*

NOT TO MISS

- VISIT THE **SVALBARD MUSEUM** IN LONGYEARBYEN THAT HAS AN EXCELLENT INTERACTIVE EXPOSITION AND EXPLAINS THE ARCHIPELAGO'S HISTORY, NATURE, ECONOMY AND SCIENTIFIC ASPECTS. IN THE OLDEST PART OF THE CITY YOU WILL FIND THE NORTHERNMOST CHURCH IN THE WORLD. ON THURSDAYS, THE REVEREND OFFERS ALL VISITORS A CUP OF COFFEE, ACCOMPANIED WITH TRADITIONAL DANISH DESSERTS, IN FRONT OF THE SACRISTY'S FIREPLACE.
- A SHORT DISTANCE FROM LONGYEARBYEN, EROSION OF THE LONGYEAR GLACIER HAS CREATED AN ENORMOUS MORAINE WHERE AN INCREDIBLE QUANTITY OF **ANIMAL FOSSILS,** DATED BETWEEN 60 AND 40 MILLION YEARS OLD, HAVE COME TO LIGHT. THE GREEN DOG AGENCY ORGANIZES HALF-DAY FOSSIL HUNTING TOURS: IF YOU FIND ONE YOU CAN TAKE IT HOME.
- CONSIDER THE IDEA OF PARTICIPATING IN A **KAYAK EXPEDITION** (THAT LASTS 8 DAYS) IN THE **ISFJORD** TO ADMIRE THE FRONT OF THE GLACIER UP CLOSE AND TO VISIT THE HISTORICAL REMAINS OF HUMAN PRESENCE ON THE ARCHIPELAGO, FROM ABANDONED MINES TO ANCIENT HUNTING REFUGES.

FISHING IN LOFOTEN

The World Championship in Cod Fishing is a legendary challenge. Do you think you can do it?

| 140 *The aurora borealis above Lofoten's skies.* | 141 *The fishing port of Henningsvær.*

NOT TO MISS

- AN ADVENTURE IN LOFOTEN ISN'T PERFECT WITHOUT A STAY IN A *RORBUER*, THE FISHERMEN'S TYPICAL LOG CABIN.
- THE SPLENDID **VILLAGE OF Å,** ON MOSKENESØYA ISLAND, IS AN ECOMUSEUM DEDICATED TO FISHING: VISIT THE STOCKFISH MUSEUM AND THE OLDEST CODFISH OIL FACTORY IN NORWAY.
- IN BORG, ON VESTVÅGØY ISLAND, THE **LOFOTR VIKINGMUSEET** HOSTS IMPORTANT REMAINS OF VIKING ARCHITECTURE AND OFFERS THE EXPERIENCE OF SPENDING A DAY LIKE VIKINGS, INCLUDING A TRIP IN A *DRAKKAR*.
- ON AUSTVÅGØTA ISLAND, THE **POLAR LIGHT CENTER** STUDIES VARIATIONS IN MAGNETIC CURRENTS THAT CAUSE THE AURORA BOREALIS AND ORGANIZES NOCTURNAL EXCURSIONS GUIDED BY SCIENTISTS TO ADMIRE THE PHENOMENON.

"Lofoten's cathedral": around here, that's what the high wooden grids used to dry codfish in the wind are jokingly called. Besides, they are a part of the landscape like the sea, the granite cliffs and snow-covered peaks of this fabulous archipelago that extends into the Atlantic for 250 kilometers, north of the Arctic Circle. Here people have fished for over 1000 years and it is here that, every year, during their migration to the Barents Sea between February and April, millions of codfish pass through, transforming Vestfjorden, which jets out right in front of the town Svolvær, the archipelago's capital, into what sea lions call "the best stocked fish market on the planet." It's no chance that Lofoten is the place where, on the second weekend of March, the World Championship in Cod Fishing takes place, a fantastic occasion to challenge around 600 expert fishermen. Even if you don't feel up to accepting this challenge, that's okay. Because fishing around these islands is an exciting experience, even if you leave the thrill of competition out of it: once the cod season has gone, in September, sardine season starts along with – only for photography – whales and orcas. Then, year round, Lofoten offers adventures on boat safaris that cross the Maelström gorges, the violent ocean current that have earned the strait that separates Moskenesøya and Værøy Islands the prize as the most treacherous in the world.

When to go *Thanks to the Gulf Stream, Lofoten's climate is milder in respect to other destinations at the same latitude. The warmest months are July and August, with an average temperature of 12° C. You can watch the aurora borealis between September and March.*

How long to stay *1 week. A fishing trip lasts around 4 hours.*

Organization *Many local tour operators offer stays in fishing villages, fishing trips and boat safaris. Among these, we recommend Nusfjord, Lofoten Fisherman Adventures and Aqua Lofoten Coast Adventure.*

Advice *For a gourmet stop, go to Lofotmat (Dreyersgate 60, Henningsvær, tel. +47-97-717059) that serves zero-kilometer specialties: cod, halibut and mollusks, obviously.*

Internet site www.lofoten.info

KAYAKING THE OUTER HEBRIDES

Close encounters with seals, dolphins and puffins in the Barra Bay and Bishop Islands, one of Scotland's best-kept secrets.

| 142 *The Shiant Isles, a refuge for puffins and razorbills.* | 143 *Kisimul Castle in Barra.*

To get to Barra – or Barraigh, as its 1000 inhabitants call it, all of Gaelic ancestry – you come in ferry from Oban, on the Scottish coast, or from Glasgow by plane, and the schedule depends on the tide. Yes, because Barra's airport is the only one on the planet that is serviced with regular flights with a beach as a runway, and landing is a heart-racing experience. Besides, there's no better way to start a kayaking adventure that, in at a week's time, allows you to explore the wild paradise of the southernmost Outer Hebrides, from Barra with its fjords populated by 2 dolphin species all the way to Vatersay, Sandray, Pabby, Mingulay and Berneray that compose the Bishop Isles archipelago. You cross extraordinary marine scenery, caves and rocky shores that are home to 2 species of seals, bays of transparent water and cliffs reaching 200 meters high where colonies of puffins, guillemots and razorbills nest in the summer. And, as a surprise, you discover ancient costal constructions. Like Kisimul Castle, rented to the MacNeil Clan at the price of 1 sterling and a bottle of whiskey a year.

Internet site www.isleofbarra.com.

NOT TO MISS

- IN LATE JULY, BARRA HOSTS THE **FÈIS BARRAIGH,** A FESTIVAL DEDICATED TO MUSIC AND GAELIC CULTURE.
- THE PICTURESQUE CAPITAL OF THE ISLAND **CASTLE BAY** GETS ITS NAME FROM KISIMUL CASTLE. HERE, AFTER A HARD DAY'S ADVENTURING, STAY AT THE DUNARD LODGE.
- OFF THE COAST OF THE HEBRIDES, IT IS EASY TO SEE **ORCAS, BLUE WHALES AND HUMPBACK WHALES.**
- BARRA IS STUDDED WITH IRON AGE ARCHEOLOGICAL SITES AND REMAINS OF CELTIC CIVILIZATIONS: THE ***MENHIR* DOMINATING BREVIG BAY** IS SPECTACULAR.

When to go *From May to September, weather permitting.*

How long to stay *A complete itinerary to all the islands takes 14 days but shorter trips for beginners are organized.*

Organization *Considered one of the top wilderness experiences in the United Kingdom, this adventure is proposed by Clearwater Paddling in Barra, with lodging in tents in deserted bays.*

DIVING CRUISE IN PORT SUDAN

Shipwrecks, never before seen coral and schools of manta rays and hammerhead sharks: discovering the uncontaminated Red Sea along the Sudan coasts.

Sharm el-Sheikh and Hurghada are on the Red Sea. Even children now know that. Instead, only a handful of scuba divers with refined taste know that, today, the Red Sea is above all Port Sudan. As a destination – in a country today divided in two and that has only recently found a fragile peace – it offers a few dusty roads and asphyxiating heat. But, facing one of the most beautiful coral reefs in the world, it is the departure point for phenomenal cruises. Nearly 1500 people immerse themselves in its waters every year (just as many as in Sharm in a lazy week) and every immersion is a fantastic adventure. Traveling north, you stop to admire the shipwreck of the Umbria, an Italian warship bombarded by the British Royal Navy in 1940 and that today rests 30 meters deep on the Wingate Reef, still in prime condition, with all its 360,000 tons of bombs and a unique ecosystem developing around the metal. While, just beyond, near the Sanganeb lighthouse, the reef explodes into sensational forms and colors with gigantic umbrella coral and curious florescent coral that set the scene for parrotfish, surgeonfish, gray reef sharks, giant groupers and turtles. The most unforgettable spot, finally, is Sha'ab Rumi, where you encounter great schools of barracudas and manta rays. And even the terrible hammerhead shark.

Internet site http://www.thescubasite.com/Scuba-Diving-in-Sudan/scuba-diving-in-sudan

NOT TO MISS

- IN 1963, THE LEGENDARY JACQUES-YVES COUSTEAU BUILT THE CONSHELF II IN SUDANESE WATERS, AN UNDERWATER RESEARCH CENTER 10 TO 26 METERS DEEP TO STUDY HUMANS IN PROTRACTED UNDERWATER CONDITIONS. TODAY, YOU CAN DIVE TO SEE WHAT IS LEFT OF THE STRUCTURE AT **SHA'AB SUEDI.**
- DIVING AT **BLUE BELL** WILL GIVE YOU THE SO-CALLED "TOYOTA SHIPWRECK." IN 1977, A CARGO SHIP HEADING FOR THE SAUDI MARKET STRUCK THE REEF AND SANK. THE EFFORTS TO RECOVER ITS CARGO HAVE ONLY DESTROYED THE CARS ON THE SEABED: SEEING AN "UNDERWATER PARKING LOT" IS QUITE STRANGE.
- AFTER THE CRUISE, MAKE AN EXCURSION INTO **SAWAKIN,** 45 KILOMETERS SOUTH OF PORT SUDAN. BUILT IN CORAL ROCK, THE OLD CITY (TODAY ABANDONED) WAS ONE OF THE OLDEST PORTS ON THE RED SEA, PROBABLY CORRESPONDING TO THE LIMEN EVANGELIS, THE PORT OF GOOD HOPE, IN THE PTOLEMAIC ERA.

| **144** *The ghost city Sawakin.* | **145** *Red Sea coral is unparalleled.*

When to go *From October to June.*

How long to stay *1 week.*

Organization *In Sudan, Italian companies have the most experience in diving in the area and have boats based in Port Sudan. Among these, Don Questo Sudan, with one boat, and Felicidad II Sudan, are the only in the area that have a hyperbaric room aboard. Both propose diving 1 or 2-week diving cruises.*

Advice *Choosing the period to organize a cruise depends on your scuba priorities: visibility is better between February and early May; if you want to have close encounters with hammerhead sharks, come between December and June, while October is the perfect month for swimming with enormous schools of manta rays.*

KAYAKING MASOALA

Paddling (and walking) in Madagascar's most extraordinary and secret national park for a journey of great exploration.

| 146 *A red ruffed lemur in the Masoala forest.*

Masoala Biome is the main attraction at Zurich Zoo: a Madagascan forest populated by 30 animal species, all endemic to the island, has been recreated under a 11,000 square meter dome. Although an exceptional structure, it represents an infinitesimal part of the original, because the peninsula's Masoala National Park, extending over 236,000 hectares if virgin forest, coastal swamp, mangroves, deserted islands and 100 square kilometers of marine park in the northeastern part of the country holds 2% of the planets animal and vegetal species (as well as, in all probability, the highest number of those still unclassified), is the most extraordinary protected area of that giant evolutionary laboratory that is Madagascar. However, all you have to do is search for "Masoala" on Google Maps to realize that it is, in fact, inaccessible. Without even saying it, the only way of visiting it is coming by sea in a kayak, entering here and there along the waterways that cross the peninsula, in an adventure that is just as original as it is unforgettable: experience close encounters with 10 species of lemurs and – if you're lucky – with a fossa, a carnivorous mammal similar to a puma, and with other extremely rare and extremely beautiful animal species, like the blue coua, a bird with a bare blue oval around its eyes, and with the Madagascan sunset moth with its rainbow wings.

Internet site www.masoala.org.

NOT TO MISS

- THE FOREST NEVER SLEEPS, AND THERE IS NOTHING MORE EXCITING THAN A **NIGHTTIME SAFARI** TO OBSERVE THE NOCTURNAL HABITS OF ANIMALS LIKE THE SCOTT'S SPORTIVE LEMUR, DISCOVERED HERE IN 2008.
- SHARPEN YOUR SIGHTS TO SEE THE SMALL AND CURIOUS SPECIES FOUND HERE, FROM FROGS TO GECKOES AND FISH, ALL ENDEMIC. AND DON'T FORGET TO ADMIRE THE PLANTS, FROM THE PRECIOUS EBONY AND ROSEWOOD TREES TO THE PALMS.
- GIVE YOURSELF A DAY IN PARADISE ON THE WHITE SANDS AND THE TURQUOISE SEA OF **NOSY BEHENTO** AND ADMIRE THE SUNSET ON **ANTONGIL BAY** FROM TAMPOLO VIEWPOINT.
- INSIDE THE PROTECTED AREA, **BETSIMISARAKA TRIBAL VILLAGES** GIVE YOU THE OPPORTUNITY TO DISCOVER A MODEL FOR SUSTAINABLE HUMAN INTERACTION WITH THE FOREST.

When to go *Masoala peninsula is the rainiest part of Madagascar. The driest months are April-May and September-November, but - despite sporadic downpours - the climate is pleasant from June to August, with lows around 18° C and highs of 25° C.*

How long to stay *At least 1 week, necessary for exploring the coast and making internal excursions.*

Organization *Masoala Forest Lodge proposes kayak safaris lasting 10 days between October and November with lodging in all-comfort camps, brief treks, snorkeling the coral reef and relaxing on deserted beaches. In the other dry season months, shorter excursions are organized.*

Advice *Since the trip takes place along the coast with a calm sea and up short river tracks, the kayak safari is for those who have no previous experience with kayaking. Don't forget to bring a pair of binoculars for observing the forest animals and a good insect repellant (but don't worry: Masoala is a malaria-free zone).*

IN THE MERGUI ARCHIPELAGO

Sailing through the 800 islands of virgin archipelago in the Andaman Sea, inhabited by "sea gypsies."

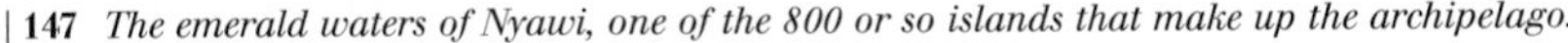
| **147** *The emerald waters of Nyawi, one of the 800 or so islands that make up the archipelago.*

NOT TO MISS

- A TREK INTO THE **LAMPI ISLAND** FOREST, EXTENDING OVER 16,800 HECTARES AND DECLARED A NATURAL RESERVE: THERE IS ALSO FAMILY OF ELEPHANTS WHO LIVE HERE. ON THE NEARBY **KUBO ISLAND** THERE IS A LARGE ENCAMPMENT OF SALON BOATS.
- AS ITS NAME SUGGESTS, **CAVERN ISLAND** IS A STRING OF SEA-LEVEL CAVES AND CLEFTS BIG ENOUGH FOR A FASCINATING EXPLORATION ABOARD A SMALL BOAT.
- DON'T MISS A VISIT (AND A FEW PURCHASES) AT A PEARL FARM: EVERY YEAR OVER 100,000 PEARLS ARE HARVESTED HERE.
- IT IS WORTH THE EFFORT TO BRING AN UNDERWATER CAMERA - WITH A MACRO LENS - FOR **SNORKELING** IN THE REEF IN THE PART WEST OF **WA ALE ISLAND.**

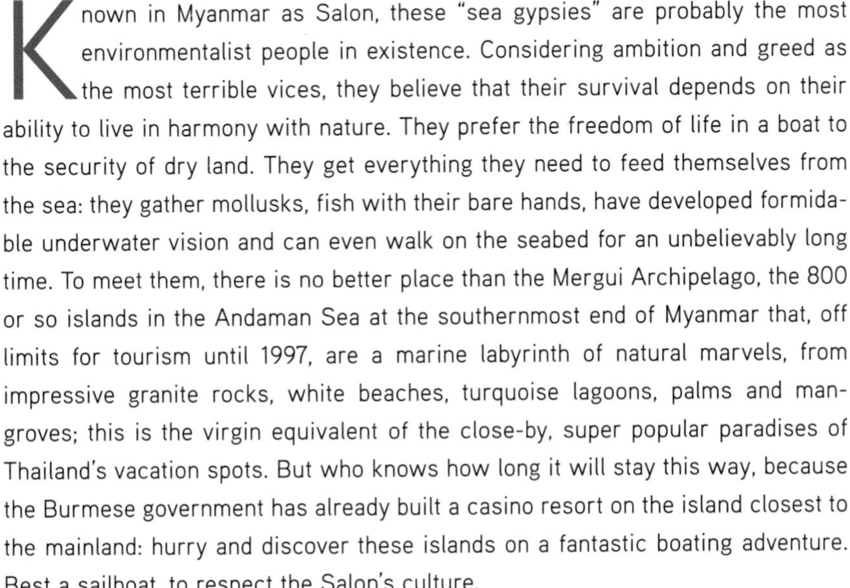

Known in Myanmar as Salon, these "sea gypsies" are probably the most environmentalist people in existence. Considering ambition and greed as the most terrible vices, they believe that their survival depends on their ability to live in harmony with nature. They prefer the freedom of life in a boat to the security of dry land. They get everything they need to feed themselves from the sea: they gather mollusks, fish with their bare hands, have developed formidable underwater vision and can even walk on the seabed for an unbelievably long time. To meet them, there is no better place than the Mergui Archipelago, the 800 or so islands in the Andaman Sea at the southernmost end of Myanmar that, off limits for tourism until 1997, are a marine labyrinth of natural marvels, from impressive granite rocks, white beaches, turquoise lagoons, palms and mangroves; this is the virgin equivalent of the close-by, super popular paradises of Thailand's vacation spots. But who knows how long it will stay this way, because the Burmese government has already built a casino resort on the island closest to the mainland: hurry and discover these islands on a fantastic boating adventure. Best a sailboat, to respect the Salon's culture.

When to go *From November to April, during the dry season.*

How long to stay *1 week.*

Organization *Of the Burmese tour operators that propose sailboat or motorboat charters and diving cruises in the Mergui, we recommend Mergui Tours, Ayuda Myanmar Travel and Asia Whale. It is also possible to organize cruises from Kawthaung: the passenger port is a short distance from the Thai border. To visit the Mergui, you need a special permit from the Burmese government, obtainable in 7-14 days through a charter company.*

Advice *Make sure there are enough masks and fins for everyone aboard. Even better if the boat has a tender or a kayak to explore the mangrove canals.*

Internet site www.myanmar-tourism.com

KOMODO, THE ISLAND OF DRAGONS

Unexplored until 100 years ago, this archipelago of the Lesser Sunda Islands is the reign of the largest and most ferocious living lizard.

| 148 *A Komodo lizard can reach up to 3 meters in length.*
| 149 *Idyllic beaches characterize the Komodo National Park.*

NOT TO MISS

- AT SUNSET, ANCHOR YOUR BOAR IN **MASANGGA BAY.** THE SURROUNDING MANGROVES ARE POPULATED BY A COLONY OF THOUSANDS OF FLYING FOXES. SINCE THEY ARE REALLY BATS, THEY ARE NOCTURNAL ANIMALS AND, WHEN THE SUN GOES DOWN, ALL TAKE FLIGHT TOGETHER TO HUNT FOR FOOD: IT IS A SPECTACLE JUST AS SINISTER AS IT IS FASCINATING. IF YOU STOP FOR THE NIGHT, YOU'LL BE AWOKEN AT DAWN BY THEIR RETURN IN MASS.
- ON KOMODO, **PANTAI MERAH,** A BEACH WITH ULTRAFINE, ROSE-CARAMEL COLORED SAND IS AN UNFORGETTABLE SIGHT. ITS PECULIAR COLOR IS DUE TO THE PRESENCE OF FORAMINIFERA IN THE WHITE SAND, PROTOZOA WITH A MICROSCOPIC RED SHELL.
- THE CANAL WITH STRONG CURRENTS, CALLED **THE ALLEY,** IS ONE OF THE MOST SPECTACULAR DIVING SPOTS IN THE PARK. IT IS EASY TO SEE PELAGIC FAUNA AND, BETWEEN SEPTEMBER AND DECEMBER, DENSE GROUPS OF GIANT MANTA RAYS.
- AFTER TREKKING, GO TO THE CAFETERIA AT THE **LOH LIANG VISITOR CENTER:** THE COFFEE (FROM JAVA) IS GREAT TO SIP WHILE WATCHING THE LIZARDS LAZING ABOUT UNDER THE RANGER HOUSE OR FIGHTING AMONGST THEMSELVES EMITTING FRIGHTFUL GUTTURAL SOUNDS.

Internet site www.komodonationalpark.org

Held in the New York Public Library and dated 1507, the Lenox Globe is one of the oldest terrestrial world maps in existence. It is also the only one that, along the coasts of eastern Asia, has the Latin phrase: Hic Sunt Dracones ("Dragons are here"). Maps at that time, when the European powers began their race to explore far off seas, were very approximate and took more into account the voices heard in ports than direct observations. Nevertheless, tales were told of monstrous beings in an archipelago in the Sunda Sea until 100 years ago, when a Dutch scientific mission landed on Komodo Island and classified the infamous dragon as Varanus komodoensis, the largest living lizard. Today, together with the nearby Rinca and Padar Islands, a handful of other little islands and the surrounding sea, Komodo is a national park, instituted above all to protect evolution's strange 4000 member "dragon" population. You come here precisely to see - from a safe distance - these reptiles that grow up to 3 meters long and weigh 70 kilograms; they are agile and fast despite their dimensions, equipped with big, sharp teeth and noted for being ferocious carnivores. Even if they aren't able to instantly kill and devour a Java deer or a water buffalo (their natural prey), their bite is deadly because it causes septicemia: 15 varieties of harmful bacteria have been identified in their saliva.

In truth, you will discover that although these terrible animals are the island's superstars (and finding yourself just a few meters way, during a trek guided by a ranger, is a thrilling sensation), a trip to Komodo offers much, much more. First of all, arriving in Labuan Bajo, the sleepy little city on the end of Flores Island that is the access point to the park – itself reachable by plane from Bali, the bustling capital of Indonesian vacations – is like moving the hands of time back a few decades, before the era of tourism. Then, a ride on a *phinisi,* a traditional fishing boat, from enchanting deserted beaches to stunning coral reefs swarming with colored fish that are perfect for snorkeling and diving, all the way to the great heights and wide clearings of Komodo and Rinca, where we find vegetation like that of the African savannah, a result of the long, scorching dry season, alternated with haggard forest groves. Even if 4000 people live here in a handful of villages on stilts along the shores, nearly besieged by the lizards that devour sheep at night, the Komodo National Park is like a land "off the map," with its internal contradiction of being an infernal paradise. In November 2011, following an online survey called New Seven Wonders, the "dragon islands" were included in the list of the natural wonders of the world. Ever since the results of the survey were published, a record increase in tourism has been registered: more than 40,000 people now come here annually. However, in any case, this is much less than the number of people looking for sand and sun that arrive in nearby Bali each and every day.

Internet site www.komodonationalpark.org

| **150 and 151** *The archipelago's islands are surrounded by coral reefs swarming with colorful life forms: ideal for scuba diving and snorkeling.*

When to go *Between April and December, during the dry season.*

How long to stay *From 3 days to 1 week (with a couple of days for relaxing on the beach).*

Organization *Once you are in Labuan Bajo, on Flores Island, you can go to the port and rent a* phinisi *(with a 2-person crew) from local fishers for 1,000-1,500,000 Indonesian Rupees a day (80-120 Euro), including food. For diving or a more comfortable stay, contact Komodo Resort: on Sebayur Island, inside the park, it offers splendid beach bungalows, boat rides to the most interesting places and 4-5 day cruises.*

Advice *In Loh Liang and Loh Buyaya, the parks' visitor centers for Komodo and Rinca, respectively, each have 3 guided treks: short, medium and long. Both of the long treks (that last 1 hour 30 minutes) are preferable because they offer the best possibility to observe the lizards, better in the early morning when they are more active and the sun isn't too hot. Take a good supply of water.*

Curiosities

- *The Komodo lizard is the only terrestrial animal able to reproduce though parthenogenesis, i.e. even if its eggs aren't fecundated.*
- *These "dragons" eat about once a month, devouring 3/4th their bodyweight in one sitting. They spend the rest of their time perfectly still, or almost, under the sun, digesting.*
- *Spread out in 4 villages, the archipelago's 4000 inhabitants are Muslim fishers, descendants of those who arrived here in the 19th century when the sultan of the nearby Sumbawa instituted a penal colony here.*

DIVING SAFARI IN RAJA AMPAT

Sailing the satellite archipelago of Papua Island on an extraordinary journey that also helps protect sea life.

An impressive identity card: 1606 fish species, 603 corals (75% of all known species, 10 times as many as those in the Caribbean), 57 rare crustaceans from the stomatopod order, 13 marine mammals and 5 endangered tortoise species. And this is only under sea level in Raja Ampat, the archipelago of the "Four Kings" that extends for 50,000 square kilometers off the northwestern coast of Papua and is made up of around 1600 islands, mostly uninhabited and covered in virgin forest. Scientists consider Raja Ampat the epicenter of the planet's marine fauna, engine of a fundamental "reproduction chain" that, thanks to strong ocean currents, transports coral larvae from its reefs to the Pacific Ocean, contributing to the repopulation of distant marine landscapes, damaged due to global warming and human activities. So, conserving the archipelago's biodiversity (that incudes seven protected marine areas) is the object of an ambitious international project. And contributing to it is an unforgettable experience because Raja Ampat's life – including the small human communities that live there – depends on the income generated by a careful, environmentally sustainable tourism. The only thing left to do is to come here on an ethical sailboat cruise and take spectacular dives, admiring tiny life forms, like the colorful nudibranchs, swimming with manta rays with a 5-meter "wingspan" and living like Robinson Crusoe on primordial beaches.

Internet site www.diverajaampat.org

NOT TO MISS

- IN THE COASTAL CITY **SORONG,** THE ACCESS PORT TO RAJA AMPAT, SPEND HALF A DAY IN PASAR REMU, THE BIGGEST AND MOST COLORFUL MARKET OF IRIAN JAYA, THE INDONESIAN PART OF PAPUA ISLAND.
- KNOWN AS **"THE PASSAGE,"** THE STRAIT BETWEEN THE WAISAI ISLANDS AND GAM IS A SALT-WATER RIVER WITH PERFECTLY VERTICAL WALLS THAT HOST A FANTASTIC SAMPLE OF SOFT AND NUDIBRANCH CORALS.
- A **NOCTURNAL IMMERSION IN PULAU MISOOL** ALLOWS YOU TO SEE SPECIES LIKE THE WOBBEGONG SHARK AND THE RARE EPAULETTE SHARK THAT USE THEIR FINS TO WALK ON THE SEAFLOORS AND AMBUSH SCHOOLS OF BATFISH.
- GO TO **GAM** ISLAND TO FOR A FOREST TREK "HUNTING" ORCHIDS AND BIRDS-OF-PARADISE, WATCHING THE MALE'S ELABORATE MATING DANCES DURING THE MATING SEASON.

| **152-153** *There are about 1600 little islands that make up the Raja Ampat archipelago.*

When to go *From October to May.*

How long to stay *1 week.*

Organization *For an ethnic experience, the Raja Ampat Homestays association organizes stays in the local community and guided activities like diving, snorkeling, trekking, kayaking and rock climbing of the granite cliffs.*

Advice *The Papua territory is infested by anopheles mosquitoes, carriers of a Lariam-resistant strain of malaria, the drug commonly used as a prophylaxis. We advise preventive therapy using Malarone or doxycycline.*

ON THE RING OF FIRE

A sea expedition between the Kamchatka Peninsula and the Kurile Islands to discover extreme environments and Cold War memories.

The celebrated Ring of Fire gives proof of its fearful presence in many places on the edges of the Pacific plate – from San Francisco, California, unfortunately situated on the San Andreas Fault, in Japan, Java and Sumatra, to name just a few – but it is only in Russia's far-east, near the remote Kamchatka Peninsula, that it shows its reckless nature daily. Here, the intense volcanic and geothermal activity constantly shapes a sensational landscape, while, just off the coast, it causes impetuous underwater currents resulting in the fact that ocean here and the adjacent Okhotsk Sea are among the richest in fish and marine mammal life in the world. The first to explore these lands and seas was, in 1741, the legendary Danish navigator Vitus Bering and, during the Cold War, thousands of kilometers away from prying eyes, the gigantic Soviet war fleet was stationed here. It goes without saying, Kamchatka and the Kurile Islands, still contested between Russia and Japan, were off-limits until the dissolution of the Soviet empire and, even today, their position at the end of the world makes them a destination for true adventurers. And, since this destination is already quite original in itself, its worth it to exaggerate, boarding a cruise ship that from Petropavlovsk-Kamchatski, the peninsula's administrative capital, leads to the even more remote Komandorski Island, part of the Aleutian archipelago and declared a natural reserve because it hosts vast colonies of seals, sea lions, sea puffins and other birds, to then continue – along a route that allows you to see whales and orcas –

| 154 *Kamchatka's brown bear feeds on migratory fish in coastal rivers.*

NOT TO MISS

- JUST NORTH OF PETROPAVLOVSK-KAMCHATSKY, **AVACHA BAY** IS ONE OF THE WIDEST NATURAL PORTS IN THE WORLD. HERE - NOW FORGOTTEN - MANY SOVIET SUBMARINES FROM ARE SILL ANCHORED.

- ON BERING ISLAND, IN THE **KOMANDORSKI NATURAL RESERVE,** THERE IS AN INTERESTING MUSEUM THAT IS HOME TO THE ONLY EXISTING COMPLETE STELLER'S SEA COW SKELETON, A GIANT MARINE MAMMAL SIMILAR TO THE SEA COW AND DISCOVERED DURING VITUS BERING'S FIRST EXPLORATION IN 1741 AND HUNTED TO EXTINCTION JUST 30 YEARS LATER.

- IN THE KURILE ARCHIPELAGO, **ATLASOVA** IS DOMINATED BY ALAID THAT, WITH ITS 2340 METERS, IS THE HIGHEST VOLCANO IN THE REGION. THE ISLAND WAS HOME TO A FISHING VILLAGE THAT WAS COMPLETELY SWEPT AWAY BY A TSUNAMI IN 1952; TODAY IT IS INHABITED BY A DENSE COLONY OF SEA OTTERS AND TENS OF THOUSANDS OF BIRDS: A PHOTO OF THE SPLENDID SPECTACLE OF HARLEQUIN DUCKS TAKING TO FLIGHT ALL TOGETHER WHEN A DINGY PASSES IS A MUST.

| 155 *The volcanic zone and parks were declared World Heritage Sites by UNESCO in 1996.*

to the Kurile Islands. Lined up like a marvelous necklace to the Japanese Hokkaido Islands, they are home to unruly volcanoes, magical forests and tundra, a rich habitat of arctic fauna to explore on a trek or, in a dingy, up the rivers whose banks can reveal brown bears hunting salmon. To conclude such an exhilarating trip, once you are back on land you should go into Kamchatka's heart of fire. Or to the "philosophic" freeze of the city of Magadan, on the Okhotsk Sea: here you can visit the remains of Kolyma, the most terrible of Soviet gulags.

Internet site www.kamchatka.gov.ru

When to go *From mid-May to mid-July for the cruise, but - if you're not afraid of arctic temperatures - Kamchatka offers grand emotions in every season.*

How long to stay *The cruise lasts 13 days, but plan for at least another week to visit Kamchatka's mainland.*

Organization *There are about a dozen navigation companies that organize cruises around here, but the Australian Aurora Expeditions, that has a 54-passanger ship, is noted for their scientific and ecotouristic approach, the quality of their land and dingy excursions as well as for their services and activities aboard, including workshops held by noted photographers specialized in nature photography. Among the local operators that have marine and terrestrial activities in Kamchatka, we recommend Kamchatka's Vision and Kamchatka Lost World Tour.*

Advice *This is a journey that should be planned well in advance: the modalities for obtaining tourist visas at Russian consulates are often complicated, especially when the destination is the extreme east since access to some places (like the Kurile Islands) is subject to particular restrictions.*

THE HUMPBACK WHALE OF FREDERICK SOUND

A whale watching adventure (and not only) in the incredible scenery with the sea, glaciers and the mountains of Alaska's southeastern Inside Passage.

Usually called hunchback whales, *Megaptera novaeangliae* win the prize for most exuberant cetacean. Thanks to their well-developed pectoral fins, they are able to do acrobatics: the jump straight up, slap one another in elaborate spins and show off with spectacular flips. They can also orally communicate with their "voices," or rather extremely long, intense, articulated sounds made through their noses. The feed on krill and small fish and, as if they weren't already original enough, they have developed a fishing technique known in technical jargon as bubble-net thanks to which they trap their food in a spiral net of air bubbles. Observing hunchbacks is an exciting experience, above all if they are in pods with tens or even hundreds of members. This is what happens in Frederick Sound, a leg of the sea as wide as 60 kilometers in Alaska's famous southeastern Inside Passage where between 500 and 1000 hunchbacks gather during the summer, along with a vast population of orcas, seals and sea lions. Beyond whale watching, the charm of Frederick Sound lies in its grandiose landscapes forged by incessant glacial activity, with snowcapped Costal Range Mountains that rise up to 3000 meters above sea level. Plus, you can only come here by air or by sea, with ferries that travel along the legendary Alaska Marine Highway.

Internet site www.travelalaska.com

NOT TO MISS

- ON THE WRANGELL NARROWS, AT THE NORTH END OF FREDERICK SOUND, **PETERSBURG** IS THE CENTER OF NORWEGIAN CULTURE IN ALASKA. THE 3000 RESIDENTS GAVE LIFE TO THE LARGEST HALIBUT FISHING PORT IN THE STATE AND LIVE IN CHARACTERISTIC WOODEN HOUSES DECORATED IN *ROSEMÅLING*, THE COLORFUL DESIGNS OF RURAL SCANDINAVIAN TRADITION.
- JUST A FEW KILOMETERS FROM PETERSBURG, **LECONTE GLACIER** IS THE STATE'S SOUTHERNMOST SEA GLACIER. ITS FRONT - FROM WHICH THE ICEBERGS FLOATING IN FREDERICK SOUND BREAK - CAN BE EXPLORED IN A MOTORBOAT OR KAYAK TRIP.
- EXTENDING OVER 69,000 SQUARE KILOMETERS, **TONGASS NATIONAL FOREST** COVERS THE ENTIRE INSIDE PASSAGE: IT IS THE LARGEST PROTECTED FOREST IN THE UNITED STATES AND HOME TO THE NATIVE TLINGIT, HAIDA AND TSIMSHIAN TRIBES AND OFFERS AN EXTRAORDINARY OPPORTUNITY TO TREK TO THE WILDEST OUTLANDS.

| **156-157** *The hunchback whale is able to perform amazingly acrobatic jumps.*

When to go *From June to September.*

How long to stay *Whale watching lasts 1 day, but you need a week for a full adventure in Frederick Sound.*

Organization *Petersburg and Juneau, Frederick Sound's main inhabited centers, can be reached by ferries that travel the Alaska Marine Highway System through the Inside Passage. Of the local operators propose whale watching excursions, cruises of various length, kayak adventures and fishing trips, we recommend Alaska Sea Adventures in Petersburg and Gastineau Guiding Company in Juneau.*

Advice *After an adventure in Frederick Sound, head south and stop in Ketchikan, the American capital for salmon fishing. Here you can participate in the curious tour with masks and fins proposed by Snorkel Tours: immerging yourself into the algae forests of this icy sea, you will discover a "tropically colored" marine fauna that incudes nudibranchs, crustaceans and starfish.*

ALONG THE COASTS OF BAFFIN ISLAND

By ship (and dingy) to discover the legendary island of the Inuit, phenomenal white landscapes and the "big five" of arctic animals.

| 158 *Polar bear cubs weigh less than 1 kilogram at birth.*
| 159 *The Inuit still dress in animal skins.*

NOT TO MISS

- IN 1899, THE NORWEGIAN EXPLORER OTTO SVEDRUP BAPTIZED **GRISE FIORD,** "PIG FIORD," FOR THE SOUND OF THOUSANDS OF WALRUSES BARKING. BUT 141 INUIT ALSO LIVE IN THIS MAGNIFICENT FIORD, THE NORTHERNMOST PERMANENT COMMUNITY ON THE PLANET. THE SUN NEVER SETS HERE FROM APRIL TO OCTOBER.
- EXTENDING BETWEEN THE NORTH OF BAFFIN ISLAND AND **BYLOT ISLAND,** AN IMPORTANT BIRD SANCTUARY, THE SIRMILIK NATIONAL PARK ("GLACIER PLACE" IN INUIT), IS AN ICEBERG FACTORY, IN A MANNER OF SPEAKING. ON LAND, IT SUPPORTS A VAST POPULATION OF ARCTIC FOXES AND RABBITS, BOTH WITH WHITE FUR.
- IN ORDER TO BUILD AN IGLOO, THE BLOCKS MUST BE *APUTI*, AN INUIT TERM THAT MEANS "PERFECT SNOW": LEARN TO RECOGNIZE IT DURING A STAY IN AN INUIT COMMUNITY LIKE THE SMALL **KIMMIRUT** IN THE SOUTH OF THE ISLAND. FOR A JOURNEY INTO THE CULTURE OF ARCTIC PEOPLES, CONTACT THE GREAT ADVENTURE COMPANY IN EDMONTON.
- THE INUIT ARE AN ARTISTIC PEOPLE: TO DISCOVER THE BEAUTY OF THEIR HANDMADE GOODS, GO TO NUNATTA **SUNAKKUTAANGIT MUSEUM IN IQALUIT** AND, THERE IN THE CAPITAL, THE NUNAVUT ARTS & CRAFTS ASSOCIATION ORGANIZES THE ALIANAIT ARTS FESTIVAL, DEDICATED TO THE ARTS, MUSIC, THEATER AND CINEMA OF THE "EXTREME NORTH" BETWEEN LATE-JUNE AND EARLY-JULY.

Paul Nicklen was born in Saskatchewan Province, Canada and is just over 40 years old. In 1995, after a carrier as a conservation biologist, he picked up photojournalism, publishing his reportages in National Geographic and becoming one of the great masters of natural photography of all time. Or, better yet, the greatest, when it comes to taking pictures of our planet's least hospitable areas. He himself defines his a "Polar Obsession" (that is also the title of his latest book, published in 2009) that – he says – came to him during his childhood, which he spent on the ice in a remote Inuit community of Baffin Island: "I've never seen another culture more patient than the Inuit. They live in a difficult world and, like polar bears, know how to wait." Nicklen made this quality his own, fundamental when photographing animals in their natural environment and, thanks to it, he is able to show a wide public the marvels of polar regions but also bring attention to the problem of how this world is disappearing due to global warming caused by human activities. Curiously thumbing through his stunning images, you discover that his "polar obsession" can be quite contagious. Try it, you might just get the urge, on a whim, to head towards this cold, white land of adventure, starting right here in Paul Nicklen's very own Baffin Island.

As large as Germany - itself a part of Nunavut, the Canadian province as large as western Europe and recently instituted in 1999, being recognized as the ancestral territory of the Inuit people – Baffin is the least densely populated territory on the planet. Most of it is located above the Arctic Circle, is perennially covered in ice and the closest land is Greenland, separated by Davis Strait. It goes without saying, it is very, very cold here (the average annual temperature is -8° C) but, in exchange for its harsh climate, you will enjoy the warm hospitality of its people, because Inuit culture is deeply based on sharing and a sense of community. The island settlements – including Iqaluit that, with just over 7000 residents, is the capital of Nunavut - are connected to each other and the rest of the world only by air and sea, so the best way to discover the island's exceptional arctic environment is by circling it in a ship that, in turn, becomes a base for taking dinghies into the profound fiords and for exploring the satellite islands, also taking the opportunity to experience a night ice camp or a dogsled or cross-country ski excursion into the monstrous Auyuittuq National Park, whose name in Inuktitut, the Inuit language, means "the land that never thaws." Surprisingly varied, Baffin's white landscapes are the habitat for the animals that are usually referred to as the Arctic's "big five": the polar bears, musk oxen, walruses, nattiq (or ringed seal) and whales. Of the last, rare species like the sociable white whale, or beluga, that lives in large pods and, despite this animal's considerable dimensions, it is known as the "sea canary" for its chirping sounds. And, moreover, like Greenland's whale or the arctic whale that, lacking a dorsal fin and reaching up to 20 meters in length, is second only to the blue whale in the entire animal kingdom. Among the cetaceans, however, the superstar in Baffin is the narwhal – with its incisor tooth in the shape of a spiral that grows up to 3 meters in length and is as sharp as a sword – that, since the beginning of time, has alimented – all over the planet – the legend of the unicorn. The largest concentration of marine fauna (and polar bears) are found, in spring and summer, on the *sinaaq*, the Inuit term that defines the enormous ice floes that float in the Arctic Ocean at Baffin's northern tip; instead, all you have to do is go into the island a bit to observe the enormous herd of caribou that, with around 750,000 members, is the most common terrestrial mammal in the western

| **160** *Baffin Island owes its name to the English explorer William Baffin, who landed here in 1615.*

| 161 *Baffin Island is cut by the Arctic Cordillera.*

arctic. However, the island's most widespread species (this time marine) is the ringed seal, and it is so present – numbering around 2 million exemplars – that it is absolutely the fundamental base for the equilibrium of the complex arctic ecosystem, being the main source of food for polar bears and the Inuit alike. Every year, the island people hunt less than 30,000 seal, a perfectly sustainable number. And it couldn't be otherwise, because the Inuit know, and have know for millennium, what is the right amount to take from nature: the main guiding principle in their lives is called *Avatittinnik Kamatsiarniq*, a concept roughly translatable as "respect and care for the earth, animals and the environment." A guiding principle that should be the main concern for everybody, everywhere, not just up here at the icy poles of the planet.

Internet site www.nunavuttourism.com

When to go *From April to September.*

How long to stay *Cruises last between 10-15 days.*

Organization *Of the tour operators that organize summer cruises along the coasts of Baffin Island (and through the legendary Northwest Passage), we recommend Adventure Canada and The Great Canadian Travel Company. The French Compagnie du Ponant is also quite good.*

Advice *Before leaving for Baffin, stay a couple of days in a large Canadian city to buy an arctic wardrobe. Don't skimp on a good pair of perfectly waterproof trekking shoes with good thermic insulation.*

Curiosities

- *Many refer to the Inuit as Eskimos, but they consider it offensive. In Inuktitut, the word* Inuit *means "human beings" and the singular is* Inuk.
- *Over the course of history, the narwhal tooth has always been a desired object: in the 16th century, Queen Elizabeth I of England bought one for 10,000 pounds, then equivalent to the price for a castle and Elizabeth II's scepter was forged with the tooth of this fabulous unicorn of the sea.*
- *Despite its goofy appearance, the walrus is able to dive several hundred meters in the search for mollusks, its favorite food. It can consume up to 4000 in a single meal. But his animal is itself considered a gastronomic delight: called* igunaq *in the Inuit language, dried walrus meat is a local specialty. It has the vague aftertaste of aged cheese.*

WHALE WATCHING IN EL VIZCAÍNO

Overlooking the Sea of Cortés, Baja California's Los Cabos is a marvelous natural "amusement park" for many whale species.

| 162 *Direct contact with grey whales in San Ignacio Lagoon.*
| 163 *The Arco is the unmistakable rock formation at the southern tip of Cabo San Lucas.*

The blue whale is the largest living animal. It grows up to 30 meters in length weighing up to 200 tons: its tongue, by itself, weighs as much as an elephant, its heart as much as an SUV. They feed only on krill, ingesting between 4 and 8 tons each day. Registered in the Red List of endangered species, this majestic whale is also the most rare marine mammal. There is no better place to observe it on the planet than the Sea of Cortés and, more precisely, the lagoons of El Vizcaíno and coasts of Los Cabos, on the tip of the narrow Baja California peninsula. Thanks to the Mexican government, that had already prohibited cetacean hunting in 1933, these animals have found a sanctuary here, spending their winters and reproducing undisturbed. Or almost, since every day tens of boats leave from Cabo San Lucas to bring tourist here to observe teh extraordinary marine fauna that, along with the blue whale, also includes a great number of grey whales, sperm whales, fin whales, sea lions and dolphins, just to mention the superstars of one of the riches seas in the world, populated by 900 species of marine vertebrates and 2000 invertebrates. By some sort of eye for an eye, mainland Baja California has a fascinatingly harsh desert landscape dotted with cacti, yucca, agave and (also) inhabited by rattlesnakes and scorpions. That, unlike blue whales, it would be better to never meet at all.

Internet site http://visitloscabos.travel

NOT TO MISS

- DECLARED A WORLD HERITAGE SITE BY UNESCO, THE **EL VIZCAÍNO BIOSPHERE RESERVE** HAS BEAUTIFUL LANDSCAPES LIKE THE WILD BEACHES OF BAHÍA SANTA INÉS AND THE EVEN MORE REMOTE PUNTA CHIVATO, PERFECT FOR RELAXING AND SNORKELING.
- NEAR **LOS CABOS** IT IS EASY TO SEE WHALES DURING KAYAKING EXCURSIONS, TREKS OR 4X4 OR 4-WHEELER ADVENTURES ALONG THE COAST. FOR OFF-ROAD DESERT EXPERIENCES, CONTACT BAJA OUTBACK OR BAJA WILD IN SAN JOSÉ DE LOS CABOS.
- TAKE A BREAK IN THE CALM AND LUXURIOUS **PRANA DEL MAR ECORESORT:** BETWEEN THE DESERT AND THE SEA, IT WAS DEVELOPED ACCORDING TO ENVIRONMENTAL SUSTAINABILITY CRITERIA AND OFFERS, AMONG OTHER THINGS, ORGANIC FOOD, YOGA COURSES, SURFING LESSONS, WHALE WATCHING EXCURSIONS AND HORSEBACK RIDING.

When to go *From mid-January to mid-March.*

How long to stay *Whale watching excursions take 1 day, but stay 1 week to explore Los Cabos.*

Organization *In Cabo San Lucas and San José de Los Cabos, the main tourist centers of the Baja California, there are numerous operators that offer whale watching excursions. However, if you want a special adventure, book a 1-week whaling cruise or a Searcher Natural History Tour: the American owner, Art Taylor, is a scientist that has dedicated his life to studying cetaceans.*

Advice *Book the morning excursions because that's when whales are most active. Even if it is hot, take waterproof jackets with you on the boat: they will protect you (and above all your camera) from the whales' splashing.*

DIVING THE GREAT BLUE HOLE

Traveling (underwater) to the center of the Earth, in one of the most spectacular diving sites in the world. According to Jacques-Yves Cousteau.

Internet site www.travelbelize.org/scuba

Seen from a plane (or satellite) it looks like a perfect circle, a kind of "Caribbean eye" with a dark blue pupil, staring up at the sky and surrounded by a magnificent turquoise lagoon. The first to reach its depths, in 1971, was the explorer Jacques-Yves Cousteau, declaring it one of the ten most spectacular diving sites in the world. Thus it's no chance that the Great Blue Hole – located at the center of Lighthouse Reef, about 70 kilometers off the coast of Belize – is a national monument, an unparalleled jewel of the largest coral reef in the western hemisphere.

Deep 125 meters with a 330 meter diameter, the Great Blue Hole is a system of chalky caves collapsed into the sea at the end of the last ice age that, dropping

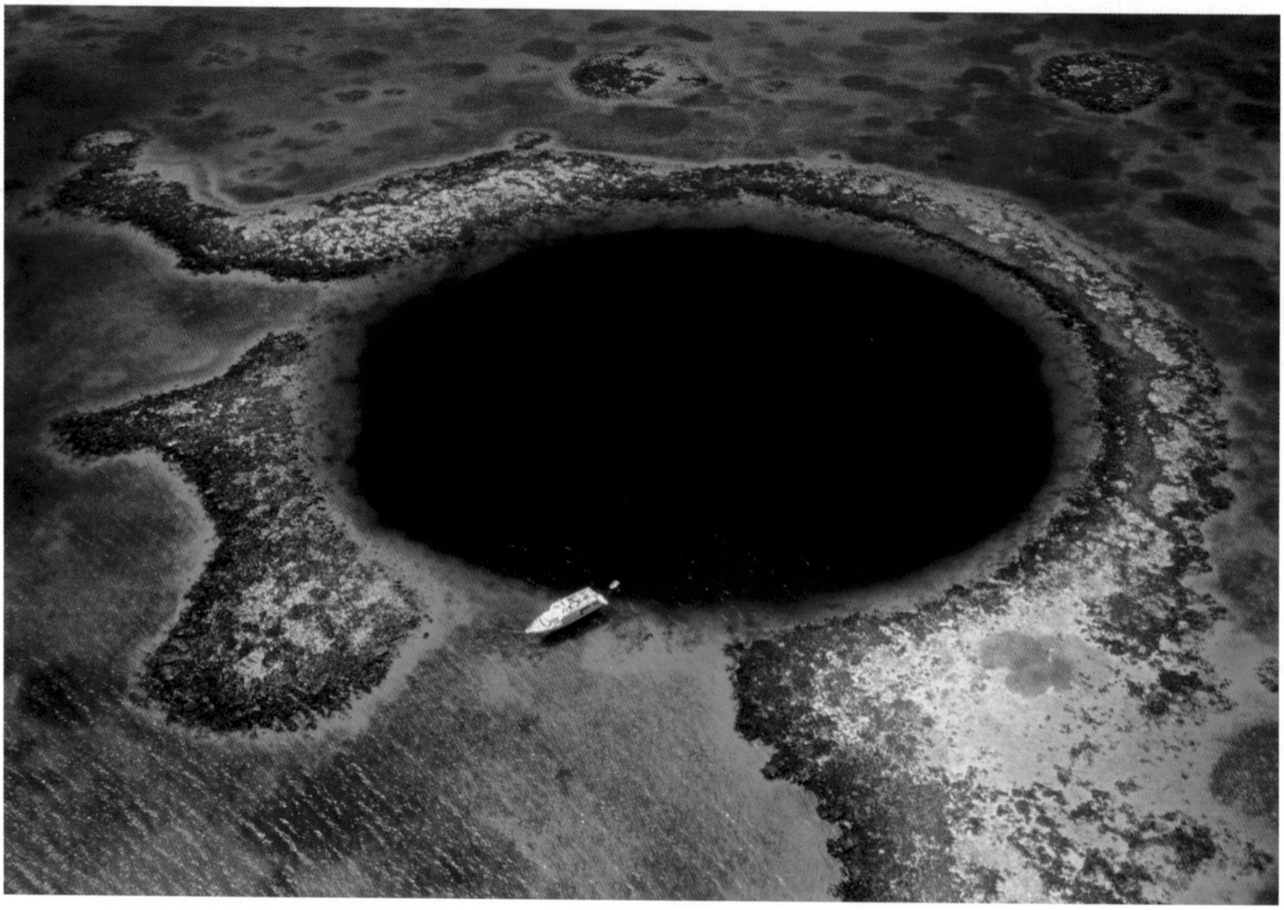

| **164** *The Great Blue Hole is an underwater sinkhole.*

| **165** *Large rocky stalactites characterize the depths of the Great Blue Hole.*

down 30 meters, reveals the earth's complex geologic architecture, made up of a labyrinth of stalactites up to 6 meters long, impressive columns and smooth walls decorated with sponges and gorgonians. Even if it is possible to encounter a few curious sharks that, every now and then, adventure into this submerged cathedral, the Great Blue Hole is characteristically scarce in marine life. So a dive here has the charm of a mystical voyage into the Earth's primitive origins, to a time before animals dominated the planet.

When to go *The best period is the dry season, between March and May. Avoid August to October because of the danger of hurricanes.*

How long to stay *You only need 1 day to dive the Great Blue Hole, but we recommend 1 week to explore Belize's coral reefs.*

Organization *Diving centers in Ambergris Caye propose immersions in the Great Blue Hole: we recommend Aqua Scuba Center di San Pedro. Owned by director Francis Ford Coppola, the Turtle Inn Resort in Placencia offers 7-day diving safaris from Alexandra Cousteau, National Geographic's Emerging Explorer and granddaughter of the legendary Jacques-Yves Cousteau.*

Advice *Diving the Great Blue Hole is a job for underwater experts and can be dangerous. Make sure the gear provided by the diving center is in perfect working order.*

NOT TO MISS

- IN ORDER TO OBSERVE THE MARINE FAUNA, IT IS SUFFICIENT TO MAKE SHALLOW DIVES ALONG THE CRATER'S EXTERNAL EDGE: THE REEF IS RICH WITH COLORFUL TROPICAL FISH AND SOME OF THE WORLD'S BEST EXAMPLES OF PARROTFISH.
AND, JUST OFF THE COAST, MANTA RAYS, GROUPERS, TURTLES, BARRACUDAS AND SHARKS OF THE *CARCHARHINUS LONGIMANUS* SPECIES, ALWAYS ACCOMPANIED BY THEIR PILOT FISH.
- MORE SPECTACULAR DIVING SPOTS ARE FOUND JUST OFF THE COAST OF **AMBERGRIS CAYE** AND INCLUDE UNDERWATER CAVES AND CANYONS.
- AT NIGHT, RELAX IN ONE OF THE LITTLE BEACH RESTAURANTS IN **SAN PEDRO,** THE "CITY" NEAR AMBERGRIS CAYE: PURE *CARIBBEAN STYLE* FUN!

GALÁPAGOS CRUISE

A cruise following in Charles Darwin's footsteps, to discover the harsh landscapes and animal species in the laboratory of evolution.

| 166 *Numerous seal colonies characterize the Galápagos beaches.*
| 167 *There are 13 large islands that make up this volcanic archipelago.*

NOT TO MISS

ESPAÑOLA, THE SOUTHERNMOST ISLAND, IS PROBABLY THE MOST HOSPITABLE AND CHARMING. HERE YOU CAN FIND THE ONLY NESTING SITE OF THE GREAT WAVED ALBATROSS IN THE WORLD AND YOU CAN TAKE FANTASTIC SNORKELING ADVENTURES IN THE CLEAR WATERS OF GADNER BAY: JUST A FEW METERS FROM THE SHORE, YOU ARE 100% GUARANTEED TO HAVE CLOSE ENCOUNTERS WITH MARINE MAMMALS.

UNDER THE SCORCHING SUN, THE CLIMB UP 379 STEPS ON THE ESCALERA TRAIL TO THE SUMMIT OF THE **VOLCANO OF BARTOLOMÉ ISLAND.** THIS WALK IS SPECTACULAR AND ALMOST "MARTIAN." PLUS, THE SUGGESTIVE PEAK OF LAVA ROCK ON ONE SIDE OF THE ISLAND IS THE BEST SPOT FOR OBSERVING THE ARCHIPELAGO OF PENGUINS.

GO TO THE **EL CHATO RESERVE,** ON SANTA CRUZ ISLAND, TO OBSERVE AN EXCEPTIONALLY GREEN LANDSCAPE AND GREAT GATHERINGS OF GIANT TORTOISES LAZING IN THE MUD. THIS HELPS THEM TO REGULATE THEIR BODY TEMPERATURE AND PROTECT THEMSELVES FROM THE MOSQUITOS.

NAVIGATING THE CANAL THAT SEPARATES ISABELA AND FERNANDINA, KEEP YOUR CAMERA READY BECAUSE WHALES AND ORCAS GATHER HERE. ON **ISABELA,** TREK ALONG THE LAVA CANAL OF MORENO POINT TO OBSERVE **CERRO AZUL,** ONE OF THE MOST ACTIVE VOLCANOES IN THE ARCHIPELAGO, BORDERED BY A LAGOON COAST POPULATED WITH FLAMINGOES.

From Quito, capital of Ecuador, it takes a 3-hour plane ride to reach the Galápagos: think ahead and ask for a window seat to get a taste, from the sky, of the panorama of the craziest archipelago in the world. Literally. That way you'll have a phenomenal view of the 13 main islands, next to the 6 smaller ones and the 42 tiny ones, that clamored into the history of science (and humanity) when, in 1859, the naturalist Charles Darwin handed over *On the Origin of Species* for print, where he postulated the gradual and continual evolution of living species, the descent of all organisms from a common ancestor and finally selection, actuated through the "survival of the fittest" in the struggle for existence. For Darwin, come ashore here from the *Beagle* in 1935, everything started with the observation of the 13 species of finches that inhabit this island. Now, from above, you will instead start with an extraordinary and contradictory vision of the whole. Because the Galápagos are wild and prehistoric and, at the same time, are dramatically effected by the presence of humans, since naturalist tourism has made its permanent residents now 40,000, mostly together in the city of Puerto Ayora, and a rate of demographic growth judged unsustainable. And because the Galápagos, before even arriving, are well noted: if you get past the paradox, the feeling is like the déjà vu you get when you first

| **168** *The marine iguana can stay underwater for about 30 minutes, but must recover body heat by laying on the rocks.*

see New York's skyscrapers, made familiar by many films. You will recognize the island of San Cristóbal where, in 2001, the oil tanker Jessica shipwrecked (while bringing fuel for "your" cruises) it what could have been the mother of all disasters. And then, you will get the feeling of an agonizing wait when you see Española Island, where couples of blue-footed boobies show off in incredible mating dances in the winter, or absolute marvel in the presence of the majestic volcanoes on Isabelle and Fernandina Islands: everyone's dream is to see the spectacle (reserved for a privileged few) of the climb to the crater that iguanas do once each year in order to lay their eggs. Finally, only from above will you have the possibility of seeing all the Galápagos, because the strict regulation of the National Park that protects them makes just 8% of the area accessible, even if this tiny fraction already contains 70 terrestrial locations and 74 marine areas that are open to international tourism. Upon landing, near the airport on Baltra Island, you will already be able to observe your first terrestrial iguanas and, before boarding a cruise ship, you absolutely must visit the main headquarters of the Darwin Foundation open to the public, on Santa Cruz Island, and instituted in 1959 in celebration of the 100th anniversary of the publication of Darwin's *On the Origin of Species*. Here you can also touch the shells of giant tortoises, the Galápagos tortoises who gave this archipelago its name and that can weigh up to 300 kilograms and live between 150 and 200 years, while nearby you will encounter the archipelago's curious flora when you observe the *opunta,* huge cacti related to the prickly pear that gradually assumed the shape of a tree to keep its fruits from the iguana's voracity. But it is only during a cruise that you will be able to fully appreciate the Galápagos' natural environment, enchanted by this paradise in the form of an inferno with a harsh and inhospitable landscape of black lava that shines under the ruthless sunlight and where innocence and perversity are irremediably intertwined. In this open-air laboratory, you will observe "monstrous" animal species, like the only species of marine iguana, descendant from a terrestrial species extinct over 100 million years ago, able to stay underwater for half an hour to feed on algae and then recovering body heat on the lava rock shores, while blowing salt-frost from its nostrils.

Or like the only species of penguins and seals adapted to a tropical climate. Or even more superb natural curiosities, like the numerous species of birds, from the majestic Galápagos falcon to the celebrated Darwin finches. Of the latter, there is even one that has developed an incredible vampire behavior and, with its sharp beak, sucks blood from the poor boobies' necks.

Internet site www.galapagospark.org

When to go *Although most naturalistic tours are planned between December and May, when the sea is calm and the temperature is pleasantly warm, consider going in July and August too, when the avifauna is most active and it is possible to see whales too.*

How long to stay *Cruises last between 11 and 15 days.*

Organization *When choosing an operator for a Galápagos cruise, favor those that have small boats (access to the best naturalistic spots is limited to groups of maximum 16 people at a time and, on some islands, like Genovesa, landing is permitted to boats transporting a maximum of 40 passengers) and that have a naturalist aboard. Among these, we recommend Enchanted Expeditions, the American Row Adventures that also offers camping in tents and kayak adventures, and Natural Habitat Adventures that works in close contact with the WWF and also proposes specific itineraries for lovers of naturalist photography.*

Advice *If you are passionate about diving, consider the idea of booking a cruise with Dive the Galápagos!, the only tour operator authorized to offer this kind of adventure in the archipelago.*

Curiosities

- *Although they are classified as one single species, Galápagos giant tortoises are divided into to 11 subspecies (the only example of the 12th subspecies,* Geochelone Abingdon, *died in the Darwin research center in summer 2012) and thus are quite interesting from a evolutionary point of view. Curiously, however, Darwin largely ignored them, noting simply that they made great soup...*
- *Darwin was not the first European to set foot in the Galápagos. Exactly 300 years before, in 1535, the Spanard Tomás de Berlanga, bishop of Panama, baptized them the Archipelago de Colón in honor of Christopher Columbus. This is still the official name today.*
- *The Galápagos flightless cormorant is one of the rarest birds in the world. Its population, presently only on the coasts of Isabela and Fernandina Islands counts just 900 members. It is the only of the 29 cormorant species that has lost the ability to fly: despite the fact it is a large bird, its wingspan is a full third shorter than any of its "cousins."*

| **169** *Galápagos giant tortoises can weigh up to 300 kilograms.*

170 *Fatu Hiva, volcanic in origins, has peaks 1000 meters high.*

CARGO BOATING THE MARQUESAS ISLANDS

Push off (along with postal packages) for a cruise from Papeete to Fatu Hiva – and back – in one of the most remote atolls in the world.

Love them or hate them. And real travelers cordially hate cruises. But even the purest adventuring spirits are willing to make an exception to this iron rule to sail on the boat that connects Tahiti to the Marquesas, the remote volcanic islands famed for being the last lands populated by man. Because *Aranui III* (the third ship of the "dynasty" with this name, since 1980 it is the only means of regular transport for the archipelago) is a postal cargo ship that crosses the border between the Marquesas indigenous and the rest of the world: it takes basic necessities there – from cement to sugar, from toys to beer – and loads coconuts, copra and noni fruit that their economy depends on. *En passant,* it also takes passengers, in duly no-frills comfort, although the ship has a pool, a small store, a library and a restaurant that serves better than average food: the luxury is in the scenery it crosses, making stops in 14 islands, each of

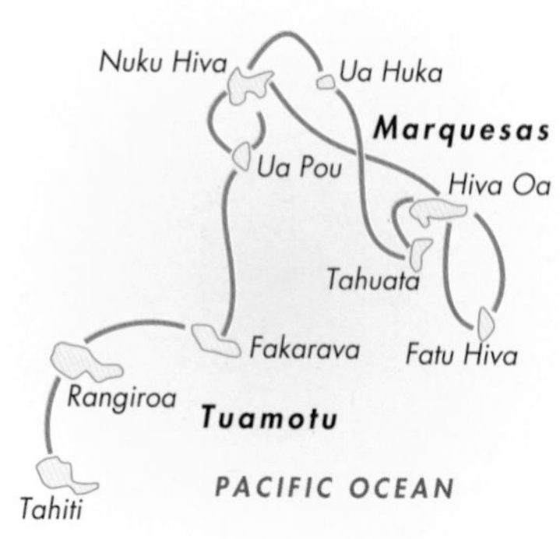

Internet site www.tahiti-tourisme.pf

which, already by its name, perfectly incarnates the dream of an adventure in the South seas.

The first contact with the Marquesas is with the high volcanic peaks of Ua Pou, the island loved by Robert Louis Stevenson, then the magnificent bay of Nuku Hiva, protagonist in a story by another maestro of adventure, Herman Melville. And, before arriving in Fatu Hiva, the super green island that is the center of Marquesas culture, at over 1000 kilometers from Papeete, the *Aranui III* touches destinations like Hiva Oa, that was Paul Gauguin's splendid refuge for years, and Ua Huka, that counts 300 residents and about 1000 wild horses, an itinerary that has earned it the nickname "Ship to Heaven."

When to go *From March to October, during the dry season.*

How long to stay *The cruise takes 14 days.*

Organization *Managed by the Compagnie Polynesienne de Transport Maritime, the cargo boat* Aranui III *departs from Papeete (Tahiti) on the first and third Saturday of the month, except in January. Every cruise offers the presence of a scholar aboard who, in the evenings, entertains passengers with conferences of the Marquesas' natural environment and culture.*

Advice *Forget your "usual" cruises: aboard, even the captain wears flip-flops and, it goes without saying, informal attire is obligatory.*

NOT TO MISS

- TAKE A SWIM AT **HAKAUI FALLS** IN NUKU HIVA AND SNORKEL IN **TAIOHAW BAY,** RICH WITH VOLCANIC CRATERS.
- GO ON A **JEEP SAFARI ON HIVA OA,** THROUGH COCONUT AND VANILLA PLANTATIONS AND VIRGIN FORESTS, TO ADMIRE THE *TIKI,* THE MYSTERIOUS STONE TOTEMS THAT REPRESENT POLYNESIAN DIVINITIES.
- STOP IN FATU HIVA FOR ETHNIC SHOPPING: BE SURE TO BUY *TAPA,* FABRIC WITH A FIBER OBTAINED FROM TREE BARK, AND *MONOI,* OIL MADE FROM SANDALWOOD, COCONUT AND TIARE FLOWERS THAT - APPARENTLY - HAS APHRODISIACAL POWERS.
- AS PART OF THE TUAMOTU ARCHIPELAGO - AND THE CRUISE'S LAST STOP - **RANGIROA** IS THE VASTEST CORAL ATOLL SOUTH OF THE EQUATOR: IT IS HOME TO A MAGNIFICENT LAGOON WITH 415 ISLANDS (*MOTU,* IN TAHITIAN) AND IS THE POLYNESIAN CAPITAL OF BLACK PEARL CULTIVATIONS.

| **171** *Fatu Hiva is characterized by abundant vegetation thanks to the rich rains that distinguish the island.*

SAILING THE WHITSUNDAY ISLANDS

At the heart of the Great Barrier Reef there is a paradise of 74 islands (and just as many smaller ones) that is the amusement park for any sea dog.

Daydream Island, Hart Reef, Whitehaven Beach: even the names of some of Whitsunday Islands' destinations sound like paradise when reading the nautical map. Add to that the fact that since this archipelago, in the heart of Australia's Great Barrier Reef, also includes Hamilton Island – famous worldwide because a few years ago it was the object of an internet contest promoted by the Minister for Tourism of the Australian state Queensland that offered the "most beautiful job in the world," working as this marvelous island's lighthouse guardian – the suspicion that this is the planet's best marine "amusement park" becomes a certainty. Sailing, on a rented boat best adapted to your navigational experience, or on an organized cruise aboard a sailboat that vaguely resembles (although with an infinite number of added comforts) the Endeavor, the vessel the explorer James Cook took to this area on Easter Sunday in 1770, baptizing the leg of the sea between the coast of Queensland and the archipelago White Sunday, you can take what really is a dream vacation. There are 74 Whitsundays, as they are amicably called by Australians, plus just as many smaller islands and coral reefs, seven of them are island resorts (modeled with in the most unbridled luxury and romanticism imaginable, apt for gourmets, families, sports fanatics or those with a rigorous sense of eco-sustainability) while all the others are uncontaminated naturalistic jewels, many of which are protected parks or natural reserves. Navigating this spectacular labyrinth - taking obligatory stops onto

| **172** *Whitehaven Beach is about 7 kilometers long.*

NOT TO MISS

- DURING LOW TIDE, ANCHOR IN TONGUE BAY AND GO TO HILL INLET WITH A TENDER: FROM HERE YOU CAN ADMIRE THE MOSAIC OF SEA COLORS FROM **WHITEHAVEN BEACH** AND THEN ENJOY A LITTLE SWIM IN THE INTIMATE BETTY BEACH.
- ON THE NORTHEASTERN SIDE OF HAYMAN ISLAND, **BLUE PEARL BAY** IS PERFECT FOR SNORKELING OR DIVING. HERE, IN THE SHALLOWS, THERE IS AN EXQUISITE SELECTION OF FISH AND, ON CASTLE ROCK REEF, YOU CAN ADMIRE MARVELOUS CORALS AND GIGANTIC GORGONIAN SEA FANS.
- BETWEEN THE WHITSUNDAY ISLANDS, SOUTH MOLLE AND HOOKE, THE **NGARO SEA TRAIL** IS A MARITIME AND TERRESTRIAL JOURNEY TO DISCOVER SITES SACRED TO THE NGARO ABORIGINES, THE ARCHIPELAGO'S ORIGINAL INHABITANTS. ON LAND, A NETWORK OF TRAILS LEADS THROUGH THICK TROPICAL FORESTS, SPLENDID CLEARINGS, UP PANORAMIC PEAKS AND INTO CAVES ONCE USED AS BURIAL SITES.
- AFTER SAILING, TREAT YOURSELF TO THE LUXURY OF A **SEAPLANE RIDE** OVER THE ARCHIPELAGO. THIS IS THE ONLY WAY TO TRULY ADMIRE THE CURIOUS FORMS OF ITS BARRIER REEFS: AMONG AUSTRALIANS, IT IS NOW FASHIONABLE TO ASK SOMEONE'S HAND IN MARRIAGE WHILE FLYING OVER HEART REEF, PERFECTLY SHAPED LIKE A HEART. CONTACT AIR WHITSUNDAY OR GLS AVIATION.

| **173** *Whitehaven Beach was elected the beautiful beach in all Australia.*

land to admire the green landscapes - is a rewarding experience. Each person will find his or her own secret beach, surrounded by seas with enchanting shades of blue and green. And, of them all, don't forget a stop at the "white paradise" Whitehaven Beach that extends over more than 7 kilometers of bleach-white sand on the island that gives the archipelago its name and was elected Australia's most beautiful beach.

Internet site www.tourismwhitsundays.com.au

When to go *The climate is enjoyable all year round: the lowest temperatures are in July-August (23° C on average) and the rainiest period is between January and March, with temperatures between 28° C and 30° C.*

How long to stay *1 week.*

Organization Bareboating *is the term used to indicate cruises where you are the skipper, renting the vessel best adapted to your needs from specialized operators, from sailboats of various dimensions to catamarans and motored yachts. Of the agencies that offer charters (with or without skipper), we recommend Whitsunday Escape and Queensland Yacht Charters. For an organized adventure aboard a tall ship, contact Whitsunday Sailing Adventures, while adventures aboard smaller boats that have participated in legendary races - and for sailing lessons - contact ProSail.*

Advice *If you are a good sailor, the perfect conditions for sailing are in March-April and September-October, with southeast winds at 15-20 knots. To discover all the archipelago's secrets, buy the book 100 Magic Miles.*

| 174 *There are about 300 little islands that make up Palau's "Floating Garden."*

DIVING CRUISE THROUGH ROCK ISLANDS

OCEANIA

It's called Palau's "Floating Garden" and offers you unforgettable dives. Hunting for remains, with sharks and... jellyfish.

Millions delicately floating like ballerinas through the transparent water in horizontal lines. They are little, peach-colored jellyfish and are not dangerous to humans: they live in what the Palauan natives call *Ongeim'l Tketau,* a lake interconnected with the ocean through a series of fissures and underground canals that are at the heart of Eil Malk, one of the pearls of Rock Islands. This Micronesian sub-archipelago is made up of a handful of uninhabited islands that emerge like emeralds from the sea in the form of sugar cakes, so extraordinary they've earned the name of "Floating Garden," other than being the destination that, for all those passionate about diving, is the crown jewel in any underwater "carrier." Even if it is all too easy (you can leave your oxygen tank and respirator on the boat), even the most hardcore scuba divers consider swimming with these special jellyfish an unforgettable experience. Yet, around Rock Islands there are exceptional experiences everywhere: here, every immersion is an adventure, into underwater caves and tunnels, coral reefs that perfectly drop in vertical walls and a concentration of marine life that has few parallels on the planet, counting over 700 coral species and 1500 fish species, from small to large, including a vast quantity of sharks, here protected by the most severe marine legislation in the world. And, if that wasn't enough, in the turquoise lagoons that surround the Rock Islands, you'll find 75 wrecks of Japanese and American ships and planes sunk here during WWII, when this archipelago between the Philippines and the Pacific Ocean, then under Japanese control, was theater of the American Navy's Operation Desecrate One. On the sheet metal of these wartime dinosaurs a particular ecosystem has developed, with species that are quite different from those that live in the nearby reefs.

Internet site www.visit-palau.com

NOT TO MISS

- AT THE ENTRANCE TO **CHANDELIER CAVE** (ITSELF THE MOST SENSATIONAL SPOT FOR CAVE DIVING), YOU'LL FIND A LAGOON POPULATED BY MANDARIN FISH THAT, DUE TO THEIR COLOR - AND FOR THEIR ELUSIVE BEHAVIOR - ARE A KIND OF HOLY GRAIL FOR UNDERWATER PHOTOGRAPHERS.
- SOME DIVING CENTERS OFFER COURSES FOR FOLLOWING THE MONITORING OPERATIONS OF THE GREAT SCHOOLS OF MANTA RAYS THAT, BETWEEN FEBRUARY AND MARCH, COME TO REPRODUCE IN THE SO-CALLED "GERMAN CHANNEL," OF THE SHORES OF THE ROCK ISLANDS.
- RECENTLY FOUND IN 2000, THE REMAINS OF THE AMERICAN WARSHIP ***USS PERRY*** ARE FOUND AT 75 METERS DOWN AND EXPLORING THEM IS AN ADVENTURE RESERVED FOR THE MOST EXPERT DIVERS. WITHIN ALMOST EVERYONE'S REACH, INSTEAD, IS THE DIVE INTO THE ***CHUYO MARU,*** A JAPANESE CARGO SHIP IN GREAT CONDITION.
- DON'T FORGET THAT THE ARCHIPELAGO IS ALSO MAGNIFICENT ABOVE SEA LEVEL: TAKE A **KAYAKING TOUR** THROUGH THE LAGOONS OF ROCK ISLANDS AND DISCOVER MICRONESIAN CULTURE ON **KOROR ISLAND** BY VISITING **ETPISON MUSEUM,** HOME TO A NOTABLE ETHNOGRAPHIC COLLECTION AND ACTIVE IN CONSERVATION PROJECTS FOR THE ARCHIPELAGO'S PELAGIC SPECIES.

When to go *With a constant average temperature of 27° C, the climate is perfect all year round. More rainfall, although not bothersome, is registered between June and October.*

How long to stay *1 week.*

Organization *Koror, the main island of Palau's archipelago, is the departure point for the rest of the Rock Islands. Of the many specialized operators that propose diving cruises in motorboats or sailboats, we recommend Sam's Tours and Neco Marine: both provide technical assistance for* National Geographic *photographers during their underwater reportages in Palau.*

Advice *In Palau, scuba divers are in safe hands: the personnel at the diving centers are prepared and the equipment provided is always perfect. In Koror, there are modern health services and the public hospital has two hyperbaric chambers. We recommend buying specific diving insurance with Divers Alter Network.*

| **175** *Jellyfish in Lake Ongeim'l Tketau.*

CRUISING ANTARCTICA

From Ushuaia, through Drake Passage, for an unforgettable adventure to the icy shores of the continent at the end of the world.

If it were music, it would be Mozart. If it were art, it would be Michelangelo. If it were literature, it would be Shakespeare. We're not exaggerating: these are the perfect comparisons to describe the indescribable Antarctica, the marvelous land at the end of the world that, already imagined by the ancient Greeks, was touched by man for the first time only in 1821. It doesn't belong to any country and is the only continent without a stable population (a group of scientist live here, but never for a whole year). 98% of its vast territory is covered in ice, thick 1600 meters, on average. Plus, it is the only continent without significant flora or mammals, reptiles and amphibians. Finally, it isn't possible – at least if you're not part of a scientific expedition – to travel in Antarctica, in the strict sense of the term. You'll have to "settle" for a glimpse of its coasts during the austral summer's "infinite days." But even like this, coming here on a cruise that leaves from Ushuaia, the remote Argentinean outpost that is the world's southernmost city, the Antarctic experience is life changing for every traveler. Starting with the trip through Drake Passage between Cape Horn and the Antarctic Peninsula, in what are the most treacherous waters in the world, to the close encounters with the Falkland Islands

| 176 *Cruises through Antarctic ice generally depart from Ushuaia.*

NOT TO MISS

- KNOWN AS THE SERENGETI OF THE SOUTH, **SALISBURY PLAIN** IN SOUTH GEORGIA ISLAND IS A NATURALISTIC PARADISE: ALONG WITH KING PENGUINS, THESE PLAINS SUPPORT AN INCREDIBLE POPULATION OF AVIFAUNA THAT INCLUDE 30 SPECIES AND DENSE COLONIES OF FUR SEALS.
- IN SOUTH GEORGIA, YOU HAVE TO PAY HOMAGE TO THE EXPLORER SIR ERNEST SHACKLETON'S TOMB AND VISIT THE **GRYTVIKEN SETTLEMENT** THAT IS HOME TO A MUSEUM DEDICATED TO ANTARCTIC EXPLORATIONS, AN OLD WHALING STATION, A CHURCH AND A RESEARCH CENTER WITH ABOUT 20 RESIDENT SCIENTISTS.
- LEAVING SOUTH SHETLAND, **DECEPTION ISLAND** IS KNOW FOR ITS COLONIES OF *PYGOSCELIS ANTARCTICA* PENGUINS AND ANTARCTIC TERNS AND OWES ITS SPECTACULAR MORPHOLOGY TO AN EXPLOSIVE ERUPTION. WHAT WAS ONCE THE VOLCANO'S CRATER IS NOW A NAVIGABLE BAY, ACCESSIBLE THROUGH A NARROW ICE PASSAGE. GET YOUR COURAGE UP: PUT ON A WETSUIT AND JUMP IN, THE BAY WATERS ARE WARMED BY INTENSE GEOTHERMIC ACTIVITY.
- IT'S A FACULTATIVE EXCURSION AND NOT INCLUDED IN THE PRICE OF THE CRUISE. BUT A **KAYAKING EXPERIENCE IN THE ANTARCTIC SOUND FIORD,** COVERED IN ICEBERGS, IS AN ADVENTURE THAT, BY ITSELF, MAKES THE WHOLE TRIP WORTHWHILE.

| 177 *Icebergs and marine mammals are constantly present on South Shetland Islands.*

and South Georgia Island and its impressive colony of 100,000 king penguins.

When you come near South Shetland Islands, you'll be enchanted by the abundance of majestically peaceful icebergs that turn shades of intense blue in the sunlight and the stunning abundance of marine mammals, from the curious and sociable minke whales to the well-known orcas, all the way to noisy communities of aggressive leopard seals. And if the fauna at the end of the world will leave you breathless, a visit to the powerful glacial tongues jetting precariously into the sea is priceless: you can bet that when you disembark from the ship and taking your first step onto the forgotten continent of Antarctica, you'll feel just like Neal Armstrong when he first stepped out onto the barren landscape of the moon.

When to go *In the austral summer, from late November to early March.*

How long to stay *Cruises last 10 to 22 days, on average.*

Organization *There are about 80 tour operators that belong to the IAATO (International Association of Antarctica Tour Operators) that sets the rules for behavior and environmental sustainability for Antarctic journeys. We recommend those that organize cruises aboard smaller ships because they can enter into the fiords and, in general, get closer to the coast. Besides, based on international directives, landings are limited to 100 passengers at a time, so you'll have to wait your turn on a large ship. Of the operators with a lot of experience and a multiplicity of Antarctic proposals, we recommend Antarpply Expeditions and Quark Expeditions: both have scientists aboard, dinghy excursions and at least two landings a day, once you get to the Antarctic Peninsula.*

Advice *A cruise in Antarctica is expensive, okay. But you should also plan for extra expenses, if needed, to update your photographic equipment as much as possible, preferably with a 500mm lens. Once you are home, you'll be glad you did.*

Internet site www.coolantarctica.com

ON 2 WHEELS

HORSEBACK AND BICYCLING ARE MUCH MORE THAN TWO MEANS OF TRANSPORTATION. THEY HAVE THE MAGICAL ABILITY OF MAKING US FEEL, SPEAK...

George-Louis Leclerc de Buffon, one of the sharpest French illuminists, considered horses to be man's most noble conquest. Regarding what we could define as a steel horse (or its version with an engine, a motorcycle: its no chance that riders are called centaurs) a man of great intelligence like Albert Einstein, in a letter to his son, wrote: "Life is like riding a bike. To keep your balance, you must keep moving." If an adventure on a horse – or a camel, or even an elephant, because in this section we've thought of it all... – and on two wheels requires that extra quid of ability to enjoy the trip, it is precisely the added effort that makes it unforgettable. Whether it be living like a cowboy in cinematographic American scenery of Monument Valley or with the Gauchos of Pampa Argentina, be it peddling along the mind-blowing Pyrenees circuits of the Tour de France or slaloming between the holes of Cuban carreteras all the way to the western province of Pinar del Río, the land of tobacco, each of the journeys proposed in this section promises a true revolution in our way of experiencing geography – and keeps that promise.

AND 4 PAWS

ETHNOGRAPHIC JOURNEY
WILDLIFE WATCHING
TREKKING
ROCKCLIMBIG
BICYCLING
MOTORCYCLING
FERRYBOAT
HORSEBACK
CAMEL RIDING
ELEPHANT RIDING

... AND OBSERVE THE WORLD
FROM A SPECIAL PERSPECTIVE,
WITH AN ADOLESCENT ENTHUSIASM
FOR WHAT SURROUNDS US.

ON 2 WHEELS AND 4 PAWS

CHOOSE THE RIGHT EMOTION

JOURNEY	PG	TIME ZONE	WHEN TO GO	NOT TO MISS
Iceland - Mountain Biking Geysers and Volcanoes	184	GMT 0	June-September	*Thingvellir National Park*
Norway - Along the Rallarvegen	186	GMT+1	July-October	*Nærøyfjord*
France, Spain - Pyrenees Tour	188	GMT+1	May-September	*Vall de Boì*
Namibia - On Horseback in Fish River Canyon	192	GMT+1	May-September	*Fish River Lodge*
Russia, Kazakhstan, Mongolia - On the Altai Mountains	194	GMT+7/+8	May-November	*Mount Belukha*
China - In the Taklamakan Desert	198	GMT+8	August-September	*Tonggzubasti*
Thailand - With Elephants in the Golden Triangle	200	GMT+7	November-March	*Thai Elephant Conservation Center*
Vietnam - Along the Ho Chi Minh Trail	202	GMT+7	November-March	*Hué*
Australia - The Bicentennial National Trail	204	GMT+10	April-October	*Kilkivan*
Australia - Western Australia by Motorcycle	207	GMT+8	May-September	*Pinnacles, Nambung National Park*
United States - In Monument Valley	210	GMT-7	May-September	*Hunts Mesa*
Cuba - The Far West of Pinar del Río	212	GMT-5	December-April	*Cueva di Santo Tomàs*
Argentina - In the Pampa with the Gauchos	214	GMT-3	November-March	*San Antonio de Areco*

| **182-183** *A horseback tour in Navajo Territory in Monument Valley is the most authentic occasion for experiencing a Western vacation.*

DON'T FORGET	A CLASSIC BOOK FOR EVERY JOURNEY
Swimsuit	*Jón Kalman Stefánsson*, Heaven and Hell
Road map	*Erlend Loe*, Naïve. Super
Waterproof clothing	*Gianni Mura*, The Last Kilometer
Brimmed hat	*Thomas Pynchon*, V.
Binoculars	*Colin Thubrom*, The Lost Heart of Asia
Windbreaker	*Bruce Sterling*, Taklamakan
Camera	*Rita Ringis*, Elephants of Thailand: Myth, Art, and Reality
High socks	*Denise Chong*, The Girl in the Picture
Change of socks	*Bruce Chatwin*, Songlines
GPS	*Bill Bryson*, In a Sunburned Country
Camera	*Cormac McCarthy*, Blood Meridian
Driver's license	*F. Ortiz*, Cuban Counterpoint: Tobacco and Sugar
Boots, hat, poncho	*J.L. Borges*, Martín Fierro

| **184-185** *The Jokulsarlon, that literally means "frozen lake lagoon," is considered one of Iceland's natural wonders.*

When to go *In the summer, between June and September, when temperatures are comfortable and the days long.*

How long to stay *Local operators organize mountain biking from the capital Reykjavík that can last between 1 and 6 days, but enthusiasts who want to challenge the fatigue and the climate's temper can also study itineraries of 2 weeks or more.*

Organization *Mountain biking is now so widespread that more and more supporters are gathering on the official site of the Icelandic Mountain Bike Club, where general advice on equipment and travel organization. Among the agencies based in Reykjavík, Opus Adventures is one of the most popular, offering tours varying in length and difficulty.*

Advice *To restore muscles back from all the peddling, there is nothing better than a swim in one of the island's many natural geothermal pools. The most famous – also considered a wonder of the world by* National Geographic *– is the so called Blue Lagoon near the capital.*

MOUNTAIN BIKING GEYSERS AND VOLCANOES

Between ice and fire through the most spectacular panoramas of a disturbed earth, challenging wind and severe weather.

In March 2012, when ashes from a spectacular volcanic eruption brought panic to the skies of Europe, closing many airports, the most serious problem for non-Icelanders was decently pronouncing the name of the volcano Eyjafjöll and, even worse, the volcano above it, Eyjafjallajökull. But that event was, substantially, a synthesis of the fascination of this volcanic island that emerged from the Atlantic 20 million years ago, a fact that makes it, proudly for its 300,000 inhabitants, the planet's youngest country, other than one of its most tormented lands. Situated on the Mid-Atlantic Ridge, Iceland is characterized by frequent volcanic and geothermic activity, shaping its landscape along with its powerful glaciers. The climate is temperate, relative to its latitude near the Arctic Circle, but its isolation has not certainly helped its human settlements, so much that the island was only inhabited by colonies of hermitic Irish monks until the 9th century, when the first Norwegians arrived. Today, it still gives visitors the impression of a primordial and inaccessible land, beyond the few villages scattered mostly along the coast.

And it is precisely this wild nature that attracts the most adventurous travelers here every year, adventurers who often chose to face the narrow Icelandic streets on a mountain bike at a speed that allows them to enjoy the panorama more than if they were on a motorized vehicle. The itineraries are generally rather challenging, but Iceland rewards your effort with uncommon warmth. And for those who dream of watching a volcanic eruption, maybe two steps away from a glacier, this is a unique occasion: here there is an eruption every 5 years on average.

Internet site www.iceland.is

NOT TO MISS

● **SNAEFELLSJOKULL NATIONAL PARK,** NAMED AFTER THE NEARBY GLACIER, RISING ABOVE 1400 METERS, HAS LUNAR LANDSCAPES AND WILD NATURAL ENVIRONMENTS. SETTING DOWN YOUR BIKE, IT OFFERS GREAT TREKKING THROUGH LAVA FIELDS AND CRATERS, AS WELL AS OFFERING BIRD WATCHING OPPORTUNITIES.

● WELCOMED INTO UNESCO'S WORLD HERITAGE SITES IN 2004, **THINGVELLIR NATIONAL PARK** IS ONE OF THE MOST SYMBOLIC PLACES IN ICELAND'S HISTORY. NOT FAR FROM THE CAPITAL, IT IS IMMERSED IN AN UNFORGETTABLE VOLCANIC PANORAMA, BUT IT WAS ALSO HOME TO ONE OF THE FIRST PARLIAMENTS IN THE WORLD, INSTITUTED IN 930 B.C.

● **AFJÖRDUR**, AFJÖRDUR, THE LARGEST SETTLEMENT IN THE AREA OF THE WESTERN FIORDS, IS FAMOUS FOR ITS CULTURAL LIVELINESS AND ARTISTIC WEALTH, OTHER THAN THE PRESENCE OF MANY MUSICIANS AND COMPOSERS WHO HAVE CHOSEN IT AS THEIR IDEAL REFUGE.

EUROPE

ALONG THE RALLARVEGEN

From glaciers to fjords: the historical road parallel to the most treacherous track of the Bergen-Oslo railway is a sensational cycling trip.

In 1894, the Norwegian Parliament overwhelmingly voted in favor of constructing a railway line to connect Bergen, in the west, to Christiania (Oslo's old name) in the east, crossing the high mountain range that, up until then, had divided the country in two. It was the most ambitious project in Europe: all the construction materials had to be transported into the mountains in carts pulled by horses during the brief and whimsical northern summer so, first of all, 2400 naval officers were employed as workers to build a service road. Inaugurated in 1909, the railway still operates, while the Rallarvegen, or "old navy road" is today a national monument and open only to 2-wheeled traffic.

 The section of the Rallarvegen that curves along Lake Uste.

| 187 *Hardangerjøkulen Glacier in Hardangervidda National Park.*

84 kilometers long, it is nearly parallel to the railway at the edges of Hardangervidda National Park between the cities Haugastøl and Flåm, the gateway to the marvelous fjord region, passing through Finse (where Norway's highest rails station still sits at 1222 meters) and the remote outpost Myrdal. Considered the most spectacular cycling itinerary in the country, over 20,000 athletes ride it every summer: the effort of climbing to over 1300 meters to then descend, headlong, to sea level is amply rewarded by the beauty of the landscape.

Internet site www.visitrallarvegen.no

When to go *From 15 July to 1 October.*

How long to stay *You can comfortably cover the road in 3 days, but plan for at least 3 more days for excursions in the area.*

Organization *The Rallarvegen can be done independently: near the departure station of Haugastøl and along the course you can book refuges, cottages, B&Bs and comfortable hotels that offer bicycle renting services and technical assistance. Of these, we recommend Hotel Finse 1222, member of Norway's Historical Hotel Association. In the summer, Norwegian Railways (Norges Statsbaner AS) add a bike car to trains between Bergen and Oslo.*

Advice *The Rallarvegen is a challenging road, above all around Flåmsdalen Valley, with a 857 meter climb and 21 dizzying curves in under 20 kilometers: consider walking it and enjoy the sumptuous forest scenery with waterfalls.*

NOT TO MISS

- THE EPIC OF THE CONSTRUCTION OF THIS RAILWAY IS TOLD IN THE INTERESTING **RALLAR MUSEET,** IN THE PICTURESQUE BURG OF FINSE.
- INSIDE HARDANGERVIDDA NATIONAL PARK, **BLÅISEN GLACIER** IS THE DESTINATION FOR A SPECTACULAR 4-HOUR TREK LEAVING FROM FINSE. THE WHITE LANDSCAPE IS SO UNREAL THAT IT WAS EVEN THE SET FOR PLANET HOF IN THE SCIENCE FICTION CLASSIC *THE EMPIRE STRIKES BACK.*
- FACING A BROOK AT 1310 METERS, **FAGERBUT** IS THE MOUNTAIN OF THE RUSTIC HOMES THAT WERE HOUSING FOR THE RAILWAY CONSTRUCTION WORKERS. TODAY THERE IS A REFUGE-CAFÉ PERFECT FOR A GOURMET STOP.
- ONCE IN FLÅM, DEDICATE A DAY TO A CRUISE ON THE **NÆRØFJORD,** THE WILDEST BRANCH OF THE FAMOUS SOGNEFJORD, THE "KING OF FJORDS," LISTED AS A WORLD HERITAGE SITE BY UNESCO.

PYRENEES TOUR

From the Atlantic to the Mediterranean, passing the legendary Col du Tourmalet on a two-wheeled trip following the champions of the Tour de France.

| 188 *A panorama over Fabrèges Lake, at 1241 meters, in the Pyrénées-Atlantiques Department.*

NOT TO MISS

- THERE ARE MANY FORMIDABLE DESTINATIONS IN THE PYRENEES PARK, SO MANY THAT IT IS WORTH THE EFFORT OF LEAVING YOU BIKE TO DISCOVER THE MARVELS OF THE **VALLÉE D'OSSAU,** WITH ITS CLIFFS AND THE BEST OBSERVATION POINT OF THE MOUNTAIN PREY, OR THE TRAIL THROUGH THE GLACIAL LAKES IN THE **VALLÉE DE LUZ,** ON FOOT.
- AFTER A CHALLENGING SECTION, TAKE A DAY TO RELAX IN **BAGNÈRES-DE-LUCHON,** THE MOST WELL KNOWN THERMAL IN THE PYRENEES. HERE, THE MAIN ATTRACTION IS THE VAPORARIUM: CARVED INTO ROCK, IT IS THE ONLY NATURAL HAMMAM IN EUROPE.
- THE PYRENEES BOAST A SURPRISING CONCENTRATION OF VILLAGES OF AN EXCEPTIONAL NATURAL AND CULTURAL INTEREST.
- MAGICAL MOUNTAIN SCENERY SURROUNDS THE **VAL DE BOÍ,** ONE OF CATALONIA'S TREASURES. A WORLD HERITAGE SITE, ITS EIGHT CHURCHES (AND A CHAPEL) ARE THE MASTERPIECES OF ROMANIC ART IN ARCHITECTURE, SCULPTURE AND PAINTING.

"Murderers!" Crossing the finish line, a dead exhausted Octave Lapize greeted the organizers of the 1910 Tour de France with this word. The legendary cyclist - who would go on to Paris to win that year's competition - was the first to ride the Col du Tourmalet road, the highest in the entire Pyrenees Range: 19 kilometers uphill with a 1404 meter variation in altitude, and Lapize had to walk, bike in hand, most of the section that was then on a dirt road full of holes. But, despite that first experience - and a section that, in French cyclist jargon, is defined as "hors catégorie," i.e. exceptional - the Col du Tourmalet has become a classic part of the Tour de France and is often borrowed for the nearly as famous Vuelta de España. Besides, there is no cyclist enthusiast that would miss the live TV broadcast of the so-called "Pyrenees Stages," the hardest, most exciting and dramatic part of the circuit. In the same way, there is no amateur cyclist that doesn't want to try to ride it to then stop, in recollection, in front of the Géant de Tourmalet, the monument to the heroes of this sport, erected on the peak at an elevation of 2115 meters. If you set aside the agonizing rush and ride the itinerary with due tranquility, crossing the Pyrenees from the Atlantic to the Mediterranean is one of the most extraordinary cyclist adventures in Europe.

| **189** *The Col de l'Aubisque, along with the Tourmalet and the Galibier, is one of the Tour de France's legendary "climbs."*

Certainly, besides the Col du Tourmalet, you should go over other exceptional passes like the nearby Col d'Aspin and Col de Peyresourde, and the Prort de la Bonaigua, the highest pass on the Spanish side of the mountain range. But the beauty of these landscapes amply reward the challenge of an itinerary that, from St. Jean de Luz, a short distance from the mundane Biarritz, leads to the Costa Brava, crossing nature's masterpieces, from Iraty's forests, Europe's largest beech grove, to the Pyrenees National Park with its crystalline lakes, its granite peaks its forests and, in Spanish Catalonia bordering Andorra, the wild Cadí-Moixeró National Park, where Pablo Picasso stayed to find inspiration. You'll be spoiled for choice of places to stop along a journey that goes through enchanted bergs and splendid thermal spots, that often traces the ancient pilgrimage route to Santiago de Compostela or gastronomic itineraries – from the Route du Formage between Ossau and Iraty in Basque Country, where you can taste alpine cheeses, to the wine road in Lot – or leads you to discover ancient traditions like the *fiestas* that explode with incredible vitality even in the remotest Spanish villages. Finally, although this is above all a green journey through valleys and mountains, don't forget to pay homage (and fully enjoy) the ocean and the sea that mark the beginning and the finishing line of this trip. The habitués of this crossing say that stepping into the Atlantic makes for a lucky journey. And that, at the end, there is nothing more gratifying than swimming under the Mediterranean sun.

Internet sites www.tourisme-midi-pyrenees.com and www.spain.info

| 190 *The Col du Tourmalet, a mythical place for cycling.*
| 191 *The entire crossing of the Pyrenees is quite challenging and generally only a section is traveled at a time.*

When to go *From May to September.*

How long to stay *10 days to 2 weeks (with breaks).*

Organization *Although it is possible to cross the Pyrenees independently, there are many specialized tour operators that organize groups and offer bike rental services, hotel booking and technical assistance along the way, including luggage transportation. We recommend Vélo Loco and Best of the Pyrénées.*

Advice *Always bring a rainproof jacket. Especially on the French side, the Pyrenees' climate is humid and, even in August, it rains 10 days out of 31!*

Curiosities

According to myth, the name Pyrenees is derived from Pyrene, the beautiful daughter of the King of Cerdanya, who Hercules asked married. When her father refused, she escaped and died tragically. Hercules buried her under a pile of rocks: thus was formed the Pyrenees Range.

Some cite the abnormal phenomenon of magnesium, others say that the Arc of the Covenant is hidden in these mountains, but the fact is that the tiny Pyrenees town of Bugarach is considered the only place that would survive the end of the world, predicted by the Mayans for 2012. Nothing actually happened, but property prices skyrocketed and the berg got some good publicity.

If the Col du Tourmalet is a "milestone" in the history of cycling, it owes it not only to the champions that have climbed it but also to those who told their stories. For this reason, a monument was also erected for Jacques Goddet, the most famous French sports journalist and founder of L'Équipe.

ON HORSEBACK IN FISH RIVER CANYON

AFRICA

A journey in Far West style in southern Africa, to experience – far from everything and everyone – the continent's geological granite masterpieces.

| 192 *Fish River is 650 kilometers long and the most spectacular part, the Canyon, spreads over 160 kilometers.* | 193 *The horse is one of the best "means" for exploring the marvels of Fish River Canyon.*

According to a native Nama legend, the giant serpent Koutein Kooru created Fish River Canyon, digging out the rock with his coils, while geologists trace its formation back to violent telluric and erosive phenomena that started 650 years ago, in the era when the supercontinent Gondwana divided. The landscape of the so-called "African Grand Canyon" is certainly legendary – extending 160 kilometers and as deep as 500 meters – and is second only to its American cousin. The most part of the 3000 excursionists that visit it every year face the terrible challenge (also due to the temperature) of doing it on foot, but here the most rewarding adventure is going on horseback, a tour that allows you not only to cross its entirety, from the town of Hobas at the sulfuric spring Ai-Ais, admiring the unreal shades of color of its rocky stratification and the spots of Aloe dichotomoa, a curious tree that the bushmen used to build their bows and arrows, but also to go further, to the Karoo Plains, all the way to the border with South Africa. It is in this territory, characterized by a mind-blowing variety of succulent plants, that you can see the little wild Nambian horses, a species that has adapted to living in the desert's extreme conditions.

Internet site www.namibiatourism.com.na

NOT TO MISS

- A DIP IN THE NATURAL JACUZZI POOLS OF **PALM SPRING AND AI-AIS,** RESPECTIVELY IN THE NORTH AND THE EXTREME SOUTH OF THE CANYON. THE FIRST OWES ITS NAME TO THE DATE PALM THAT, IT IS SAID, SPROUTED FROM THE DATE CORES LEFT BY TWO GERMAN SOLDIERS WHO, HAVING ESCAPED FROM A SOUTH AFRICAN PRISON, HID HERE FOR 2 YEARS UNTIL THE END OF WWII.
- SPEND A NIGHT AT THE **FISH RIVER LODGE:** IT IS THE ONLY STRUCTURE BUILT IN A SPECTACULAR POSITION ON THE CANYON'S EDGE. IN A LUXURIOUS MODERN-CHIC FLAVOR AND WITH PERFECT SERVICE, IT'S WHAT YOU WILL BE LOOKING FOR AFTER YOUR TIRING JOURNEY.
- LEAVING THE CANYON, ENJOY THE RIDE IN THE DUNES OF THE **AUSSENKEHR NATURE RESERVE.** HERE, ON THE BANKS OF THE ORANGE RIVER, STOP IN THE VILLAGE OF AUSSENKEHR: SURPRISINGLY, YOU WILL DISCOVER A LAND OF VINEYARDS. A PERFUMED SAUVIGNON BLANC IS MADE FROM THESE GRAPES.

When to go *From May to September.*

How long to stay *Between 6 and 11 days.*

Organization *Of the local operators that organize horseback tours in the canyon lasting between 6 and 11 days (with 20-30 kilometers covered each day), we recommend Namibia Horse Safari Company and Chameleon Holidays & Travel.*

Advice *Prepare yourself for an out of this world adventure: you probably won't encounter anyone along the way. Nor do cell phones work.*

ON THE ALTAI MOUNTAINS

In the mountain paradise of Central Asia, on a horseback adventure following the proud Kazak nomads, masters of the art of falconry.

If the father of a falconer dies the day before the first snows of November – according to the Kazaks – it is useless to wait for his son for the funeral: he'll be on the Altai Mountains with his golden eagle because the first snows announce the corsac hunting season, the fox of the steppes. And there is no better fur than that for lining heavy felt coats and hats that make up traditional Kazak dress. Besides, the art of falconry is the supreme symbol of this people's identity: they were the ones that introduced it to the Arabs and into China and, as the story goes, in the 12th century, Kazaks were Genghis Khan's personal guard, chosen from the best warriors of the falconry regiment. Up to the age of 10, every Kazak learns from his father how to capture a baby golden eagle and train it to hunt, caring for it like you would a son. Or rather, like a daughter, because the Kazak chose the more aggressive females of these large and fast birds of prey, with wingspans of over 2 meters and a flight speed that can reach 280 kilometers per hour. Following a Kazak on horseback (because they are also great riders) during the summer training of golden eagles to hunt foxes, marmots and rabbits or while they take their herd of sheep, yaks, horses and Bactrian camels to graze on the Altai Mountains, sleeping in ger, the large felt tents that are also their "mobile homes," is a life-altering experience. It will allow you to live in the natural setting of the so-called "Golden Mountains" that extend over 2000 kilometers between the Gobi Desert and the Himalayas, in one of the most remote and harshest territories in Central Asia between Russian Siberia, Mongolia and, to a lesser extent, Kazakhstan and China. Made up of peaks over 4000 meters high, glaciers, mountain lakes, rushing rivers, conifer forests and green prairies, the Altai Mountains are alienating and nobody knows them better than the Kazaks.

Internet site http://planet3000.voila.net/altai/altai_home_en.html

NOT TO MISS

● IN RUSSIAN TERRITORY, **MOUNT BELUKHA** IS SACRED TO THE KAZAKS AND WHERE THEIR CIVILIZATION ORIGINATES. EVEN ON HORSEBACK, THE CLIMB TO ITS GLACIER IS CHALLENGING (IT TAKES 2 DAYS OF TRAVEL FROM TUNGUT), BUT THE SCENERY IS EXCEPTIONAL.

● ALTHOUGH LAKE TELETSKOYE IS ONLY ACCESSIBLE WITH A SPECIAL PERMIT (DUE TO THE SPACE RUBBLE THAT FELL HERE, AT ONLY 80 KILOMETERS FROM THE TELETSKOYE SPACE STATION IN KAZAKHSTAN), **BIYA RIVER,** ITS ONLY BAYOU, IS ONE OF THE MOST POPULAR TOURIST DESTINATIONS - WELL, KIND OF - IN THE ALTAI MOUNTAINS: HERE RAFTING TRIPS ARE ORGANIZED.

● IN MONGOLIA, **ALTAI TAVAN BOGN NATIONAL PARK** OFFERS THE OPPORTUNITY FOR BIRD WATCHING ON THE BANKS OF KHOTON, KHURGAN AND DAYAN LAKES AS WELL AS FOR SEEING RARE ANIMAL SPECIES LIKE ARGALI, MARAN, THE CENTRAL ASIAN RED DEER OR EVEN THE ELUSIVE SNOW LEOPARD.

● A SHORT DISTANCE FORM KHOTON LAKE, TAKE A REST IN THE WILDEST SPA ON THE PLANET, **THE RASHANY IKU UUL HOT SPRINGS.** NEAR THE POOLS OF WATER AT 33°-36° C, YOU CAN LODGE IN A *GER* CAMP.

| **194-195** *The word Altai in Turkish and Mongolian means "Golden Mountains."*

When to go *From May to November.*

How long to stay *2 weeks.*

Organization *A horseback tour of the Altai can be organized from the Mongolian capital Ulaanbaatar with local operators like Altai Expeditions, Blue Wolf Travel, Kazakh Tour and Mongolia Horseback Riding. Or, leaving from Novosibirsk, in Russia, with Ecotours Russia and K2 Travel.*

Advice *If you decide to travel on the Russian side of the Altai, skip right over the capital of the Gorno-Altajsk Republic, which is the worst place that the Soviet regime could have ever built, and use Barnaul as a starting point, a city with 750,000 residents that is the capital of the adjacent Altai Territory: inhabited by a German community during the Tsarina of Catherine the Great, this university town is considered Siberia's hidden jewel.*

| **196** *A Kazak ger in Mongolian territory of the Altai region.* | **197** *Two falconers participate in the Kazak Eagle Festival.*

This people was recognized as the Altai Republic by Russia, extending over 92,600 square kilometers with Gorno-Altajsk as its capital, including Mount Belukha, Siberia's highest, while the 80,000 Kazaks who live in Mongolia represent a strong Muslim minority in a nation of Lamaist Buddhsts. In reality Islam "à la Kazak" is, in a certain sense, very flexible. Oral histories are the preferred method of passing down principles over reading the Koran, and there is a basic equality between men and women, who don't wear veils. Able riders, women are the protagonists of one of this people's most curious festive traditions, where they are the ones who chase down their husbands, on horseback: once they reach them they loudly whip them in a kind of settling of scores for his misgivings over the course of the last year. The "Revenge of the Wives" is one of the highlights of the Kazak Eagle Festival that is held every October in the shadows of the Tavan Bogd massif, in the fable-like landscape of the Bayan-Ölgii Region, in Mongolia. The Kazaks come from all over Altai to show off their eagle hunting skills: you should go to...

Curiosities

- *It was the Altai people who brought horses to Mongolia, and today with 2 million heads, this country has the biggest breeding capacity on the Asian continent.*
- *Falconers consider their art part of the Altai's ecological equilibrium. The corsac hunting season, an endangered animal, ends on 20 February as to not disturb their reproductive season. Regarding the golden eagles (that live 35 years on average), they are freed after 10 seasons in captivity.*
- *Kazaks also hunt wolves, for their furs, but for the Mongols this is taboo: they consider the descendants of the blue wolf, the mythical ancestors of Genghis Khan, and it is said they host his spirit, so much that sighting a wolf is good luck in Mongolia.*

| 198 *A tourist camel caravan affronts Taklamakan's dunes, western offshoots of the Gobi Desert.*

IN THE TAKLAMAKAN DESERT

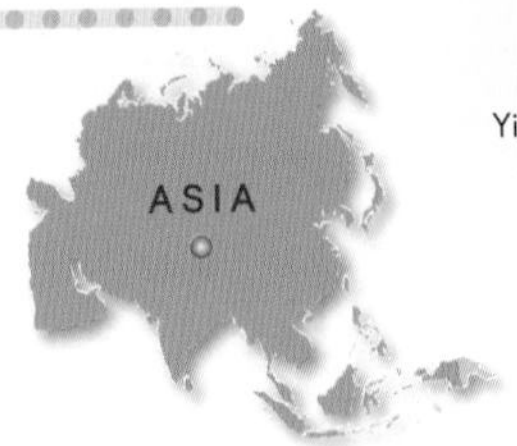

Forget the jeep: you need a Bactrian camel to really discover the desert crossed by legendary Silk Road.

In the ancient *Turcoman* language, Taklamakan means "Sea of Death." And, although it cannot compete with the planet's great deserts – it is 900 kilometers long and 400 kilometers wide – over the centuries, the testimony of those who have crossed it have always been marked with horror: in this gibbous and desolate plain, temperatures drop below -35° C in the winter, while in July they burn over 50°. When the *buran* whips up around noon, the wind blows at speeds up to 250 kilometers per hour, burying caravans in a sand and gravel storm to the extent that, according to local legend, the dunes cover famous villages and entire lost tribes. Yet, the Taklamakan was one of the obligatory steps of the Silk Road. On its edges, some of the most ancient caravan centers of Central Asia are found, from the celebrated Kashgar to the oases of Hotan and Turfan, each with its own market that recalls the stories (maybe not true, but no less fascinating for this) narrated in Marco Polo's *Books of the Marvels of the World.* Today part of the turbulent autonomous province of Xinxiang, mostly populated by Muslim Uighurs, Taklamakan has been, in a sense, dominated by Chinese

When to go *From August to September.*

How long to stay *1 or 2 weeks.*

Organization *In order to arrive in Kashgar, the starting point for a Taklamakan journey, consult the information relative to the Karakorum Highway in this volume. There are a few Uighur operators based here that propose camel tours that last between 3 and 17 days. We recommend Adbul Wahab Tours and Uighur Tours.*

Advice *Plan your trip so that you are in Kashgar and Hotan on Sunday, when both these towns host some of the biggest and most interesting markets in Central Asia.*

determination, building a highway in record time. However, to really experience the suggestive Silk Road with the due patience – discovering the extraordinary settlements of Islamic peoples with long beards and blue eyes and even more remote evidence of Buddhism, once diffused in the area – you need to at least partially go down the Taklamakan's invisible roads with what has always been the most trusted means of caravan transportation: the Bactrian camel. With two hump and thick fur, they walk up 80-meter dunes and fair much better than automobiles, especially when the *buran* blows.

Internet site www.cnto.org/silkroad-xinjiang.asp

NOT TO MISS

- THE LITTLE TOWN **YINGSAR** IS FAMOUS FOR ITS ARTESIAN PRODUCTION OF UIGHUR KNIVES, WHILE THE NEARBY **YARKHANT** – THAT WAS THE CAPITAL OF THE UIRGHUR CAPITAL OF SEIDIYE – HOSTS SPLENDID MOSQUES.
- A SHORT DISTANCE FROM HOTAN AND SURROUNDED BY POPPIES, **TONGGZUBASTI** IS ONE OF THE FEW REMAINING VILLAGES IN THE TAKLAMAKAN. ALL OF THE BUILDINGS WERE BUILT IN MUD AND THE LIVING CONDITIONS ARE EXTREME AND PRIMITIVE. IT IS SAID THAT THE INHABITANTS ARE MEMBERS OF ONE OF THE MYTHICAL TRIBES LOST IN THE DESERT.
- KNOWN AS THE GRAND CANYON OF THE TAKLAMAKAN, **TIEN SHAN** HAS SPLENDID SCENERY, WHILE THE RED ROCK WALLS ON THE NORTH SIDE OF THE MUZAT RIVER, ABOUT 40 KILOMETERS FROM THE CARAVAN CENTER OF KUCHA, IS DOTTED WITH TENS OF CAVES THAT HOST BUDDHIST REMAINS DATED BETWEEN THE 3RD AND 8TH CENTURIES.
- FROM THE TURFAN OASIS, VISIT THE RUINS OF THE **ANCIENT YARGUL** THAT, FOUNDED IN THE 1ST CENTURY B.C., WAS PROBABLY THE FIRST TAKLAMAKAN SETTLEMENT, INHABITED UNTIL THE 8TH CENTURY WHEN IT WAS RAVAGED BY THE TROUPS OF GENGHIS KHAN. A PART OF THE TOWN WALLS AND DEFENSIVE STRUCTURES, BUDDHIST STUPA, MOSQUES, TOMBS AND A SURPRISING UNDERGROUND IRRIGATION SYSTEM REMAIN.

199 *The Tien Shan Range extends over 2800 kilometers.*

WITH ELEPHANTS IN THE GOLDEN TRIANGLE

Are they the royal symbol of Thailand or only a tourist attraction? It's up to you, on an ethical adventure with these majestic Asian pachyderms.

NOT TO MISS

- EVERYDAY AT 9:40 AND 13:10, YOU CAN SEE ELEPHANTS SWIMMING AT THE THAI ELEPHANT CONSERVATION CENTER: THEY ARE EXPERT SWIMMERS (EVEN IF IT IS HARD TO BELIEVE, THEIR CLOSEST RELATIVE ARE DUGONGS) AND THEY AMUSE THEMSELVES SPRAYING EACH OTHER WITH THEIR TRUNKS.
- THE CENTER IS HOME TO AN ELEPHANT HOSPITAL, A NURSERY AND THE ROYAL STALLS WITH SIX SPLENDID ALBINOS OWNED BY THE KING OF THAILAND, BHUMIBOL ADULYADEJ. THEY ARE TRAINED TO CARRY THE LEADER IN OFFICIAL CEREMONY PARADES.
- WITH ITS PICTURESQUE NATURAL LOCATION, ON THE HILLS INHABITED BY THE KEREN TRIBE, THE CHIANG DAO ELEPHANT TRAINING SCHOOL OPENS ITS DOORS FOR PARTICIPATING IN THE TRAINING SESSIONS AND ORGANIZES WALKS AND RAFTING ON BAMBOO RAFTS ALONG THE PING RIVER.

| **200** *A* mahut *washes an elephant in Chiang Dao.* | **201** *Elephant riding.*

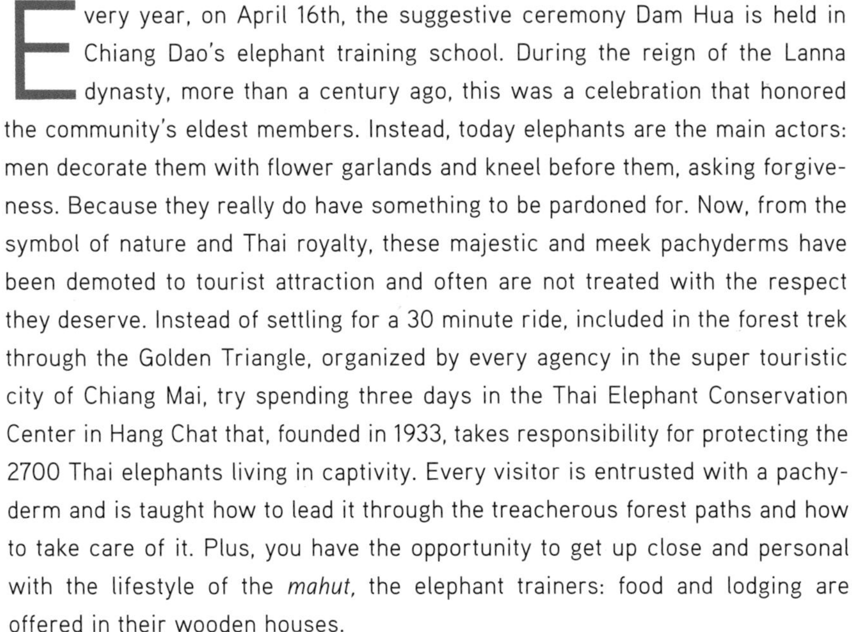

Every year, on April 16th, the suggestive ceremony Dam Hua is held in Chiang Dao's elephant training school. During the reign of the Lanna dynasty, more than a century ago, this was a celebration that honored the community's eldest members. Instead, today elephants are the main actors: men decorate them with flower garlands and kneel before them, asking forgiveness. Because they really do have something to be pardoned for. Now, from the symbol of nature and Thai royalty, these majestic and meek pachyderms have been demoted to tourist attraction and often are not treated with the respect they deserve. Instead of settling for a 30 minute ride, included in the forest trek through the Golden Triangle, organized by every agency in the super touristic city of Chiang Mai, try spending three days in the Thai Elephant Conservation Center in Hang Chat that, founded in 1933, takes responsibility for protecting the 2700 Thai elephants living in captivity. Every visitor is entrusted with a pachyderm and is taught how to lead it through the treacherous forest paths and how to take care of it. Plus, you have the opportunity to get up close and personal with the lifestyle of the *mahut,* the elephant trainers: food and lodging are offered in their wooden houses.

When to go *From November to March.*

How long to stay *From 1 day to 1 week.*

Organization *Next to the Thai Elephant Conservation Center, within 50 kilometers of Chiang Mai, there are other places where you can ethically experience these pachyderms.*
We recommend Elephant Nature Camp, a sanctuary that hosts tens of exemplars saved from accidents or violent situations to favor their return to freedom and organizes forest treks that last 2, 7 or 14 days.

Advice *If you prefer a "softer" approach, book a stay at the luxurious Anantara Golden Triangle Resort & Spa in Chiang Saen, near Chiang Rai: immersed in the jungle, the complex hosts an Elephant Camp managed in collaboration with the Golden Triangle Elephant Foundation and organizes treks guided by* mahut *and river swimming with elephants.*

Internet site www.thailandelephant.org

| **202-203** *The trail mostly travels through mountain landscapes on the border with Laos.*

NOT TO MISS

● IN HANOI, PAY HOMAGE TO **HO CHI MINH** AT THE **MAUSOLEUM** THAT HOSTS HIS REMAINS AND IN THE MUSEUM DEDICATED THE TRIUMPHS OF COMMUNISM NARRATED WITH INCREDIBLY KITSCH FLAVOR: PROPAGANDA IN TECHNICOLOR!

● EXPERIENCE EXOTIC **THAI HOSPITALITY** IN A HANDFUL OF STILTED VILLAGES IN THE NORTHERN MOUNTAINS, TASTING THEIR FOOD AND WITNESSING THEIR ELABORATE TRADITIONS TIED TO THEIR ANCESTORS' BELIEFS.

● STOP IN **HUÉ,** VIETNAM'S ANCIENT CAPITAL, TO ADMIRE THE TOMBS AND ROYAL PAGODAS. THEN CROSS THE FAMOUS WARTIME BORDER AT THE 17TH PARALLEL AND HEAD TO **HAI AN** THAT, FOUNDED BY JAPANESE MERCHANTS IN THE 16TH CENTURY, IS THE COUNTRY'S MOST ROMANTIC CITY.

● IN THE CU CHI DISTRICT, NOT FAR FROM HO CHI MINH CITY, YOU CAN VISIT THE LEGENDARY **TUNNELS DUG BY THE VIETCONG.** THEY ARE A KIND OF MAN-SIZED ANT COLONY (OR ALMOST, SINCE YOU HAVE TO CRAWL IN SOME PARTS) THAT WERE USED AS HIDING PLACES, STOREHOUSES AND EVEN AS FIELD HOSPITALS FOR THE SOLDIERS FIGHTING AGAINST SOUTH VIETNAM FORCES.

ALONG THE HO CHI MINH TRAIL

Forests, mud and excitement in a mythical motorcycle adventure through the history of the Vietnam War.

"One of the great achievements of military engineering": this is how the American National Security Agency defined the Ho Chi Minh Trail during the Vietnam War. 1600 kilometers long, this trail allowed troops and ammunitions to be transported between Hanoi and Saigon, now Ho Chi Minh City, supplying fundamental logistic support to the people's army of North Vietnam and the Vietcong resistance in the south. Even if it was the symbol of the most disastrous wartime chapter in United States history at the time, today the trail is still shrouded in myth. Since 2000, the country can boast the Ho Chi Minh Highway, a useful costal throughway that unites the capital, in the north, to the rampant metropolises in the south: but don't be confused, because the trail by the same name dedicated to the patriotic father is still mostly hidden in the forest among the mountains along the border with Laos. And traveling it is anything but easy, but allows you to discover remote locations with a formidable natural beauty, villages surrounded with a chessboard of rice paddies and inhabited by around 30 ethnic minorities. And, above all, distant – in kilometers and decades – from the most visited tourist destinations in Vietnam. To be philologically correct (also because you can only travel the entire distance on 2 wheels: some parts are too narrow for automobiles), you have to adventure along the trail in the just as mythical Minsk, the 125cc motorcycle that, although still produced in Vietnam, is a Soviet-era vintage bike. But before departing you should know that, scenery a part, you shouldn't expect an *Apocalypse Now* experience, but the disarming hospitality of the most smiling people of Southeast Asia.

Internet site www.ridehochiminhtrail.com

When to go *From November to March. In this period the average temperature in the north is 17° C (10° C in the mountains) and 27° C in the south.*

How long to stay *To cover the entire trail between Hanoi and Ho Chi Minh City you need at least 16 days.*

Organization *Specialized in adventurous journeys and ethical and sustainable tourism, the operators of Activetravel Vietnam and Explore Indochina propose itineraries along the entire trail, between Hanoi and Ho Chi Minh City, or just a part of it. Every tour includes Minsk rental, a guide, a mechanic and all food and lodging for 90 Euro a day.*

Advice *This is not a trip for beginners: prepare yourself to drive at least 160 kilometers a day on make-shift roads, full of obstacles like rivers, mud, steep slopes and slaloms between chickens and water buffaloes.*

THE BICENTENNIAL NATIONAL TRAIL

5330 kilometers long, through all the country's landscapes and the longest marked trail in the world, heroically blazed on horseback.

"He was excessively generous, loved to joke and was a volcano of energy." This is how Dan Seymour is described by those who met him. Born in the Canadian state of Alberta in 1923, he died at 78 in Dorrigo, in the north of New Southern Wales. Dan was a pioneer down to his bones: after various peregrinations in the Far West and taking sail as a cabin boy for the United States Merchant Marines, he emigrated to Australia in 1950, where he worked for 20 years in the outback. At the beginning of the 1960s, he met R.M. Williams at a rodeo, an eccentric bushman who had become a millionaire and founder of the Australian Trail Horse Riders Association. The two hit it off rat first glance and, when Williams told him his dream of blazing a horse trail that crossed Australia north to south following the pioneers, Dan volunteered for the challenging task. So, leaving in February 1972 from Ferntree Gully, in Victoria, with two horses a donkey and Bluey, his faithful German shepherd, 21 months later – having flanked the entire Great Dividing Range, the 4th longest mountain range in the world – Dan arrived in Cooktown, in the tropics of Queensland. He had ridden over 5000 kilometers. Thus the National Horse Trail was born, even if it would take years to map the itinerary, dividing it into 12 sections of 400-500 kilometers each, indicating each kilometer with a sign as well as write and publish a careful guide on each

NOT TO MISS

- ALONG SECTION 2 OF THE BNT, STOP IN **RAVENSWOOD.** TODAY ITS HAS JUST 160 INHABITANTS AND IS ALMOST A GHOST TOWN, BUT AT THE END OF THE 1800S IT WAS THE CENTER OF THE AUSTRALIAN GOLD RUSH. ITS BUILDINGS ARE A PART OF NATIONAL HERITAGE AND THERE IS STILL A FASCINATING PUB IN THE HISTORICAL IMPERIAL HOTEL.
- WITH A BORDER-TOWN ATMOSPHERE, **KILKIVAN,** IN QUEENSLAND, IS ONE OF THE RARE TOWNS CROSSED BY THE BNT. HERE, EVERY YEAR IN APRIL, THERE IS AUSTRALIA'S LARGEST **COWBOY GATHERING:** OVER 1000 HORSES PARTICIPATE IN THE PARADE.
- BETWEEN EBOR AND ABERDEEN, SECTION 8 CROSSES A SERIES OF MOUNTAIN FORESTS, WETLANDS AND FIVE NATIONAL PARKS. PLAN A VISIT TO DISCOVER THE FLORA AND FAUNA, BETWEEN GIANT FERNS, RARE MARSUPIAL SPECIES AND TESTIMONIES TO ABORIGINAL CULTURE, GUIDED BY DISCOVERY RANGERS.
- THE VAST MOUNTAIN REGION OF **KOSCIUSZKO** NATIONAL PARK IS DOMINATED BY MOUNT KOSCIUSZKO (2228 METERS), AUSTRALIA'S HIGHEST. ACCESSIBLE ON HORSEBACK, THE PEAK MARKS THE BEGINNING OF SECTION 11 OF THE BNT THAT, IN TURN, INTERSECTS WITH THE GRANDIOSE EXCURSIONIST ITINERARY OF THE ALPINE WALKING TRACK, IN THE STATE OF VICTORIA.

| 204 *A forest waterfall in Brisbane.*

| **205** *A cyclist wades across a swamp near Jervis Bay in New South Wales.*

section. In 1988, the festive celebrations for Australia's bicentennial coincided with the completion of his efforts and there could have been no better occasion for renaming this trail – the perfect symbol of the nation's spirit – The Australian Bicentennial National Trail. Rightly a source of pride for all Australians, this is the longest marked trail on the planet. Its kilometer zero is in Cooktown and the official finish line is in Healesville, about 60 kilometers from Melbourne, after crossing the entire country, north to south, over 5330 kilometers of trail. It connects 18 national parks and 50 protected forest reserves with spectacular scenery through tropical forests, gorges, mountain peaks and valleys, dry desert plains of red sand and enters into some of the most remote and uncontaminated parts of this stunning country. Naturally, most excursionists travel only one of its 12 sections, or even just a fraction of one, and today there are only around 20 brave souls who have accomplished the entire herculean itinerary. Even if conceived for horseback travel (and, let's say, its "variations": there are those who have travel on donkeys or camels), recently some parts have become popular destinations for mountain bike enthusiasts, while others are more adapted for foot trekking. On September 17th, 2012, the ultramarathoner Richard Bowles crossed the finish line in what, after Dan Seymour's endeavor, will remain inscribe in the history books forever as the most legendary adventure on the Australian National Trail: he crossed the entire trail in five months, surviving (among other things) the torrid heat and deep mud of its tropical forests as well as freezing snowstorms on its mountain ranges, he even risked being horned by a bull and swept away by a rushing river. Thanks to ample media coverage, all Australians anxiously followed him step by step throughout his long trip. And, jokingly, they even nicknamed him the "Australian Forest Gump."

Internet site www.nationaltrail.com.au

| 206 *The outback in the Upper Hunter Valley, Australia's cowboy and horsing capital.*

When to go *The BNT crosses very diverse climates, latitudes and altitudes, however the best season for most of the trail is between April and October.*

How long to stay *As long as you can!*

Organization *Although well marked - and even if you have a detailed guide: there is a large volume for each of the 12 sections - the BNT is so varied that some of its parts are comfortable walks that you can do independently, while others are dangerous and should only be done with an expert guide. Given its extension, there is no tour operator in the world that proposes trips along the entire course, so its best to consult the official tourism site of the various states that it crosses for organizing a horseback adventure. Only in Victoria - that includes most of section 1, accessible in late spring and in the autumn - the BNT has been subdivided into 11 parts, each possible to do in 1 or 2 days.*

Advice *Bring a GPS tracker with you and compare your coordinates with the ones that appear in the guide often.*

Curiosities

The starting line for the BNT, Cooktown, is a small town (with just over 2000 residents) built precisely on the spot where Captain James Cook landed in Australia in 1770. It is at the mouth of the Endeavor River, named in honor of his vessel.

Recently, during an exploration of the Queensland forests for the documentary Searching for Bigfoot, *a TV troupe from Animal Planet recorded sounds defined as "the most reliable proof" of the existence of the mythic primate that Australian tradition calls the* Yowie. *Be warned: you could be the first to see it, crossing sections 1 and 2...*

Upper Hunter Valley, at the beginning of section 9, is one of the biggest horse-breeding centers in the world. Just in Scone, there are 65 stables of prized purebloods and the most prestigious horse show in the world has been organized here since 1947.

WESTERN AUSTRALIA BY MOTORCYCLE

On 2 wheels – and dusty red tracks – to taste freedom and the landscapes of an Australia that is still a land of pioneers.

For experts in Australian adventure, it is simply Kim. Instead, on geographical maps, it is Kimberley, a region (larger than Germany but with only 40,000 inhabitants) that, even for Australians, is the icon of the wilderness, of pioneering spirit and the experience – challenging and exciting – of the outback, that landscape of fire-red earth that doesn't look like part of our planet. This Far West, that also hosts one of the richest diamond mines in the world as well as fantastic national parks like Purnululu or Bungle Bungles and the Windjana Gorge, is "just barely" a part of the state of Western Australia that, with its capital Perth, is the fabled "last frontier" for tourism here. In line with the adventurous character of this immense territory (and its hospitable inhabitants), Western Australia gives its best if explored by motorcycle, along the dusty internal roads to discover deserts, gorges and secret valleys that conceal rivers, waterfalls and colorful and

| **207** *An old livestock trail, Gibb River Road extends over 660 kilometers.*

curious flora, or along the coasts, dotted with dream beaches, like the ones on Dampier peninsula in the north, or Monkey Mia, where you can experience swimming with dolphins, all the way to Ningaloo and its barrier reef protected by UNESCO and accessible – literally – with a couple of stokes from the mainland. And if there are almost an infinite amount of possible itineraries in this extreme Australian paradise, a long crossing of Kimberley's arid north to the green lands in the south, near Perth, lets visitors experience all Australia's climates and ecosystems. Including the majestic tree-monument of the celebrated Southwestern Forest and Margeret River, one of the sweetest and epicurean wine zones in Australia.

Internet site www.westernaustralia.com

When to go *From May to September.*

How long to stay *You need at least 1 month to cross Western Australia from north to south, but you can plan a 1-2 week motorcycle trip in each of the state's regions.*

Organization *Traveling Western Australia by motorcycle is very popular and there are various operators in the state that propose guided itineraries or motorcycle rentals with technical assistance along the route. We recommend Kimberley Trail Bike Tours, in Kimberley, and Down Under Motorcycle Tours in Perth, who offer trips on legendary Harley-Davidsons.*

Advice *Live this experience with the courageous pioneering spirit, but don't' forget to bring a GPS. Because it's easy to lose yourself in this immense wildlife...*

NOT TO MISS

- TRACED BY HERDS OF LIVESTOCK, THE **GIBB RIVER ROAD** THAT, OVER 660 KILOMETERS OF DIRT ROAD, CONNECTS WYNDHAM AND DERBY IN THE KIMBERLEY REGION, IS THE MOST CHALLENGING AND LEGENDARY OF ALL THE OUTBACK ROADS IN AUSTRALIA. ITS LANDSCAPES, ALONE, MERIT A TRIP FROM ONE END TO THE OTHER.
- NORTH OF DAMPIER PENINSULA, THE **ROCK WALLS NEAR BURRUP** HOST THE MOST IMPORTANT COLLECTION OF CAVE PAINTINGS IN AUSTRALIA. HERE, EVEN THE MOST ANCIENT PICTOGRAMS, DATED TO THE LAST ICE AGE AROUND 60,000 YEARS AGO, ARE EXTRAORDINARILY ELABORATE AND TELL OF A COMPLEX SYSTEM OF MYTHS OF THE ABORIGINE'S ANCESTRAL "DREAMTIME," NARRATED IN BRUCE CHATWIN'S *THE SONGLINES.*
- A TRIP ALONG **INDIAN OCEAN DRIVE,** THE SPECTACULAR COASTAL DRIVE ALONG THE SO-CALLED CORAL COAST, WILL TAKE YOU THROUGH UNCONTAMINATED MARINE LANDSCAPES AND COSTAL DESERTS WITH GOLDEN SAND DUNES: DON'T MISS THE FANTASTIC LUNAR SHELL AND SANDSTONE FOSSILS OF **PINNACLES** IN **NUMBING NATIONAL PARK.**
- ALONG WITH THE PLEASURES OF WINE AND FLORA WITH MORE THAN 8000 SPECIES OF FLOWERING PLANTS (INCLUDING 400 ORCHIDS), THE **SOUTH WEST REGION** OFFERS SURFING BEACHES AND, BETWEEN MAY AND SEPTEMBER, ITS WATERS ARE A HOTSPOT FOR WHALE WATCHING.

| **208** *The rocky pinnacles of Nambung National Park.* | **209** *Cape Leveque, on the northern edge of Western Australia.*

IN MONUMENT VALLEY

On horseback through sandstone masterpieces and red sand dunes in the iconic valley that was the setting for John Ford's classic westerns.

NOT TO MISS

- MOST VISITORS COME HERE TO ADMIRE THE SUNRISE AND SUNSET, BUT YOU SHOULD ALSO **STAY OVERNIGHT:** MONUMENT VALLEY IS ONE OF THE RARE PLACES IN THE UNITED STATES WHERE THERE IS NO LIGHT POLLUTION FROM ARTIFICIAL SOURCES AND THE STARTS ARE CLEARLY VISIBLE ALL THE WAY TO THE HORIZON.
- WITH ITS FRAGILE APPEARANCE, THE VERY HIGH AND VERY THIN PINNACLE SHAPE OF **TOTEM POLE** IS ONE OF THE MOST CURIOUS ROCK FORMATIONS IN TSE' BII' NDZISGAII ("ROCK VALLEY," THE NAVAJO NAME FOR MONUMENT VALLEY). PHOTOGRAPH IT AT SUNDOWN, WITH THE RED SAND DUNES IN THE BACKGROUND.
- CONSIDERED THE VALLEY'S HIDDEN TREASURE, **HUNTS MESA** IS ACCESSIBLE THROUGH KEYENTA ONLY ON GUIDED OFF-ROAD TOURS, DEDICATED TO LANDSCAPE PHOTOGRAPHY ENTHUSIASTS. MONUMENT VALLEY SAFARI ORGANIZES THESE EXCURSIONS.
- MANAGED BY A NAVAJO FAMILY AND PERFECTLY INTEGRATED INTO THE LANDSCAPE, **THE VIEW** IS THE ONLY **HOTEL** INSIDE THE PROTECTED AREA. ALL OF ITS 95 ROOMS HAVE A SPECTACULAR VIEW.

When to go *From May to September.*

How long to stay *2 days.*

Organization *For a horseback adventure that lasts from a few hours to 2 days with lodging, see Sacred Monument Tours or Black's Tours. For a longer itinerary (custom tailored, with horses if desired) in the Navajo Nation Parks, contact the operator Discover Navajo.*

Advice *Stop in one the Navajo Nation's Trading Posts to buy native artifacts (silver jewelry, rugs and traditional ceramics) and cinematographic memorabilia.*

| **210** *Mitten Butte, the unmistakable film silhouette.*
| **211** *A guided horseback excursion through Monument Valley.*

The question is worthy of Hamlet: did film transform Monument Valley into a legend or is it the wilderness of this landscape that made John Ford's films legendary? It's impossible to say. The best place to contemplate Monument Valley from above is the one with the sign John Ford Point, and you can bet that the director of *Stagecoach* and *The Searchers* really set up his camera in that spot to shoot the memorable scenes of his great westerns, so it almost seems obvious to watch an assault on a stagecoach or a clash between cowboys and Indians right there, among the flaming sandstone masterpieces Mitten Butte and Merrick Butte. It's true that Monument Valley existed way before John Ford, but he gave it to the world, ripping it from its separated existence in a remote angle of the Navajo Reserve, on the border between Arizona and Utah (and 70 kilometers from Kayenra, the nearest inhabited center), to make it the icon par excellence of the epic West. Today, this magnificent valley studded with monumental square hills called *mesas* or buttes that are the result of millenniums of erosive activity is the most visited and photographed of the Navajo Nation's so-called tribal parks. To be philologically correct, you should experience it on horseback, accompanied by a Navajo that will show you, next to the cinematographic natural monuments, the interesting aspects of Native American culture, from ancient and mysterious petroglyphs to a suggestive pueblo, an ancient troglodyte settlement of the legendary Anasazi people that were the Navajo's ancestors.

Internet site http://navajonationparks.org/htm/monumentvalley.htm

| 212 *The sweet panorama of the Valle de Viñales, with typical mogotes in the background.*

THE FAR WEST OF PINAR DEL RÍO

NORTH AMERICA

By motorcycle (or even with a sidecar) and then on horseback to discover the west of the island, the marvelous land of the world's finest tobacco.

There are 60,858 kilometers of Cuban roads. Of this, about half isn't asphalted and all of them are literally Swiss cheesed with holes. Plus, if you consider that, outside Havana, traffic is mostly made up of the *campesinos'* little carts, old trucks that carry cane sugar and *guaguas,* collective buses (little more than rusty heaps) full of people, including riders on the roof, then it goes without saying that the most fun means of transportation for an Cuban on the road adventure is, without a doubt, a motorcycle. And, of the "Cuban centaur" adventures, the most epic and curious is the one that leads... to the west of the island, precisely, to the province of Pinar del Río, 170 kilometers from the capital. Although there are other zones dedicated to tobacco cultivation on the island (that, together with tourism, is the main source of currency, precious for the Cuban state), here the plantations extend over 40,000 hectares and produce a fine variety used for the *capa,* the outside part of these celebrated cigars. But not only: in the heart of the province, in Valle di Viñales – protected by UNESCO for its extraordinary natural and cultural landscape – the tobacco fields are alternated with characteristic and scenic limestone rock formations called *mogotes* and clearings that host the entire, rich collection of Cuban botany, with curiosities like the *almacigo,* familiarly known as the "tourist tree" because the bark strips like the faces of vacationers exposed to the Caribbean sun. Along the little roads of Pinar del Río, then, you will discover

When to go *From December to April.*

How long to stay *1 week, including the trip to and from Havana.*

Organization *All you need is your passport and a driver's license to rent a motorcycle in Havana: often they are older bikes (it is also possible to rent a Soviet sidecar), but make sure that they are in good condition. To rent a motorcycle or for 2-wheeled tours, we recommend the operators Mototouring, and Italian company, and Cuba Motorcycle Tours, that proposes Harley-Davidson rentals and tours.*

Advice *The* mogotes *in Valle de Viñales are the perfect destination for rock climbing since some of the walls are easy enough for beginners*

villages that look like they were transported from a film on the Far West, with wooden houses and a population of cowboys, descendants from the colonies that came here from the Canary Islands at the end of the 18th century to cultivate tobacco for the Crown of Spain. They maintain the blue eyes and blond hair of their ancestors as well as an exceptional ability to ride. And, every now and then, its worth it to park your bike and go down the most dangerous roads on horseback, slowly penetrating the enchanting canyons studded with *mogotes*.

Internet site www.cubatravel.cu

NOT TO MISS

- THE ZONE AROUND VUELTA ABAJO IS KNOWN FOR ITS PRODUCTION OF WHAT COULD BE DEFINED AS THE *GRAND CRU* OF TOBACCO. HERE YOU CAN VISIT THE *TABAQUERE* COMPANIES, IN PARTICULAR THE PRESTIGIOUS **FINCA VEGAS ROBAINA IN THE VILLAGE OF JUAN Y MARTÍNEZ,** THAT PRODUCES THE BEST HABANOS CIGARS IN THE WORLD FROM LEAVES SELECTED ACCORDING TO THE STANDARDS ESTABLISHED BY ITS FOUNDER, THE LEGENDARY DON ALEJANDRO ROBAINA.
- *MOGOTES* HIDE MANY CAVES. VISIT THE **CUEVAS DEL INDIO,** WITH REMAINS OF THE TAÍNO TRIBE, AND THE ONE IN SANTO TOMÁS, THE ISLAND'S LARGEST NATURAL CAVE: YOU GET THERE THROUGH A SPECTACULAR FOREST LANDSCAPE. THEN, ON THE **MOGOTE LOS HERMANOS,** A GIGANTIC AND SUPER KITSCH MURAL WAS PAINTED (COMMISSIONED BY FIDEL CASTRO) THAT ILLUSTRATES HUMANITY'S JOURNEY FROM *HOMO SAPIENS*... TO *HOMO SOCIALISTA*.
- STAY IN THE PARTICULAR HOUSES IN PINAR DEL RÍO'S CAPITAL OR IN THE NEARBY VILLAGES TO GET A TASTE OF THE WARM HOSPITALITY OF THESE CUBAN COWBOYS, WHO WILL TREAT YOU TO A ROBUST CUISINE WITH **GUAYABITA** (THE TYPICAL, HIGH-PROOF PLEASURABLE POISON) AND POIGNANT BOLEROS SANG AT THE GUITAR.
- TAKE A HORSE RIDE TO THE VILLAGE OF **LOS AQUATICÓS,** WHERE THE LAST MEMBERS OF A COMMUNITY CONVINCED THAT THERE IS NOTHING BETTER FOR YOUR HEALTH THAN TO BATHE ONCE A DAY IN THE NEARBY RIVERS. THEY EVEN MAKE THEIR LIVESTOCK TAKE A SWIM...

| 213 *Casa del Veguero, a tobacco plantation near Viñales.*

IN THE PAMPA WITH THE GAUCHOS

Saddled in a "Criollo" horse, travel among the estancias in the provinces of Buenos Aires and Córdoba to experience the tradition of Argentinean cowboys.

There are more cows than inhabitants in Argentina. To be precise, there are 54 million bovines and 40 million humans. And – it couldn't be otherwise – this isn't the place for vegetarians: at 70 kilograms *pro capite,* Argentineans are by for the world leaders in consuming red meat. According to the story, bovines arrived here halfway through the 16th century, brought form Spain by Don Pedro de Mendoza, who also founded Buenos Aires. However, a few years later, colonization came to a standstill and the *indios* rebellion devastated the Spanish encampments, the Spaniards finding refuge in the Pampa's endless prairies. Here, where pastures were abundant and predators scarce, their animal quickly reproduced and, in just a few decades, they reached 1 million. At the time, private property didn't exist, but the *derecho de vaquería* was instituted, i.e. the right to capture livestock. The Gauchos were the ones that took on the responsibility (the term comes from Quechua and means "orphan," or

Internet site
www.confederaciongaucha.com.ar

| **214** *A gaucho using his lasso.*

| 215 *The* estancias, *typical Argentinean ranches, are often equipped to host excursionists.*

"solitary"), and invented a whole lifestyle: they captured cows and calves, feed off their meat and worked their skins. Many of them became legendary characters – some were even attributed miracles! – and today the Guacho tradition is the symbol of Argentina, just as much as the Tango, Jorge Luís Borges and the Boca Juniors soccer club. The Gauchos' temples are the *estancias*, enormous ranches in the provinces of Buenos Aires and Córdoba. They are places to visit but, above all, to live with the cowboys in the Pampa, saddled up in a Criolla horse, accompanying them on a day's work and following the enormous bovine herds and, at night, dining with them, in their typical *pulperias* or out in the open under the moonlight, in a banquet based on the traditional *asado*, Argentina's monumental red meat barbeque. No vegetarians allowed!

When to go *From November to March.*

How long to stay *1 or 2 weeks.*

Organization *To stay in an* estancia, *in order to live the Guacho traditions and explore the Pampa on horseback, choose the one most adapted to your needs (there are a few that have polo camps and schools, the equestrian sport par* excellence*). Among the operators that organize tours on horseback, we recommend Argentina Exeptión, Riding Argentina and Welcome Argentina.*

Advice *Before adventuring into the Pampa, buy gaucho equipment (boots, leather hat and the unforgettable poncho) at the Fiera de Mataderos held every Sunday in the neighborhood by the same name in Buenos Aires. The best gauchos artisans are found here.*

NOT TO MISS

- DECLARED A HISTORICAL VILLAGE OF NATIONAL INTEREST, **SAN ANTONIO DE ARECO,** AT 100 KILOMETERS FROM BUENOS AIRES, IS THE CAPITAL OF GUACHO CULTURE. ALONG WITH THE MANY *ESTANCIAS*, YOU CAN VISIT THE **MUSEO GUACHESCO RICARDO GÜIRALDES,** THAT TELLS THE HISTORY AND TRADITIONS OF THE PAMPA COWBOYS. IN EARLY NOVEMBER, THE FIESTA DE LA TRADICIÓN IS CELEBRATED HERE, WITH GAUCHOS COMPETING IN HORSE COMPETITIONS.
- PROTECTED BY UNESCO, THE *ESTANCIAS* FOUNDED BY THE JESUITS BETWEEN 1599 AND 1767 IN THE PROVINCE OF CÓRDOBA ARE BAROQUE ARCHITECTURAL TREASURES AND, THANKS TO AGRICULTURE AND LIVESTOCK, THEY CREATE A UNIQUE CULTURAL, SOCIAL AND RELIGIOUS SYSTEM IN LATIN AMERICA. YOU SHOULD VISIT THEM ALL, BUT THE ABSOLUTE MASTERPIECE IS **ESTANCIA SANTA CATALINA.**
- THE **ONGAMIRA VALLEY,** A PROTECTED NATIONAL PARK, HAS ONE OF THE MOST EXTRAORDINARY LANDSCAPES OF THE PAMPAS. CROSSED BY THE SAUCES RIVER AND STUDDED WITH *TERRONES*, GREAT MASSES OF RED SANDSTONE, THIS PRAIRIE IS A MUST FOR HORSEBACK, LEAVING FROM THE SPLENDID **ESTANCIA DOS LUNAS.**

FRESH WATER

YOU CAN NEVER STEP INTO THE SAME RIVER TWICE, ACCORDING TO ANCIENT WISDOM. RIVERS TRAVEL WITH US. AND MORE THAN US.

There probably is no more effective symbol than the river to describe movement and constant change, in landscapes like in our journey through life. Besides, there is nothing else like water, so tenacious in moving and running everywhere. So, break all barriers and chose to travel – and lose yourself – in the immense labyrinth of rivers and canals on this planet. Along fresh water routes the trip is fresh too, whether they cross Ireland's placid scenery or chose to meander through the bursting Amazon Basin, whether paddling a canoe to discover the extraordinary fauna of the Okavango Delta, northern Africa's purest treasure, or in a dingy, hoping to see a ferocious Bengal tiger in the mangroves of the Sundarbans.

In addition, our civilization was born along rivers (and lakes). It is here, in the lands made fertile from flooding that man started cultivating the earth and changing the planet to meet his needs, with results – macroscopically visible in the Amazon – that don't always put us in a good light. But from the waterways that penetrate a dense forest to the liquid highways of the Mekong Delta, every river has a great story to tell.

OURNEY

ETHNOGRAPHIC JOURNEY
WILDLIFE WATCHING
TREKKING
BICYCLING
OFF-ROAD
TRAIN
PLANE
SAILBOAT
MOTORBOAT
KAYAK
HORSEBACK

THE LANDSCAPES CHANGE
WITH THE SEASONS,
STIMULATING NEW EMOTIONS
AND NEW PERSPECTIVES
FOR OBSERVING NATURE
AND HUMAN ACTIVITY.

FRESH WATER JOURNEY

CHOSE THE RIGHT EMOTION

JOURNEY	PG	TIME ZONE	WHEN TO GO	NOT TO MISS
Ireland - Ireland's Waterways	222	GMT0	May-September	*Athlone*
India, Bangladesh - In the Labyrinth of the Sundarbans	224	GMT+5:30/+6	October-March	*Sajnekhali Tiger Reserve*
Vietnam, Cambodia - In the Mekong Delta	226	GMT+7	November-April	*Cai Be Market*
Indonesia - With the Orangutans of Kalimantan	230	GMT+8	May-September	*Camp Leakey*
Canada - On the Nahanni River	232	GMT-7	May-September	*Virginia Falls*
Botswana - In the Okavango Delta	234	GMT+2	June-October	*Moremi Game Reserve*
Guatemala - Sailing the Río Dulce	236	GMT-6	November-May	*Castillo de San Felipe de Lara*
Honduras - In a Cayuco at La Moskitia	238	GMT-6	Feb-May/Aug-Nov	*Raista and Bélen*
Venezuela - Canoeing Salto Ángel	240	GMT -4:30	June-November	*Kavak*
Brazil - On Río Negro	242	GMT-4	July-December	*Yanomami villages*
Brazil - In the Pantanal	246	GMT-4	May-October	*Fauna*

| **220-221** *The Okavango Delta in Botswana has one of the largest concentrations of fauna in Africa.*

DON'T FORGET	A CLASSIC BOOK FOR EVERY JOURNEY
Electronic badge for opening locks	*Brendan Behan,* Confessions of an Irish Rebel
Antimalarial treatment	*Amitav Ghosh,* The Hungry Tide
Mosquito repellant	*Marguerite Duras,* The Lover
Camera	*Mary Galdikas,* Orangutan Odyssey
Waterproof clothing	*R.M Patterson,* Dangerous River: Adventure on the Nahanni
Camera	*Alexander McCall Smith,* Tears of the Giraffe
Waterproof clothing	*Gabriel García Marquéz,* Love in the Time of Cholera
Antimalarial treatment	*Paul Theroux,* The Mosquito Coast
Binoculars	*Arthur Conan Doyle,* The Lost World
Waterproof container	*Ann Patchett,* State of Wonder
Yellow fever vaccination	*Jorge Amado,* Showdown

IRELAND'S WATERWAYS

On a houseboat or a canoe, discovering the internal waterways of the green island.

Internet site www.waterwaysireland.org

"If you don't like the weather, wait 5 minutes," the Irish love to say to foreigners who complain about the downpours that, around here, torrentially fall when you least expect it, disappearing just as quickly giving way to sweet rays of sun. But, if it weren't for the rain, Ireland wouldn't be the green country par excellence. Plus the water that comes from the sky is part of the show here. Few know, in fact, that a fifth of the island is "liquid," making a giant natural amusement park spread over 13 counties and extending over 1000 kilometers of navigable waterways, half of which are along the Shannon, the main river through the British Isles. Furthermore, the Gran Canal and the Royal Canal are added to this, the two majestic artificial waterways that, built in the 18th century, connecting the Shannon to the Liffey, Dublin's river – thus bringing, through commerce, Ireland into the modern age – as well as the vast systems of locks and channels between the great river and the Erne that, widening into two lakes, is Ulster's enchanting liquid highway. Since 1999, the island's internal waters are managed by Waterways

| 222 *Carrick-on-Shannon is the main departure point for cruises.*

| 223 *Ross Castle on Lough Leane is the historical home of the O'Donoghue Clan.*

Ireland, on of the first joint organizations between Northern Ireland and the Republic, and represents one of the largest ecotourism districts in Europe. You can spend entire, unforgettable weeks slowly navigating aboard a well-equipped houseboat, paddling a canoe or kayak, dedicating yourself to windsurfing or waterskiing, fishing and even swimming (if you are able to stand the water temperature, never above 18° C). And, above all, admiring the romantic rural landscapes made up of fairytale castles, pastures, clearings blooming with irises and narcissuses and ponds populated with ducks and swans, all from a new perspective. Then, in the evening, the river hamlets offer navigators refreshment and craic, traditional "indigenous" fun made with Guinness beer and Gaelic music. The latter – everyone here swears it – is the mother of bluegrass, the soundtrack to the American Far West, colonized by intrepid cowboys of Irish descent.

When to go *The nicest time to go is between May and September.*

How long to stay *In high season, boats are rented for 1 or 2 weeks.*

Organization *To rent a boat, see the Irish Boat Rental Association. You don't need a boating license or previous navigational experience. The cruise can be coupled with golf at any of the innumerable greens along the banks or a cultural itinerary.*

Advice *Before leaving, be sure to buy the electronic badge that enables you open the water locks (available at all marinas).*

NOT TO MISS

- 146 KILOMETERS LONG, WITH A SYSTEM OF 46 LOCKS, THE **ROYAL CANAL** CONNECTS DUBLIN TO THE HEART OF IRELAND AND TAKES YOU THROUGH THE COUNTRY'S HISTORY.
- IN MULLINGAR, ON THE ROYAL CANAL, VISIT THE **BELVEDERE HOUSE & GARDENS:** THIS MAGNIFICENT HOME IS SURROUNDED BY ROSE AND HIMALAYAN RHODODENDRON GARDENS AND HOSTS A ROMANTIC FOLLY OF FAKE GOTHIC RUINS.
- ON A BIGHT OF THE SHANNON AND DOMINATED BY A CASTLE, THE SPLENDID LITTLE TOWN OF **ATHLONE** IS AT THE EXACT CENTER OF IRELAND.
- WANT ADVENTURE? **LOUGH ALLEN,** ON THE BORDER WITH ULSTER, CAN BE EXPLORED IN A CANOE WHILE THE NEARBY **IRON MOUNTAINS** ARE PERFECT FOR TREKKING.

IN THE LABYRINTH OF THE SUNDARBANS

The Bengal Basin hosts the largest mangrove expanse on the planet. And it is the last sanctuary of the "man-eating" tiger.

When we're standing on their wooden boats, along the water labyrinth created by the planet's largest mangrove forest, the Sundarbans fishermen wear a mask of a human face on the back of their heads. This is the only defense they have against the fierce Bengal tiger that, it is said, only attacks cunningly from behind. Here they call them "man-eaters," and not incorrectly, because every year at least 50 villagers are killed along the banks of the Bengal Basin formed, along with the Ganges Delta, by the Brahmaputra and Meghna Rivers. If you add the fact that the world's largest delta is an area afflicted by an atavistic poverty and frequent, dramatic flooding, it is clear that this is not one of the easiest places to live on earth. Or to take a vacation to. Despite this, Sundarbans is a destination of extreme beauty, as well as the only place where the concrete possibility of actually seeing the now rare and endangered Bengal tiger in its natural habitat. Navigating along these canals, the "mobile" landscape of sandbanks, deep swamps and astounding mangroves let you observe a fragile environment, rich with beautifully curious fauna, populated by immense colonies of aquatic birds, fearsome crocodiles, macaques and chital and the spotted deer, overwhelmingly present with over 80,000 exemplars in the area. And, furthermore, stop in their unique stilted villages to observe the stoic fishermen, whose main source of sustenance are crabs. These little clawed animals, alone, constitute the highest portion of animal biomass in all the Sundarbans.

Internet sites www.westbengaltourism.gov.in and www.tourismboard.gov.bd

NOT TO MISS

- 75 KILOMETERS FROM CALCUTTA, THE VILLAGE OF **PIYALI** OFFERS A "GENTLE" INTRODUCTION TO THE SUNDARBANS. LINED WITH CANALS AND RICE PADDIES, IT HAS NICE GUESTHOUSES AND IS THE ROMANTIC DESTINATION FOR BENGAL HONEYMOONS.
- IN THE **SAJNEKHALI TIGER RESERVE,** IN INDIA, AN WATCHTOWER TO OBSERVE THESE FELINES HAS BEEN ERECTED AND IS ACCESSIBLE AFTER A 45 MINUTE WALK (ACCOMPANIED BY AN ARMED RANGER) THROUGH A THICK MANGROVE FOREST.
- THE FAMOUS WRITER AND PHILANTHROPIST DOMINIQUE LAPIERRE, AUTHOR OF *CITY OF JOY* (AMONG OTHERS), FOUNDED ***THE SOUTHERN HEALTH IMPROVEMENT SAMITY,*** AN NGO ACTIVE IN SANITARY ASSISTANCE FOR THE SUNDARBANS PEOPLE. ITS HEADQUARTERS ARE IN BANGAR AND HAS HOSPITAL-BOATS THAT NAVIGATE THE DELTA.
- IN BANGLADESH, **KATKA** IS A SANDY ISLAND RICH WITH VEGETATION (THE CLEARINGS COVERED IN ORCHIDS ARE SPLENDID) AND A BEACH ON THE SEA THAT IS JUST AS MAGNIFICENT AS IT IS DESERTED, PERFECT FOR A RELAXING SWIM.

| **224-225** *There are about 250 "man-eaters" in the Sundarbans territory.*

When to go *From October to March.*

How long to stay *3 or 4 days.*

Organization *Is possible to visit the Sundarbans independently, taking the ferry lines that connect the villages along the main canals. However, to best experience the natural environment (and to be more comfortable), you should book a guided tour on a motored launch with a cabin, that includes visits to naturalistic sanctuaries and brief treks. India, we recommend Tour de Sundarbans, managed by a young and enthusiastic team, and India Beacons Sojourn, specialized in ecotourism; in Bangladesh, see Bengal Tours.*

Advice *Malaria and dengue are only the most noted endemic illnesses carried by Sundarbans mosquitoes: you are strongly advised to get antimalarial treatments and bring a powerful insect repellant with you.*

IN THE MEKONG DELTA

Internet site www.vietnamtourism.com

Come discover a liquid world, among floating merchants, cities, villages, canals and thousands of stories on the mouth of the "Mother of Water."

In Southeast Asia, it is said that the Laotians live near the river, the Cambodians on the river and the Vietnamese in the river. Despite this apparent exaggeration, this statement couldn't be truer. After flowing for over 4000 miles from its source in the Tibetan plateau, through Burma, Laos, Thailand and Cambodia, the Mekong - whose name is derived from Mae Nam Khong, or "The Mother of Water" – opens up in Vietnam into a gigantic delta. 17 million people live here, 22% of the Vietnamese population. They produce 50% of the country's rice (Vietnam is the second rice exporter in the world), 80% of its fruit and 60% of its fish. Moreover, despite its dense population, the delta is considered a natural treasure trove, so much that in the last decade around 1000 new species have been found here. The delta's liquid landscape is so spread out that it is influenced by the tide. It is host to great cities – from Can Tho, with over 1 million inhabitants, to My Tho and Vinh

| **226** *The so-called "monkey bridges" over the Mekong canal.* | **227** *The Mekong Delta extends over 39,000 square kilometers.*

Long, all with buildings that are testimony to French colonization and Buddhist pagodas - and thousands of islands, big and small, interconnected by a labyrinth of canals and each with its own distinct personality. Like Ba Vat, where the air is dense with the sweet aroma from the artesian shops of desserts and caramel made from coconut, or like Thoi Son, with its expanses of fruit plantations and tropical flowers. Then, in the delta, you find yourself in front of one of the symbols of the rampant modernity of New Asia like the Can Tho Bridge over the Bassac River, one of the Mekong's major tributaries, that cost $342 million and, nearly 3 kilometers in length with 6 lanes, it is the biggest suspended bridge on the continent. And, a short distance away, you can admire the celestial bamboo architecture of cau khi, the "monkey bridges" no more than 30 centimeters wide, owing their name to the particular equilibrium you need to cross them.
The great majority of tourists visit the Mekong Delta on organized trips lasting 1 or 2 days, departing from the Vietnamese capital Ho Chi Minh City, but to truly understand its vastness and the extraordinary economic and cultural importance, you have to spend much more time here, losing yourself in its meandering nature, using a vast gamma of transportation, from large farriers that navigate the "water highways" to little wooden boats with flat keels that transport cargo and passengers, from motorized canoes for discovering villages of floating houses whose inhabitants live off of fishing, to rowboats, perfect for penetrating the canals lined with stilted villages and rice paddies to get the "inside experience" of the colorful and enchanting floating markets. And, again, traveling the entire length of the islands by bicycle, peddling through the coconut plantations and the immense flower cultivations, exported throughout the world. Because the delta's charm is above all in its diversity and its industriousness, discovered in the rice crêpe factories with which, on all latitudes, their famous spring rolls are made, in bucolically fascinating canals, where you won't see anyone but swan herders in their canoes and classic coned hats, or among the mangroves that are home to millions of aquatic birds.

| **228** *Bikes are also a good way to discover villages and the delta.*

| 229 *Phu Quoc Island is situated at the mouth of the Delta.*

NOT TO MISS

ALTHOUGH THE **CAI BE MARKET,** NOT FAR FROM VINH LONG, IS THE DELTA'S LARGEST, THE ONE IN **PHUNG HIEP,** IN THE SOUTH, IS MORE EXOTIC: HERE THERE IS A WHOLE SECTION DEDICATED TO SELLING SNAKES, CONSIDERED A GASTRONOMIC DELICACY AROUND HERE.

THE **TRAM CHIM NATIONAL PARK** PROTECTS THE LAST REMAINS OF THE "PLAIN OF REEDS," AN EXTRAORDINARY WET ECOSYSTEM THAT HOSTS SPANS OF LOTUS FLOWERS AND RICH WITH AVIFAUNA: HERE YOU CAN ADMIRE THE RARE SARUS CRANE, THE LARGEST VOLATILE, THAT CAN REACH HEIGHTS UP TO 180 CENTIMETERS.

INHABITED BY THE KHMER ETHNICITY, THE LITTLE TOWN OF **TRA VINH** HOSTS A SERIES OF VIVIDLY COLORED RELIGIOUS PAGODAS THAT ARE HOME TO DENSE COMMUNITIES OF MONKS.

AT THE MOUTH OF THE DELTA YOU WILL FIND **PHU QUOC,** THE BIGGEST ISLAND IN VIETNAM. FAMOUS FOR ITS PRODUCTION OF NUOC MAM, THE FERMENTED FISH SALSA USED TO SALT EVERY PLATE, IT HAS SPLENDID WHITE BEACHES FOR TAKING A FEW DAYS OFF: NOT BY CHANCE, IT IS CONSIDERED THE "TWIN" OF THE THAI PHUKET, BEFORE THE ARRIVAL OF TOURISM.

When to go *In the dry season, from November to April.*

How long to stay *1 or 2 weeks.*

Organization *Traveling in the delta independently is easy, but if you prefer a guided tour, have a local tour operator custom organize one for you. We recommend the optimal SinhBalo Adventure Travel that proposes itineraries that combine boat and bicycle trips with lodging in villages, and Viet Bamboo Travel, offering trips aboard traditional sampan.*

Advice *Take into consideration the idea of crossing the entire delta to then continue to the Cambodian capital Phnom Phen and, after, going upriver to Lake Tonle Sap. Traveling independently, you'll have to take a series of ferries (and some buses) or, alternatively, you can chose to rent a charter boat with the tour operator Blue Cruiser.*

Curiosities

The most typical dish is Elephant Ear Fish that is fried and presented vertically on a plate, held up by little bamboo sticks and accompanied with vegetables cut in the form of a lotus. It is eaten with chopsticks and dipped in a sweet and sour sauce.

Sa Dec might have the absurd nickname "Little Venice" but it is a splendid city where the writer Marguerite Duras set her novel The Lover. *To experience the literary atmosphere, visit Tran Thuy at 255 Nguyen Hue, it is a 1800s colonial home with romantic Chinese and Vietnamese furnishings.*

Of the fruit cultivated in the Delta, the king (and not only in size and weight. It is the most smelly fruit in the world and contains 43 sulfur compounds, including those present in onions, garlic and the skunk's perianal gland: a penetrating mix, comparable to the smell of rotten eggs. To make up for it, its flavor is super sweet, so much that in Southeast Asia it is considered a delicacy.

WITH THE ORANGUTANS OF KALIMANTAN

Boating along the rivers of Tanjung Puting National Park, to discover the remote habitat of these great Asian primates.

| 230 *A young orangutan.* | 231 *A Dayak village in the Tanjung Puting National Park.*

NOT TO MISS

- MANAGED BY DR. GALDIKAS' FOUNDATION, **CAMP LEAKEY** IS AN ORANGUTAN REHABILITATION CENTER IN THE HEART OF THE FOREST. EVERY DAY AT 2:00, YOU CAN WATCH THEIR MEALTIME RITE, WITH TENS OF LARGE PRIMATES THAT COME FOR A BANANA LUNCH ON TREETOP PLATFORMS.
- THE OTHER SUPERSTARS IN THE PARK ARE THE FUNNY **LONG-NOSED MONKEYS,** WITH THEIR WHITE FACES AND CHARACTERISTIC SCHNOZZLE: THEY ARE QUITE CURIOUS AND IT SEEMS LIKE THEY ANXIOUSLY AWAIT THE *KLOTOK'S* PASSAGE. MORE DIFFICULT TO SPOT ARE THE SHYER **MALAYSIAN BEARS** OR THE **CLOUDED LEOPARD.**
- ENJOY THE HOSPITALITY OF THE IBAN, THE DAYAK NATIVES WHO COVER THEIR BODIES IN TATTOOS AND LIVE IN **STILTED VILLAGES** ALONG THE RIVER.
- THE VILLAGE OF **TANJUNG HARAPAN** HAS ECOTOURISM STRUCTURES AND BRIEF FOREST TREKS CAN BE ORGANIZED TO OBSERVE BOTANICAL CURIOSITIES AND VISIT A SANDALWOOD REFORESTATION CENTER.

In Indonesian, orangutan means "man of the forest." And, although they are, among the great primates, our furthest relation – and the only one that lives on the Asian continent – they are extraordinarily intelligent and their offspring are more similar to our newborns in respect to other monkeys. The first European explorers that described them said they "lacked the word," but this didn't stop the white man from hunting hundreds of them. Since then, due to deforestation, the orangutan population has been drastically reduced: they now live in small communities in the North Sumatra, in the Sabah Forest (Malaysian Borneo) and in greater numbers in Tanjung Puting National Park, in Kalimantan. It is here that, in 1971, the Canadian primatologist Biruté Mary Galdikas first came to study their precise genetics and behaviors and, in collaboration with the National Geographic Society, brought the world's attention to their destiny. It goes without saying, this immense green lung is the destination par excellence for a close encounter with orangutans and, at the same time, takes you on the most exciting and laidback adventure in the planet's Heart of Darkness: the only way to penetrate the forest is along the network of rivers aboard a *klotok*, the traditional houseboats of the Dayak natives, on a photographic safari comfortably sitting on deck.

When to go *The driest season is between May and September, with occasional downpours and nice temperatures. However, during the rainy season, the swollen rivers give access to the parks remote areas.*

How long to stay *1 week.*

Organization *The small town of Pangkalan Bun is the home of the park's visitors' center and here you can easily rent a klotok. If you prefer to organize a tour from home, of the specialized Indonesian operators, we recommend Adventure Indonesia and BorneoEcoTour. The Orangutan Foundation International organizes exceptional trips guided by the primatologist Biruté Mary Galdikas.*

Advice *While in the presence of orangutans, scrupulously follow the guide's rules. And, due to crocodiles and other dangers, don't swim in the river for any reason in the world.*

Internet site www.orangutan.org

ON THE NAHANNI RIVER

With the midnight sun, a canoe expedition along the Nahanni River in a national park as big as Switzerland.

Pierre Elliot Trudeau was one of the most popular political figures in Canadian history. In 1970, he caused a sensation by the fact that, in an official capacity, he spent 2 weeks canoeing along the Nahanni River in the Northern Territories. Although it wasn't exactly a task included in the job of Prime Minister, he was eventually forgiven for his adventure because the river is - officially a national treasure. The national park that derives its name from the river is ne of the vastest protected areas on the planet (it is as big as Switzerland), including high mountains, tundra and expanses of permafrost, a series of sulfuric springs and conifer forests inhabited by brown bears, mountain bison, moose and caribou. And, it goes without saying, it is an extreme territory shrouded in dark legends, like the names that popular tradition, dating back to the gold rush, has given some of its most celebrated destinations, from Deadman's Valley to the Funeral Range, from Headless Creek to Hell's Gate. Canoeing the Nahanni's 322 kilometers running through the park is an *Into the Wild* experience reserved for those who have the right dose of disdain in the face of danger for enjoying the landscape marked by Canada's 4 deepest spectacular canyons until arriving, at the end of the journey, at Virginia Falls, a waterfall that is two times higher than Niagara Falls.

Internet site www.pc.gc.ca/eng/pn-np/nt/nahanni/index.aspx

NOT TO MISS

- LOCATED WHERE THE NAHANNI JOINS WITH THE LIARD AND ACCESSIBLE ONLY VIA WATER, **NAHANNI BUTTE** IS ONE OF THE MOST REMOTE SETTLEMENTS OF THE SO-CALLED CANADIAN *FIRST NATIONS*. IT IS INHABITED BY AROUND 100 NATIVES OF THE DEHE TRIBE, DISTANT RELATIVES OF THE NAVAJO.
- TREAT YOURSELF TO A THERMAL BATH IN THE DIVING POOLS OF **RABBITKETTLE HOTSPRINGS,** IN MINERAL-RICH WATERS THAT GUSH AT A CONSTANT TEMPERATURE OF 20° C. ACCORDING TO THE DEHE NATIVES, THIS PLACE IS SACRED, AND ACCORDING TO TRADITION IT IS GOOD LUCK TO LEAVE TOBACCO AND MATCHES HERE TO PLEASE THE WATER DIVINITIES.
- BOOK A **CANOE ADVENTURE** BETWEEN JUNE AND JULY, WHEN THE SUN NEVER SETS IN THIS SUBARCTIC TERRITORY!

| **232-233** *Virginia Falls drop nearly 90 meters.*

When to go *From May to September.*

How long to stay *Between 1 and 3 weeks.*

Organization *In order to canoe (or raft) down the Nahanni River, you must go through a specialized operator. Of these, we recommend Canadian River Expeditions and Black Feather that propose adventures of varying length (from 1 week to a challenging 21 days) and different levels of difficulty that include lodging in tents and trekking.*

Advice *The best way to get to the heart of the park, admiring the Nahanni's entire course, is to rent a small plane or seaplane in Fort Simpson. Of the charter companies that offer this service, we recommend Wolverine Air and Simpson Air. The latter is based at Little Doctor Lake (where it has its water runway) and manages the splendid Nahanni Mountain Lodge.*

IN THE OKAVANGO DELTA

Aboard a *mokoro,* the native Batawana's canoe, on a safari through the extraordinary aquatic world that "lives" in the Kalahari Desert.

Fed by summer rains on the Angolan plateau, the Okavango River travels through the Kalahari Desert for over 1300 kilometers until opening up, in a perfect fan shape, into an immense internal delta. With its innumerable canals, swamps lined with palms and papyrus reeds and nearly 50,000 islands, this is one of Africa's most serene, changing and estranging landscapes. The explorer Aurel Schultz, one of the first Europeans to come here, in 1897, considered the fact that all the delta's water could disappear into the desert a mystery. In reality, only a minimal part of the river "dies" in the Kalahari or feeds Lake Ngadi: the rest is freed into the atmosphere through transpiration – which means through plant leaves – rather than through evaporation. It is, in the end, an extraordinary living organism, with canals as arteries, the far-off Angolan mountains as a heart and the islands in the role of reproductive organs.

Internet site www.botswanatourism.co.bw

| 234 *Navigating a* mokoro *through the Okavango Delta.*

| 235 *Able swimmers, elephants feel just fine in the deepest waters.*

Actually, 70% of them were formed thanks to sedimentary deposits brought by seasonal floods around the anthills. The Okavango Delta supports one of the highest concentrations of fauna on the continent. With 60,000 members, the ruling species is the lechwe *(Kobus leche)*, a large antelope with red fur that has adapted to feeding on aquatic plants and escaping predators thanks to its ability to swim and hide in deep waters, and here there are enormous herds of buffalo and elephants, along with hippos, crocodiles and large felines. Plus, the delta is an extremely fragile organism, so the most ethical and fascinating way to explore it is experiencing it slowly from the inside, during a safari aboard a *mokoro*, the natives' traditional canoe.

When to go *The Delta is at the top of its game in the dry season, between June and October, but you can enjoy the area year round.*

How long to stay *1 week.*

Organization *To organize a* mokoro *safari, contact Polers Trust Seronga, an ecotourism organization born thanks to the support of the African Development Foundation and the European Union that employs native populations. Although in a traditional form, the safari canoes are made in fiberglass, an eco-sustainable material.*

Advice *Botswana is one of the most expensive countries in Africa and choosing a* mokoro *safari is the cheapest way to go. Certainly, at night you'll sleep in a tent, on island campsites, but you'll have the possibility of getting close to the delta's tribal culture. If you prefer a luxurious experience, book a stay at the Khwai River Lodge, located in a private reserve adjacent to the Moremi Game Reserve.*

NOT TO MISS

- FOUNDED IN 1915 BY THE BATAWANA TRIBE, TODAY **MAUN** IS THE ACCESS POINT TO THE DELTA AND, AS SUCH, IS BOTSWANA'S TOURISM CAPITAL AND ONE OF THE CONTINENT'S FASTEST DEMOGRAPHICALLY AND ECONOMICALLY GROWING CITIES. SPEND A COUPLE OF DAYS HERE TO BROWSE THE OPTIMAL ARTESIAN SHOPS AND TASTE THE LOCAL GASTRONOMY.
- IN THE HEART OF THE DELTA, THE **MOREMI GAME RESERVE** TAKES ITS NAME FROM THE BATAWANA TRIBAL LEADER AND OFFERS EXTRAORDINARY WILDLIFE WATCHING OPPORTUNITIES. IN ADDITION TO EXPLORING IT ABOARD A *MOKORO*, YOU CAN ALSO TAKE A 4X4 OR A PHOTOGRAPHIC WALKING SAFARI.
- ADJACENT TO THE MOREMI GAME RESERVE, **CHIEF'S ISLAND** IS THE DELTA'S LARGEST EARTH MASS AND THE ONLY ONE THAT IS NEVER SUBMERSED. COVERED IN ACACIA AND MOPANE TREES, IT IS HOME TO MANY ANIMAL SPECIES: WITH A LITTLE LUCK, YOU CAN SEE RARE SPECIES LIKE THE WHILE RHINOCEROS AND THE LYCAON.
- WITH PRICES STARTING AT $110 PER PERSON FOR 25 MINUTES, A HELICOPTER RIDE OVER THE DELTA IS A LITTLE LUXURIOUS, OKAY. BUT IT IS THE BEST WAY TO UNDERSTAND THIS AQUATIC SYSTEM'S VASTNESS AS WELL AS A RESOUNDING PHOTO-OP! OF THE COMPANIES THAT PROPOSE THIS KIND OF ACTIVITY, WE RECOMMEND DELTA RAIN SAFARIS AND GOLDEN OKAVANGO.

SAILING THE RÍO DULCE

It is only modest in length, but navigating from Izabal Lake to Lívingston, the Caribbean's "pueblo perdido," is a journey to another world.

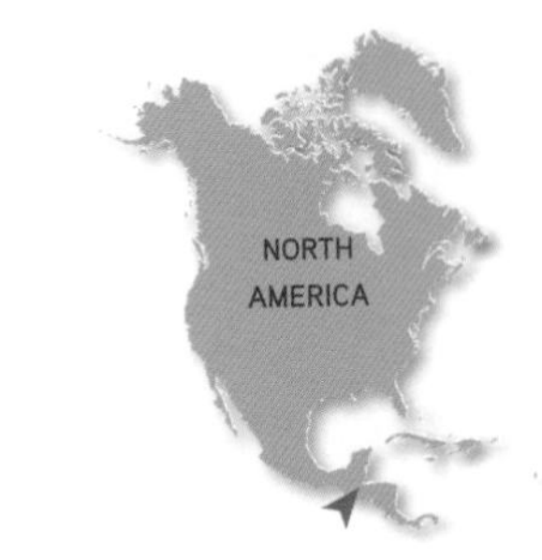

It is only 42 kilometers long and is as sweet as its name. Yet, for the indios of these parts it is the "gringos-eating river." However, more than its real dangers, Río Dulce's fame is due to the fact that it is impossible to want to go home after having visited the magical green carpet that surrounds the fishing villages along its banks and after getting used to – it doesn't take long! – the slow, dreamy rhythms of the people here, who never do today what can be done *mañana*. And you shouldn't be rushed to get to Río Dulce either, because sailing in Lake Izabal (Guatemala's largest at about 45 kilometers long and 20 wide) is itself a fantastic experience, during which you discover remains from the Mayan epoch and Spanish colonization and observe the manatees and tortoises that populate its waters. This place still has the mysterious charm of a hidden paraíso despite being connected with the modern Petén Highway that, with a bridge, unites the twin cities of El Relleno and Fronteras, rising in the exact spot where Lake Izabal flows out into the Río Dulce. And, taking the river, the sensation of finding yourself out of this world and in a far away time remains when you stop to do some bird watching in Golfete, where the basin widens, hosting little islands and banks of water hyacinths, or, to admire the high sandstone walls of the part of the river known as

NOT TO MISS

- THE MAIN HISTORICAL ATTRACTION ON LAKE IZABAL IS THE **CASTILLO DE SAN FELIPE DE LARA,** AN IMPOSING FORTIFICATION BUILD IN 1595 BY SPANISH CONQUISTADORES TO PROTECT GUATEMALA'S COMMERCIAL ROUTES FROM THE INCURSIONS OF ENGLISH OR DUTCH PIRATES.
- A SHORT DISTANCE FROM FRONTERAS, ON THE RÍO DULCE BRIDGE, STOP FOR A NATURAL HYDRO-MASSAGE (WITH HOT WATER!) AT THE **FINCA DEL PARAÍSO WATERFALL,** IN THE HEART OF THE TROPICAL JUNGLE.
- ALONG THE RIVER, STOP AT **HACIENDA TIJAX:** IT IS A MAGNIFICENT ECOLODGE IMMERSED IN THE FOREST (WITH A DOCK FOR BOATS) AND ORGANIZES KAYAK AND HORSEBACK EXCURSIONS.
- LÍVINGSTON'S MOST RESPECTED INSTITUTION IS THE **PIEL CANELA,** A GARIFUNA VERSION OF THE CUBAN BUENA VISTA SOCIAL CLUB. GO TO HEAR SOME GREAT LATIN MUSIC AND TO SIP JUERO, A COCKTAIL WITH RUM, SALT AND LEMON THAT HAS MANY - AND UNTIL NOW UNSUCCESSFUL - IMITATORS.

| 236 *Parque Nacional Río Dulce covers 130 square kilometers.*

| 237 *Castillo de San Felipe de Lara on Lake Iazabal dates back to 1595.*

El Canyon. It even becomes tangible, once you arrive at the mouth, where the green water of Río Dulce mixes with the turquoise of Amatique Bay, in the Caribbean. Here rises Lívingston, the splendid colonial city that is the center of Gariguna culture, a mestizo ethnicity between caribeños indios and Africans from the Bantu lineage brought here as slaves. Only accessible by boat, today Lívingston is a marvelous pueblo perdido, but once upon a time, right here, and across the Río Dulce, the Spanish conquest of Guatemala began.

Internet site http://riodulce.net

When to go *From November to May.*

How long to stay *4 days for the sailing cruise, but stay a little longer to explore the area.*

Organization *The local tour operator Caribbean Experience proposes sailing cruises on Lake Izabal and Río Dulce. Among the many operators that propose motorboat tours along the river, we recommend Exotic Travel Agency in Lívingston that has a nice hotel and a restaurant in the city as well as organizing transportation via sea to other locations on the Guatemalan, Belizean and Honduran coasts.*

Advice *Consider the possibility of a freshwater deviation from Río Dulce in the opposite direction during a sailing cruise in the Caribbean Sea: the river and Lake Izabal are also safer places to navigate during the hurricane season.*

| 238 *La Moskitia is characterized by a succession of mangroves, lagoons, savannah and tropical forests.*

IN A CAYUCO AT LA MOSKITIA

Due to a movie (and its name) it has a sinister fame. But - explored by boat - this remote region is one of Central America's green jewels.

Remember the film *Mosquito Coast?* Harrison Ford plays a dark lead, and the story tells of an American family that leaves their comfortable lives for the Caribbean looking for paradise but find themselves in a green nightmare. Well, the terrible setting for this film is La Moskitia, in Honduras. Not even the name is reassuring, right? However, this name isn't due to the presence of mosquitos, but to the muskets that the Spanish conquistadores used to arm one of the native tribes – who were then called Miskitos – in order to help them subdue the others. And this remote region, home to South America's second vastest forest, after the Amazon and protected as the Río Plátano Biosphere Reserve, is a formidable and relatively calm destination for an adventurous vacation. You start to suspect that Paul Theroux, the author of the novel that the film was based on, wanted to create a sinister aura precisely in order to prevent this final virgin frontier in Central America from being ruined by waves of mass tourism.

Sure, La Moskitia isn't exactly the easiest place to reach: aboard a little plane, you fly from La Ceiba to Puerto Lempira, and from there the voyage continues with the necessary slowness of traveling through its labyrinth of waterways, whether you decide to take a ferry on the *Espreso* line – only by name – or a *cayuco,* a traditional motor or row boat, to dis-

cover the magnificent tropical environment and its fauna (including birds, monkeys, alligators, manatees, ocelots and jaguars), navigating through tunnels of palms and mangroves to this splendid and completely uncontaminated Caribbean coastal area. Along with the Miskitos, another five ethnicities live in this region – the Pech, the Rama, the Sumo, the Tawakha and the Garifuna indios – and each conserves their ancient traditions that you can experience first hand for yourself while staying in the quaint villages and in the delightful eco-touristic structures.

NOT TO MISS

- LISTEN TO THE FOREST BREATHE WHILE GOING DOWN **RÍO PATUCA** IN A CAYUCO, WHERE THE TAWAKHA INDIOS LIVE IN HARMONY WITH NATURE, CULTIVATING CASSAVA, COCONUTS AND RICE.
- GET UP CLOSE AND PERSONAL WITH MISKITOS AND GARIFUNA CULTURES IN THE **PICTURESQUE AQUATIC VILLAGES OF RAISTA AND BÉLEN.** THE INDIOS ORGANIZE DANCES AND EXCURSIONS IN ROWING *CAYUCO* IN THE LAGOON. EVEN AFTER SUNDOWN, TO OBSERVE THE NOCTURNAL FAUNA.
- LEAVE THE COMFORT OF THE BOAT FOR A **TREK TO LAS MARIAS,** RÍO PLÁTANO RESERVE'S WILD MOUNTAIN ZONE: IT'S A THREE DAY WALK TO GET TO **PICO DAMA,** ALONG FOREST PATH RICH WITH ORCHIDS, OR JUST ONE TO DO SOME BIRD WATCHING IN **CERRO DE ZAPOTE.**
- PARTICIPATE IN THE **TURTLE CONSERVATION PROGRAM IN PLAPLAYA:** BETWEEN APRIL AND JULY, ALL THE INHABITANTS OF THIS REMOTE COSTAL VILLAGE SEARCH FOR THE EGGS THAT THE TURTLES LAY ON THE BEACH AND PROTECT THEM FROM PREDATORS UNTIL THEY HATCH; AFTER ONE MONTH, THEY FREE THE TURTLES INTO THE SEA.

When to go *From February to May and from August to November.*

How long to stay *1or 2 weeks, including some R&R on the Caribbean coast.*

Organization *The main tourist operator in the region is La Ruta Moskitia, an organization managed by a council of the 6 ethnicities that propose boat tours, stays in eco-lodges and themed trekking and horseback excursions: all of the proceeds go to the local community, some of Honduras' poorest. Of the other local tour operators (but with European management), we recommend Omega Tours and La Moskitia Ecoadventuras.*

Advice *In La Moskitia there are no more mosquitos than elsewhere, however this is a malarial zone. Antimalarial treatments are strongly advised.*

Internet site www.letsgohonduras.com

| 239 *There are 6 ethnicities in the La Moskitia region, with a population density of 418 inhabitants per square kilometer.*

CANOEING SALTO ÁNGEL

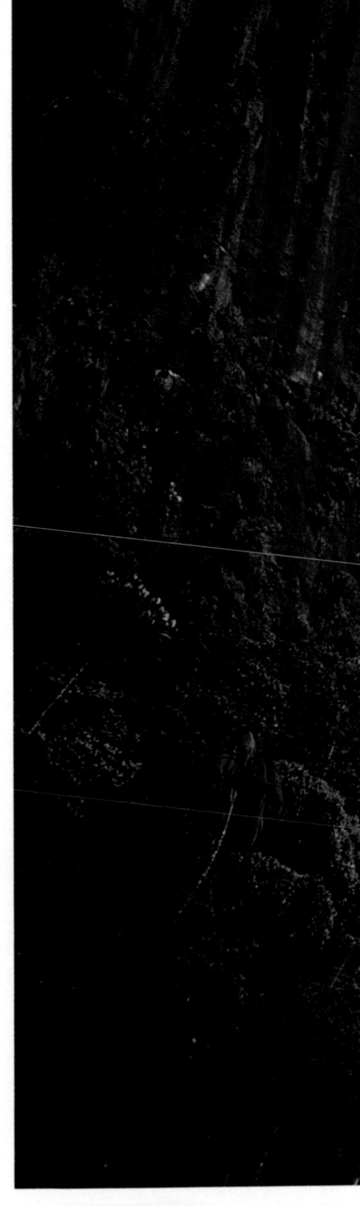

Now, as President Chávez has decided, the highest waterfall in the world is called Kerepakupai Vená. Discover it in a canoe with the Pemon indios.

In 1933, flying over the Venezuelan Gran Sabana while searching for a legendary city of gold, the American aviator Jimmie Angel saw the tallest waterfall below. At 979 meters high – the equivalent of 20 Niagara Falls – this natural wonder was called Salto Ángel is his honor and is located at the heart of one of the world's most bizarre landscapes of forests, rivers and spectacular sandstone hills with flat tops called *tepuy* in what is today the Canaima National Park. However, recently, in one of his populist and indigenist acts, Venezuela's leader Hugo Chávez renamed the falls with the arduous name Kerepakupai Vená, the name the local natives, the Pemon, originally gave it. Ideally shareable, the motivation lies in the fact that the Pemon knew this area long before Jimmie Angel's arrival. But Chávez went even further, accusing the United States of violating Venezuelan airspace – many decades later. Whatever you want to call it, the best way to admire the falls is, let's say, from an indigenous perspective. This means arriving aboard a *curiara,* the typical, large canoes used by the indios (and today equipped with a motor) on an adventure along the Acanan and Carrao Rivers, going along the monumental Auyantepui massif, all the way to where the river joins with Río Churun, in the exact spot where Salto Ángel tumbles down, creating a phenomenal rainbow. During the trip you'll experience the excitement of the forest. And, at night, you can stop in the Pemon's stilted villages and sleep there among the indios: in a hammock, lulled by the sound of the falls.

Internet site http://salto-angel.com

NOT TO MISS

- THE MAIN ACCESS POINT FOR SALTO ÁNGEL IS THE SMALL TOWN OF CANAIMA. BUT IT IS BETTER TO ENTER, LET'S SAY, THROUGH THE "SERVICE DOOR" OF THE VILLAGE **KAVAK.** INHABITED BY PEMON NATIVES AND SURROUNDED BY JUNGLE AND TEPUY, IT HOSTS SUGGESTIVE ECO-TOURIST RESORTS IN TRADITIONAL *CHURUATA* CABINS.
- TAKE A WALK TO OBSERVE THE THRIVING VEGETATION OF ORCHIDS, PALMS AND BROMELIADS ON **ISLA ORQUÍDEA.** ABOUT 1 KILOMETER LONG, IT IS RIGHT IN FRONT OF THE WATERFALL AND OFFERS AN ENCHANTING PANORAMA OVER THE AUYANTEPUI.
- MUCH MORE MODEST IN HEIGHT, THE **SALTO SAPO FALLS** OFFER A WONDERFULLY RELAXING BREAK: DIVE INTO THE NATURAL POOLS DUG OUT OF THE SANDSTONE AND ADMIRE THE PRIMORDIAL LANDSCAPE SURROUNDING YOU. THEN, ADVENTURE INTO THE WATER TUNNELS UNDER THE WATERFALL.
- BRING YOUR BINOCULARS: ALTHOUGH YOU NEED A BIT OF LUCK TO SEE AN ARMADILLO OR A JAGUAR, THE FOREST IS A KIND OF METROPOLIS POPULATED BY PARROTS AND TOUCANS.

SOUTH AMERICA

| **240-241** *Salto Ángel falls 979 meters, but you need to go between June and September, during the rainy season.*

When to go *From June to November, during the rainy season (otherwise there's no waterfall, or almost).*

How long to stay *A boat tour lasts 3-5 days.*

Organization *You can arrive from Caracas and Ciudad Bolívar to Canaima and Kamarata (Kavak) by plane. Among the many Venezuelan companies that propose canoe adventures, also combined with brief treks, we recommend Orinoco Tours, Venezuela Eco-Adventures and Angel Eco Tours.*

Advice *Before leaving, read Arthur Conan Doyle's* The Lost World: *the author – noted, among other things, as Sherlock Holme's "father" – drew inspiration from the landscapes in the Canaima National Park for this novel, a classic adventure. Freely adapted from the book, the cartoon* Up, *one of Pixar's masterpieces, tells the story of a little boy who goes to discover "Paradise Falls."*

ON RÍO NEGRO

Navigating the coffee-colored waters of the largest tributary of the Amazon River is an adventure through our planet's green paradise (and hell).

NOT TO MISS

- ON THE RIO NEGRO, MANAUS IS THE AMAZONIAN METROPOLIS AS WELL AS A PHENOMENAL HUB OF BRAZIL'S WEALTH. ITS FORTUNE STARTED AT THE END OF THE 19TH CENTURY, THANKS TO RUBBER EXPORTATIONS. ITS NUMEROUS ARCHITECTURAL MARVELS, LIKE THE **AMAZONAS THEATER** AND THE **PALACIO RIO NEGRO,** TWO GEMS FROM THE BELLE ÉPOCH, TESTIFY TO THIS FACT.
- NEAR BARCELOS, ANOTHER IMMENSE FLUVIAL ARCHIPELAGO EXTENDS, CALLED **MARIUÁ,** NOTED FOR BEING THE WORLD CAPITAL FOR ORNAMENTAL SPECIES FISHING, LIKE GIANT CATFISH AND PEACOCK BASS. FOR A FISHING EXPERIENCE ON THE RIO NEGRO, CONSULT WITH PESCAMAZON.
- TO MEET THE YANOMAMI, YOU MUST OBTAIN A SPECIAL PERMIT FORM THE BRAZILIAN GOVERNMENT. ALONG THE RIVER AND ITS TRIBUTARIES, YOU CAN FIND THE **VILLAGES OF BARÉ, KULINA, KAXINAWA, SATERÉ-MAWÉ AND TIKUNA.** THEY ARE VERY HOSPITABLE: REACH THEM UP THE RIO CURICURIARI, LINED WITH COMMUNITY HUTS FROM THE GROUP CALLED SÃO FÉLIX.
- THE NORTHERN OF THE RIO NEGRO'S HIGH COURSE IS PROTECTED BY THE **PARQUE NACIONAL DO PICO DA NEBLINA** THAT OWES ITS NAME TO BRAZIL'S HIGHEST MOUNTAIN (AT 3014 METERS). IF THIS IS HARD TO ACCESS, THE SOUTHERN PART OF THE PARK IS NOT FAR FROM SÃO GABRIEL DA CACHOEIRA: GET OFF THE BOAT HERE TO TREK INTO THE FOREST TO THE CURIOUS ROCK FORMATION KNOWN AS "LA BELA ADORMECIDA" (SLEEPING BEAUTY).

Internet site
www.visitamazonas.am.gov.br

| **242** *The Rio Negro, after flowing for 200 kilometers, joins the Amazon River near Manaus.*
| **243** *The Amazonas Theater in Praça de São Sebastião in Manaus.*

They called it "the meeting of waters" and the definite article isn't casual. There is no other place in the world like here, about 10 kilometers from Manaus, where the waters of two rivers put on such an extraordinary show. The rivers in question are the Rio Negro and the Rio Solimões: the first has coffee-colored water, due to debris and the high concentration of tannin "squeezed" from the tree trunks that it transports along its journey through the forests of Colombia and Venezuela; the second is like coconut milk, fruit of an incredible quantity of clear silt that it gathers during its trip from Peru. Before becoming one, the two rivers flow side by side for at least 15 kilometers in a chromatic coupling that looks like the eastern symbol of Ying Yang, the two opposing energies that govern nature. Besides, there is not parallel to the energy that they produce together: their union gives life to the Amazon River that, with its 6937 kilometers, is the world's greatest river, in length, in the number of tributaries (10,000!) and in the volume of its hydrographic basis. At its outlet – by then mixed into a latté – another chromatic marvel takes place, wedging itself into the blue ocean for hundreds of kilometers, another spectacle that can only be understood thanks to satellite imagery. But, going back to the beginning, i.e. at the place where black and white waters meet, the Parque Ecólogico do January has been established: among its

main attractions, there are the inlets (called igarapés, in the musical version of Portuguese spoken in Brazil), the lush rainforest (igapós) and the floating Vitória Regina plants, a species of giant lotus flowers, with leaves well over a meter long. And just think that this protected area is only a small - and popular - anticipation of what awaits you in the limitless Amazon territory. Whose name, not by chance, is already a hallucination in itself, borrowed from the myth of the Amazons, the fierce, naked warriors with their right breast severed that the Portuguese thought they saw here, tormented by the delirium of malarial fever. Besides, the Amazon is a paradise of biodiversity, with a concentration of 60% of all the planet's life forms (and it is believed that there are still 30% new ones to be found here), with around one million animal and vegetal species, including 2000 fish, 2500 birds and 3550 trees. However, at the same time, the Amazon forest is also an inferno. Because in the Amazon, more than anywhere else in the world, nature can kill you swiftly with a surucucu bite, the largest living venomous serpent (up to 3 meters long) or with a simple mosquito bite that transmits cerebral malaria; here nature can make you send you into a week long delirium with a simple spider-macaque bite, or even instantly paralyze you with a tucandera ant bite - and these are just to give a few examples of the dangers that await in this mesmerizing forest. Natural paradise and fatal hell live together as one in the Amazon. Moreover, its immense economic value, from the most obvious tree patrimony here, deforested at a rate of over 2 million hectares a year, to the rare plants and berries that are sought after by multinational pharmaceutical corporations because they may contain cures for known illnesses, or even hold the secrets for cures to sickness still unidentified by man.

A trip to the Amazon puts the traveler directly in front of strange wonders and fierce contradictions, not least those surrounding the policy of keeping many indios communities isolated - including the celebrated Yanomami - maintained by the Funai, the Brazilian department that is responsible for protecting indigenous territories and cultures – often with unclear motives – and the role that tourism has in this area. In any case, going down the rivers and, above all, along the 700 navigable kilometers of the Rio Negro, the most accessible and best-equipped to welcome visitors, is an experience that will strike you straight in the heart, whether you do it on a ferry that travels between Manaus, Barcelos and São Gabriel from

| **244** *The Anavilhanas, the world's largest fluvial archipelago, rise from the waters of the Rio Negro.*

| 245 *The Yanomami wear bamboo sticks through their nasal septum and bottom lip.*

Cachoeira (the three cities on its banks), or with a tourist launch that includes deviations along the tributaries, allowing you to discover first hand the forest and native villages where a primitive lifestyle exists side by side with the incongruent aspects of modernity. Along the Rio Negro, you can admire formidable places like the Anavihanas, the world's largest fluvial archipelago that, corresponding with the part of the river that widens to a span of 27 kilometers, is a unique and extreme ecosystem, with just over 400 islands and extending over 90 kilometers of river way. These islands are a fabulous labyrinth and may be the best symbol of the fact that, in the dangerously beautiful Amazon, it's quite easy to lose yourself. And stay lost even long after you've returned to the safety of your own home.

When to go *In the dry season (as dry as it gets), between July and December.*

How long to stay *At least 2 weeks.*

Organization *For those who love to travel independently, we recommend going to Manaus' floating port and taking a ferry up the Rio Negro, or negotiate passage on the boats that transport merchandise to the villages along the river.*
For an organized adventure, we recommend the operators Discover Brazil, Southern Cross Tours & Expeditions and Amazon Riders.

Advice *In an imposing (and potentially hostile) environment like this, it seems superfluous to warn you of the need to take malarial treatments and use a strong insect repellent; we recommend you bring an antifungal medicine and a good supply of salt supplements to compensate for liquids lost due to sweating in this extraordinarily hot and humid climate. The humidity and the frequent rains can damage photographic equipment and you should keep it in waterproof plastic covers, even better if containing silicon salt packets. Also keep your passport and plane ticket in a waterproof bag.*

Curiosities

- *According to Inpa (the National Institute of Amazonian Research), by 2020 deforestation will destroy 42% of the forest's surface. And, among the threats to the forest's survival, there is also a growing demographic pressure: over the last 20 years the population in the Amazon Basic has grown from 2 to 20 million.*

- *The Amazon Forest removes 1 ton of CO_2 from the atmosphere through photosynthesis, thus playing a fundamental role in limiting the greenhouse effect. In economic terms, the value of this "operation" is $141 dollars per hectare per year and economists have calculated that humanity owes the Amazon $35 million dollars a year.*

- *Among the most original animals that live in the Amazonian rivers, we find the boto, or red dolphin. However, native fishers detest it, because it often robs fish from their nets: according to a local legend, natives with light skin and blue eyes are boto men, and are still discriminated against in their communities today.*

| 246 *The Pantanal is the world's largest wetland.*

IN THE PANTANAL

SOUTH AMERICA

Travel in a motorized piragua in the planet's wetland fauna hypermarket. Close encounters with jaguars, anacondas and caimans.

If the idea of finding an anaconda as long as a bus at your front door doesn't scare you, or if you think that there is some sort of poetic justice for which piranhas, the most voracious freshwater fish, can be a delight fried in boiling palm oil, then you are ready for the exaggerations of a trip into the Pantanal. Although immense, this tropical wetland ploughed through a maze of 170 rivers and spread out over the Brazilian states Mato Grosso and Mato Gross do Sul cannot compete with the Amazon in size or scenery. But it wins hands down in the territorial contest, on the American continent, where it is easiest (and most exciting) to observe fauna. And what fauna it is! Although there is no reimbursement if you don't see a jaguar during a trip on a piragua, it is mathematically impossible not to have close encounters with the now rare – everywhere except here – hyacinth macaw that, with cobalt plumage and a 1 meter wingspan, is the largest parrot on the planet. And, surprisingly, it isn't the Pantanal's largest avifauna: that prize goes to the jabiru stork, measuring over 2 meters with its wings spread. Regarding dimensions, here they have much to brag about, beyond the already mentioned and common anaconda, the giant anteater, the giant otter, the capybara with its 30 kilograms is the largest rodent. And also the tapir, also known as the swamp horse, chosen by Stanley Kubrick for the first scene of *2001: A Space Odyssey* for its sheer size. But in the Pantanal the quantities are also exceptional: including invertebrates, the total amount of species rises to 150,000, while its 10 million exemplars of caimans make it so that this wetland has the highest concentration of crocodiles in the world.

Internet site www.pantanal.org

When to go *From May to October.*

How long to stay *From 4 days to 1 week.*

Organization *To enjoy the Pantanal's marvels, combining piragua navigation with brief treks, it is fundamental to contact a local tour operator. Among those with the most experience, we recommend Pantanal Nature and Pantanal Trackers. The latter is managed by Julinho Monteiro, a native that is legendary in these parts: over the past 20 years, he has specialized in tours following the tracks of jaguars in the zone of Porto Jofre.*

Advice *Surprisingly, the Pantanal is a malaria-free zone. However, the Brazilian Ministry of Health recommends a vaccination again yellow fever.*

NOT TO MISS

- ALTHOUGH THE FAUNA IS THE PANTANAL'S MAIN ATTRACTION, YOU SHOULD ALSO PAY ATTENTION TO THE FLORA, FROM LAGOONS COLORED BY SPLENDID LOTUS FLOWERS TO THE CHARACTERISTIC, AND ENORMOUS, **FLOATING ISLANDS** OF ***CAMALOTES,*** THE WATER HYACINTH WITH VIOLET FLOWERS.
- THE ONLY PAVED ROAD IN THE PANTANAL IS THE **TRANSPANTANEIRA** THAT, DESPITE ITS POMPOUS NAME, IS JUST 147 KILOMETERS LONG - WITH 122 WOODEN BRIDGES - AND CONNECTS THE LITTLE TOWN OF POCONÉ AND PORTO JOFRE, THE MAIN STOP ON THE CUIABÁ, THE PRINCIPAL RIVER IN THE AREA.
- DESCENDANTS OF THE FEW EXEMPLARS INTRODUCED IN 1535 BY SPANARDS, THE PANATANEIRO HORSE HAS PERFECTLY ADAPTED TO THE HOT, HUMID ECOSYSTEM AND TO TRAVELING LONG DISTANCES IN IT. SO MUCH THAT HERE, BESIDES BOATS, IT IS THE MAIN MEANS OF TRANSPORTATION. IN POCONÉ, THE ARARAS ECO LODGE ORGANIZES VISITS TO THE HARAS BAFO DA ONÇA, A BREEDING FARM WHERE YOU CAN TAKE **HORSEBACK EXCURSIONS** AND SPEND A DAY WITH BRAZILIAN COWBOYS.
- ALONG WITH THE LODGES AND TENT CAMPS, YOU CAN ALSO STAY IN ***FAZENDAS*** IN THE PANTANAL. IT'S AN INTERESTING EXPERIENCE BECAUSE THIS AREA IS THE MAIN CENTER OF BOVINE BREEDING, DONE USING SUSTAINABLE METHODS. THE DELICIOUS MEAT WELL EXPLAINS THE FAME OF BRAZILIAN *CHURRASCARIA.*

| **247** *The black caiman is an endangered species, even though it is the largest Amazonian predator.*

ADRENALINE

FROM HEAD TO HEAD DIVING WITH WHITE SHARKS OFF THE SOUTH AFRICAN COAST TO BUNGEE JUMPING IN NEW ZEALAND...

Here we are, finally, to the section dedicated to those who laugh in the face of danger. Here you will find extreme adventures, in one way or another. Because the limit, here, is represented by the climate, with trips aboard icebreakers, snowmobiles or on skis (like in the Canadian Rocky Mountains, where heli-skiing was invented), or in the boundless skies, aboard a hot air balloon to admire the legendary landscapes of the Wadi Rum, in Jordan, and down into the abysses of the earth, with itineraries into mysterious caves and the ocean, for close encounters with the most bloody marine predators.
And the limit, again, is defeating our fears, free climbing in Thailand or flying through the trees in the forests of Costa Rica. Or unleashing adrenaline during the experience – that lasts just a few, endless seconds – of bungee jumping in Queenstown, New Zealand, the place holding the (much earned) title of world capital for extreme sports. For some, these adventures require a healthy dose of recklessness, okay. But, in the end, like Mark Twain said: "Bed is the most dangerous place on Earth, 99% of people die in it..."

WILDLIFE WATCHING/SPOTTING
CAVING
TREKKING
BUNGEE JUMPING
ROCK-CLIMBING
ŠKRAPING
SNOWMOBILE
SKI
MOTORCYCLE

OFF-ROAD
BUS
TRAIN
ICEBREAKER
MOTORBOAT
KAYAK
RAFTING
DIVING
HOT AIR BALLOON
ELEPHANT RIDING

...NOT ONLY EXTREME SPORTS, BUT ALSO JOURNEYS TO EXPERIENCE THE MOST SPECTACULAR SNOW IN THE WORLD, THE DEPTHS OF THE EARTH AND THE WONDERS OF THE SKY.

ADRENALINE

CHOSE THE RIGHT EMOTION

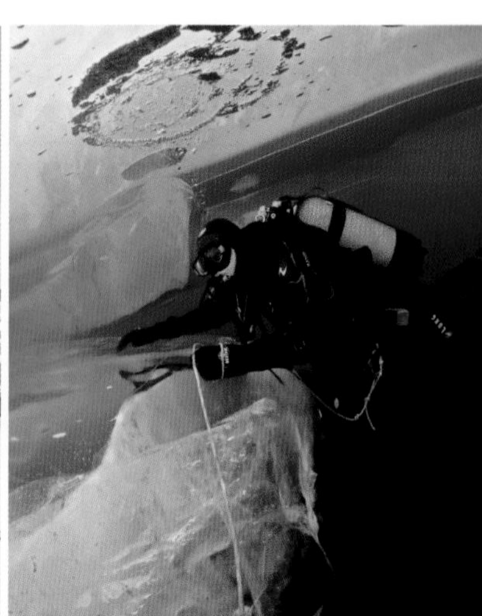

JOURNEY	PG	TIME ZONE	WHEN TO GO	NOT TO MISS
ISA - Cross-Country Skiing the North Pole	254	-	April	*Polar Arctic Base*
Finland - Emotions in Lapland	256	GMT+2	December-April	*Urho Kekkonen National Park*
Switzerland, France - At the Portes du Soleil	260	GMT+1	December-April	*La Chavanette*
Croatia - Škraping in Dalmatia	262	GMT+1	All year	*Velika and Mala Paklenica Canyons*
Zambia, Zimbabwe - Rafting the Zambezi	264	GMT+2	July-February	*Gulliver Travels Rapids*
South Africa - Caged Up in Shark Alley	266	GMT+2	June-September	*White Shark Festival*
Jordan - Hot Air Ballooning the Wadi Rum	268	GMT+2	Mar.-May/Sep.-Nov.	*Nabatee rock carvings*
Russia - On Lake Baikal	270	GMT+9	November-April	*Okhon Island*
Thailand - Rockclimbing in Krabi	274	GMT+7	November-March	*Railey Bay*
Malaysia - Down the Gunung Mulu Caves	276	GMT+8	July-Sep./Mar.-Apr.	*Deer Cave*
Philippines - The Underground River of Puerto Princesa	278	GMT+8	January-May	*Babuyan River*
New Zealand - Bungee Jumping in Queenstown	280	GMT+12	December-February	*Ledge Bunny, Nevis Gorge*
Canada - Heliskiing the Rocky Mountains	284	GTM-8	November-April	*Rocky Mountaineer Train*
United States - Rafting the Grand Canyon	286	GMT-7	April-October	*Redwall Cavern*
Mexico - In the Mayan Cenotes	288	GMT-6	October-April	*Cenote Cavalera*
Costa Rica - "Air Trekking" in Monteverde	290	GMT-6	November-May	*Selvatura Park*
Costa Rica - Sharks at Isla del Coco	292	GMT-6	June-November	*Deep Sea Submersible Tour*

252-253 *Heliskiing allows you to reach most adrenaline-driven peaks in the Canadian.*

DON'T FORGET	A CLASSIC BOOK FOR EVERY JOURNEY
Arctic clothing	*E.A. Poe,* The Narrative of Authur G. Pym
Heavy clothing	*Arto Paasilinna,* The Year of the Hare
Avalanche transreceiver	*Jean Vuarnet,* Notre victoire olympique
Mountain socks	*Predrag Matvejevic,* Mediterranean: A Cultural Landscape
Waterproof clothing	*David Livingstone,* The Zambesi Expedition
Wetsuit	*Dean Crawford,* Shark
Camera	*T.E. Lawrence,* Seven Pillars of Wisdom
Heaving clothing	*Peter Thomson,* Sacred Sea: A Journey to Lake Baikal
Climbing chalk	*Alex Garland,* The Beach
Flashlight	*C.S. Godshalk,* Kalimantaan
Flashlight	*Jessica Tarahata Hagedorn,* Dream Jungle
Life insurance	*Patrick Laviolette,* Extreme Landscapes of Leisure
Avalanche transreceiver	*Chic Scott,* Deep Powder and Steep Rock
Light clothing	*William Least Heat-Moon,* PrairyErth
Goggles and fins	*J. Eric S. Thompson,* The Rise and Fall of Maya Civilization
Long pants	*Luis Antonio Vivanco,* Green Encounters
Underwater camera	*August Gissler,* My twenty years of Cocos Island

INTERNATIONAL SEABED AUTHORITY

CROSS-COUNTRY SKIING THE NORTH POLE

Internet site www.barneo.ru

Join the exclusive Polar Club by participating in an arctic expedition with skis on your feet to the northernmost point on planet Earth.

The horizontal Everest: that is how the Italian explorer Reinhold Messner defined a trip to the North Pole. Together with his brother Hubert, they attempted to cross the ices of Siberia to Canada passing the northernmost point of the globe, but failed. Others, instead, managed to do it, so much that the honor roll of polar explorers is rather long, from Roald Amundsen, who came in 1927, aboard the aerostat Norge, on the first scientifically verified trip, to another Norwegian, Børge Ousland, who departed from Ellesmere Island in Canada in 1990 to reach the North Pole in 58 days in the first ski trek without outside support.
Contrary to Antarctica, which is a continent, the North Pole is "only" a GPS coordinate: due to wind and ocean currents, the arctic pack is an immense span of ice at least 2 meters thick that continually moves at a speed that varies between 0.1 and 0.3 km/h. This is the reason why the Arctic Polar Base, known by the acronym

| 254 *Expeditions dedicated to crossing the Arctic on skis usually take 8 to 12 days.*

| 255 *Only with a PADI Ice Diver license is it possible to experience an icy immersion.*

BARNEO and property of a Russian scientific mission, must be built and taken down every year. Accessible only by a plane departing from Longyearbyen, on the Svalbard Islands, BARNEO is also the base of operations of a few, hyper-specialized tour operators that propose (among other things) extremely expensive and well-equipped ski treks to the North Pole. From the base, it takes about 5 days – with 8-9 hours with skis on your feet, traveling about 100 kilometers in total – to reach the planet's northernmost point. Where, in keeping with tradition, the journey is celebrated with an icy caviar and champagne party.

When to go *April.*

How long to stay *The expedition lasts 8-12 days, climate permitting.*

Organization *Among the (very few) operators that organize expeditions, we recommend Polar Expeditions, which proposes ski treks, tours on husky sleds, extreme adventures like diving and parachuting at the North Pole, along with "express adventures" aboard a helicopter. Global Expedition Adventures proposes, along with ski treks, hot air balloon rallies and a cruise that lasts 2 weeks from the Russian port of Murmansk to the North Pole aboard a the Russian nuclear icebreaker Yamal.*

Advice *This is an adventure for few, and not only because it is very expensive. As soon as you start to consider the idea, get a careful medical check-up. And start training, seriously.*

NOT TO MISS

- IF YOU DON'T FEEL LIKE GETTING THERE ON SKIS, DON'T DESPAIR: A **HELICOPTER ADVENTURE** IS JUST AS EXCEPTIONAL. AMONG THOSE WHO HAVE PARTICIPATED IN THIS KIND OF ADVENTURE, WE FIND NEIL ARMSTRONG AND SIR EDMUND HILLARY, WHO BECAME THE FIRST MAN TO VISIT BOTH POLES AND EVEREST'S SUMMIT.
- IT'S CRAZY, WE KNOW. BUT THERE ARE PEOPLE WHO COMPETE IN THE **UVU NORTH POLAR MARATHON** AND RUN TO THE NORTH POLE. ACTUALLY, THERE ARE MEN AND WOMEN WHO ARE PART OF THE GRAND SLAM MARATHON CLUB, HAVING PARTICIPATED IN AT LEAST ONE COMPETITION ON EVERY CONTINENT, INCLUDING THIS ONE AND THE JUST AS EXTREME ANTARCTICA ICE MARATHON.
- IF YOU HAVE A PADI ICE DIVER LICENSE, YOU CAN PARTICIPATE IN **DIVING TOUR TO THE NORTH POLE,** ORGANIZED BY POLAR EXPEDITIONS, WHICH INCLUDES 2 DIVES A DAY FOR 3 DAYS.

| 256 *The chromatic show of the aurora borealis in the skies of Lapland.*

EMOTIONS IN LAPLAND

Cruising aboard an icebreaker, snowmobiles, dogsleds or on skis to discover the immense Arctic Circle in northern Finland.

It's an orange reflector, worn over your clothes and makes you look like the Michelin Man. But thanks to this thick suit – equipped with enormous gloves and a little opening for your face – you can treat yourself to the most exciting dive of your life, into the Baltic Sea. In the winter. You won't be able to show off your elegant free style or butterfly stroke: you'll have to settle for floating, belly up, among blocks of ice, and the sensation is more or less being an astronaut adrift in space. Then, you'll be rewarded with a cocktail made of vodka and arctic berries. It will be served in an ice glass in the most incredible open-air bar in the world, with a counter built with blocks of ice on the surface of the (obviously frozen) water, about 35 kilometers from the coast. To have brought you here will have been the captain of the Sampo, the icebreaker that, sent into retirement after 25 years of working to open routes for cargo ships in the Gulf of Bothnia, was converted into a cruise ship. With departures at least four days a week between December 21st and mid-April from Kemi harbor, in the Finnish region of Lapland, the trip lasts four hours total and is an experience in itself, accompanied by the rumble of the Sampo's 3500 gross tonnage wedging itself through the sea, shattering the thick ice crust.

Riding on the icebreaker, however, is just one of the winter adventures in Finnish Lapland that, partially residing above the Arctic Circle and with a population of 183,000 inhabitants (including Santa Claus, whose house is in the little town of

Rovaniemi) and 203,000 bustling reindeer, is a magical destination for those who love active outdoor vacations. From south to north, all of its provinces should be explored adventuring out on adrenaline safaris – that can last anywhere from one day to several weeks – on a powerful snowmobile, along the thousands of kilometers of splendid white streets, on the infinite trails that twist through dense forests or stark tundra, or even over glistening frozen lakes and rivers. Instead, for those who want to remain closer to Finnish tradition, you can participate on a nature tour of the six national parks aboard a sled pulled by either reindeer or a pack of huskies, the dogs with magnetic blue eyes that can run up to 60 kilometers a day in the snow, taking you, every evening, to enjoy your well-deserved rest in the *kotas,* the characteristic refuges of the Sami people. Furthermore, in this immense white circus, where the aurora borealis can be seen in all its splendor 200 nights a year, you can even fish by making a hole in the ice or experience the mystical northern winter along a snowshoe trek around the majestically mysterious Lake Inari, the ancient heart of Sami culture. And then, be sure to have some fast-paced fun in some of Europe's most sensational ski resorts, where the downhill season, either on skis or a snowboard, starts as early as October and goes all the way until late May, when the slopes are blessed by a full 16 hours of sunlight. Of these memorable ski resorts, an special mention goes to Suomu Resort, where snowboard enthusiasts even enjoy their very own slope that winds through a forest perfect for serious slaloming, and to Saariselkä Resort, the immense snow park with the spectacular landscapes of Urho Kokkonen National Park that also offers the possibility of lodging in Kakslaslutten, in a hi-tech version of an igloo village. You sleep under a transparent crystal dome (surprisingly warm when you are inside a sleeping bag, despite internal temperatures of -3° C) admiring the most incredibly starred skies. However, none of these exciting experiences would be complete without taking a well-deserved break in a Finnish sauna, even better if it is a *savusauna* (smoke sauna), a rustic cabin in the wild where the stove has no chimney. According to Finnish tradition, in order to increase the heat's beneficial effects, you have to smack yourself several times with a birch branch and then go outside and roll in the snow or dive into an *avanto,* i.e. a hole in a frozen lake. This time, without a suit.

Internet site www.onlyinlapland.com

| 257 *The wildest part of Lapland can be discovered on snowmobile safaris lasting one or more days.*

NOT TO MISS

● EACH YEAR, BETWEEN DECEMBER AND JANUARY, OVER 21,000 CUBIC METERS OF SNOW ARE USED TO BUILD LUMI LINNA, THE **LARGEST SNOW CASTLE IN THE WORLD.** THIS EXTRAORDINARY WHITE BUILDING IS FOUND IN KEMI AND HOSTS A RESTAURANT, A HOTEL (YOU SLEEP IN THERMAL SLEEPING BAGS ON ICE BEDS), RECREATIONAL AREAS AND A CHAPEL WHERE WEDDINGS ARE CELEBRATED. AND 200 CUBIC METERS OF ICE ARE USED JUST TO MAKE THE ARTWORK THAT DECORATES IT.

● ONE OF THE LARGEST CANINE BREEDING CENTERS IN LAPLAND IS THE **ARCTIC HUSKY FARM:** IT IS IN PYHÄTUNTURI AND HAS 90 ALASKAN HUSKIES AND 20 SIBERIAN HUSKIES TRAINED FOR SLEDDING. COME HERE FOR A SAFARI OR BRING THE KIDS TO SPEND A DAY WITH THE ADORABLE PUPPIES.

● IN SIIDA, ON LAKE INARI, VISIT **SAMI ECOMUSEUM.** IT TELLS THE HISTORY AND CULTURE OF EUROPE'S MOST "ARCTIC" PEOPLE AND THEIR SURVIVAL STRATEGIES FOR LIVING IN THE RIGID NORTHERN CLIMATE.

● AT 30 KILOMETERS LONG, **KOROUOMA,** NEAR THE SMALL TOWN OF POSIO, IS A SPECTACULAR CANYON, STUDDED WITH ICEFALLS. IT IS A PERFECT DESTINATION FOR SNOWSHOE TREKKING OR TO ICE-CLIMB. SEE THE SYÖTTEEN ERÄPALVELUT COMPANY, IN THE SYÖTTE SKI RESORT, FOR THESE ACTIVITIES.

| 258-259 *Reindeers are a valid means of transportation over the snow.* | 259 *An icebreaker in the Gulf of Bothnia.*

When to go *From December to April.*

How long to stay *From 1 to 2 weeks.*

Organization *All of the international operators specialized in arctic adventures propose trips to Lapland that include a cruise on the icebreaker and a snowmobile and dogsled safaris.*

Advice *In order to operate a snowmobile, you have to be 15 years old and have at least a tractor license. You must respect the speed limit, 60 km/h on land and 80km/h on the sea, lakes and iced waterways, or risk getting severely fined.*

Curiosities

- *Lapland crosses the border between Sweden and Finland, with the Swedish inhabitants of Haparanda and the Finnish residents of Tornio divided only by a river. And here we see the most advanced example of European integration: despite belonging to two different states (with two currencies and an hour time-zone difference), these towns have the city administration, a (bilingual) school, the healthcare system and their firefighters in common.*
- *In Finland, there are around 9000 Sami who still live in the same way as their ancestors, raising reindeer, hunting and fishing. Their language and culture are protected by a community parliament located in Inari, and are studied in the universities of Helsinki, Oulu and Rovaniemi.*
- *It is said that there are so many saunas in Finland that they could host all the countries 5,500,000 inhabitants at the same time: there is even one inside parliament in Helsinki and one 1400 meters deep inside the Pyhäalmi mine. So, no surprise: the sauna is the symbol of national identity.*

AT THE PORTES DU SOLEIL

EUROPE

On 650 kilometers of slopes in the world's largest resort, skiing is not only a sport, but a formidable white journey.

| 260 *Off-slope in the Portes du Soleil snow.* | 261 *Ski slopes overlooking Dents du Midi.*

Known as the "Swiss wall," the La Chavanette slope is both the dream and nightmare of every skier: when you find yourself at the top – at 2151 meters in elevation and exactly on the French-Swiss border – you get dizzy just looking down at that one kilometer white wall, with a 331 meter drop and, if that wasn't enough, with a series of moguls the size of an SUV. You risk the humiliation of having to go down on the lift. But don't worry: it is only one of the 27 slopes classified as "back" at Porte du Soleil's Les Crosets-Champéry Ski Resort, the largest in the world, extending over 1000 square kilometers through 14 valleys between Mont Blanc and Lake Geneva. Its numbers are impressive: 12 ski areas (seven in France and five in Switzerland), 283 slopes for a total of 650 kilometers, 119 ski lifts, ten snowparks for snowboarders and freestylers and 90 restaurants and refuges along the way. The creation of such an extraordinary snow network, which allows you to do the longest and most exciting ski safari in the Alpine Rage, was the idea of a French downhill skier Jean Vuarnet: today, at the ripe old age of 80, he is still upset about with being more famous for the brand of goggles that bear his name than for his gold metal from the 1960 Winter Olympics. Or, above all, for having made tens of thousands of skiers happy every year, experiencing "his" Portes du Soleil.

Internet site www.portesdusoleil.com

NOT TO MISS

- IN THE SECOND HALF OF MARCH, THE PORTES DU SOLEIL HOST THE COOLEST FESTIVAL IN THE ALPS CALLED **ROCK THE PISTES** AND INCLUDES FREE DAYTIME CONCERTS WITH INTERNATIONALLY ACCLAIMED ARTISTS ON STAGES SET UP ON THE SLOPES AND TENS OF *APRÉS SKI* EVENTS.
- IF MARKED RUNS AREN'T ENOUGH, YOU CAN BLAZE NEW ONES (WITH CAUTION) THROUGH FRESH SNOW. THE BEST DESTINATIONS ARE THE **NYON AND CHAMOSSIÈRE MOUNTAINS IN MORZINE AND MONT CHÉRY,** IN THE LES GETS SKI AREA.
- SUPERPIPES, BORDER-CROSS, VARIETY MODULES: FOR THOSE WHO DON'T KNOW, THESE ARE SNOWBOARD DISCIPLINES PRACTICED AT **THE STASH,** EUROPE'S FIRST 100% ECOLOGICAL SNOWPARK. IT IS FOUND IN AVORIAZ AND WAS DESIGNED BY NONE OTHER THAN JAKE BURTON, THE INVENTOR OF "SNOW SURFING." HERE YOU CAN EXPERIENCE THE THRILL OF SLALOMING BETWEEN THE TREES OF THE LES **LINDARETS FOREST.**

When to go *From December to April.*

How long to stay *1 week (at least).*

Organization *On the Portes du Soleil website you can find links to the 12 ski lodges that are a part of it (Abondance, Avoriaz, Champéry, Châtel, La Chapelle d'Abondance, Les Gets, Montriond, Morgins, Morzine, St. Jean d'Aulps, Torgon and Val d'Illiez-Les Crosets-Champoussin) to organize your itinerary. The entire circuit of this ski safari can be done both clockwise or counter-clockwise from each lodge.*

Advice *A ski journey needs the right kind of quality fuel: among the best chalets on the slopes we recommend Le Toupin on Pointe de Ripaille in Champéry (Switzerland) that serves delightful fondue and Auberge d'Alpage Chez Denis on the Plaine Dranse slope in Châtel, in the French Haute-Savoie, where you can try the raclette and the tartiflette with meat and buy Malga cheese.*

ŠKRAPING IN DALMATIA

EUROPE

In Paklenica National Park and on the Zadar archipelago to discover a new extreme sport.

| 262 *Mount Velebit's jagged rocks.* | 263 *Climbing in Paklenica National Park.*

NOT TO MISS

- EVERY YEAR, IN MARCH, THE **ŠKRAPING RACE**, IS ORGANIZED IN PAŠMAN WITH PARTICIPANTS FROM ALL OVER THE WORLD. YOU CAN CHOOSE TO COMPETE IN THE ULTRA CATEGORY (42 KM) OR LIGHT (21 KM).
- LONG 14 AND 12 KILOMETERS AND WIDE 50 AND 10 METERS RESPECTIVELY, **VELIKA AND MALA PAKLENICA CANYONS** ARE THE PARK'S MAIN ATTRACTIONS.
- EVERY SUMMER, EVERY ŠKRAPING COURSE SHOULD BE REWARDED WITH A DIVE IN THE BLUE SEA FROM THE **TKON SHORELINE,** IN PAŠMAN, FORGED INTO CURIOUS FORMS BY EROSION.
- IN ZARA, DON'T MISS A WALK ALONG THE COAST. HERE THE **MORSKE ORGULJE** WERE BUILT, A MUSICAL INSTRUMENT OF ROCK WITH 35 REEDS THAT ARE PLAYED BY THE EBB AND FLOW OF THE WAVES, CREATING A SPLENDID SOUNDTRACK FOR THE SUNSET.

The name of the newest extreme sport comes from the word in Dalmatian dialect *škrapa*, meaning sharp rock. It combines trekking, running, free climbing and a kind of *parkour* in the wild. It was invented by a Croatian athlete in 2006 and right away – thanks to the tam tam on Facebook – gained a large number of enthusiasts. It can be practiced anywhere there is rough and rocky terrain, but it's no chance that *škraping* was born in Zara territory, one of the most fascinating cities in Dalmatia. Around here, the landscapes are just as spectacular as they are arduous, whether you are on Pasman or Uglijan islands, in the "lunar" Kornati archipelago or on the mainland. Here, on the southern tip of Velebit, the Croatian's "sacred mountain," we find Paklenica National Park that, extending over 95 square kilometers, is home to deep canyons, vertiginous peaks and even a network of caves. A formidable natural gym, for those who love no-limits experiences.

When to go *Enjoyable all year round, except on the days when the Bora blows.*

How long to stay *A few hours or a week to explore the national park and the islands.*

Organization *Thanks to a network of 150 kilometers of well-marked trails, the park can be explored independently. For škraping and free climbing you should consult a specialized operator, like Zara Adventure.*

Advice *Škraping is a tiring and dangerous sport: wear a good pair of hiking shoes and bring lots of water.*

Internet sites www.tzzadar.hr and www.paklenica.hr

RAFTING THE ZAMBEZI

AFRICA

The boiling pot
Victoria Falls
Livingstone
Victoria Falls
The Vic falls bridge
Morning glory
Stairway to Heaven
ZAMBIA
Devils toilet bowl
Midnight diner featuring the muncher
Gullivers travels
Gnashing jaws of death
Commercial suicide
The three ugly sisters
Morning shave
Overland truck eater
The mother
Zambezi
The washing machine
Oblivion
Morning shower
The terminator
ZIMBABWE

In the presence of the majestic Victoria Falls, in the heart of Africa, on the planet's most exciting adventure rafting adventure.

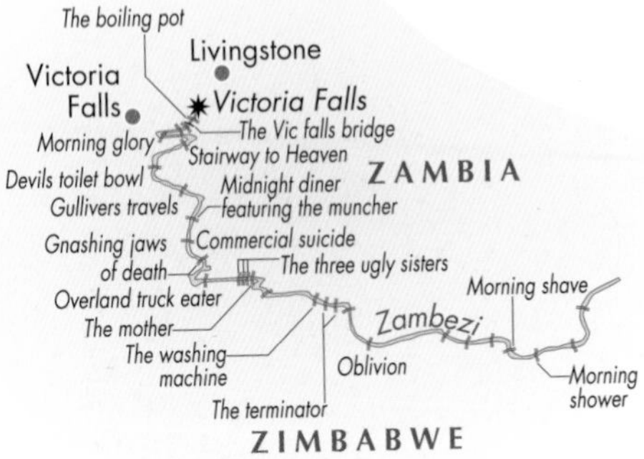

You can say that the first European to raft (even if at the time this sport hadn't been invented yet) the Zambezi was Dr. David Livingstone who, in November 1855, was accompanied by a group of Kololo natives along what they called Mosi-oa-Tunya, "smoke that thunders." He was aboard a raft, from where he could see - as he would then scribble in his notebook – "a river that rises like a fire in the savannah." That smoke, in reality, is the vaporized water that is produced by 546 million cubic meters of water that, right in the middle of the rainy season, comes crashing down from 100 meters above to form that the British explorer called Victoria Falls, in honor of his queen. Livingstone, on his part, gave the name to the location near the falls on the Zambian side of the river that, today (together with their twin Victoria Falls, in Zimbabwe) is one of the most frequented destinations on the African continent, where the people who come just to admire

| **264** *"Smoke that thunders," the fitting native name for Victoria Falls.*

| **265** *Zambezi River's rapids should be affronted between July and February, when the waters are less abundant.*

the stupefying scene are infected with rafting fever. Besides, going down the 25 rapids in quick succession between the walls of a deep basalt gorge is considered the most exciting rafting in the world.
In the rainy season, when the river is high, about half of the rapids are classified with a level 5 difficulty (where level 6 is considered beyond impossible), and they all have a name that revel the emotions they bring when going down them on a raft: try *Stairway to Heaven, Washing Machine and Gulliver's Travels,* the longest and most technical of all, itself subdivided into a series of passages that evoke the fantastic worlds of Gulliver's journeys.

Internet sites
www.zambiatourism.com/travel/places/victoria.htm
www.victoriafalls-guide.net

When to go *Between July and mid-February, when the river is lower and it is possible to run all 25 rapids.*

How long to stay *A "classic" rafting trip lasts half a day.*

Organization *In Livingstone (Zambia) and Victoria Falls (Zimbabwe) there are loads of agencies that propose rafting experiences. For an adventure along the Zambezi that lasts from 3 days to 1 week, we recommend specialized international operators like Safari par Excellence, Global Descents, Water by Nature and Zambezi Safari & Travel Company.*

Advice *In Victoria Falls, reserve a room (or go to have a beer) at Victoria Falls Hotel: in pole position over the falls, it is a colonial jewel built in 1904 when the city was finally connected to Cairo and Cape Town by the railway.*

NOT TO MISS

- IF YOU HAVE A TASTE FOR EXTREME SPORTS, HERE YOU CAN ALSO **BUNGEE JUMP,** FLYING OVER A BREATHTAKING PANORAMA OF THE RIVER UP TO THE FALLS (THAT, SUBDIVIDED INTO SEVEN SECTIONS, IS NEARLY 2 KILOMETERS LONG).
- CONSIDER A **FOOT TOUR** (OR ON TOP OF AN ELEPHANT) IN THE **VICTORIA FALLS AND ZAMBEZI NATIONAL PARKS,** RESPECTIVELY ON THE ZIMBABWEAN AND ZAMBIAN SIDES OF THE RIVER FOR OBSERVING THE FALLS AND THE RICH VEGETATION.
- GIVE YOURSELF THE LUXURY OF A TRIP ON A **STEAM TRAIN** BETWEEN VICTORIA FALLS IN ZIMBABWE AND THE ZAMBEZI NATIONAL PARK, IN ZAMBIA.
THE EXPERIENCE LASTS TWO HOURS, INCLUDING A CHAMPAGNE APERITIF ABOARD AND AN UNPARALLELED VIEW FROM ABOVE OF THE FALLS DURING SUNSET.

CAGED UP IN SHARK ALLEY

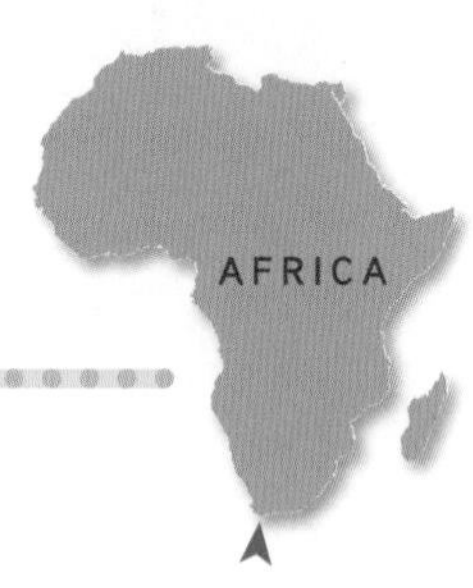

They are famed for being the killers of the sea, but white sharks aren't that mean: try it to believe it, in an emotional cage dive in Gansbaai.

It's all Steven Spielberg's fault if the white shark is famous for being the killer of the seas. In reality, it is almost impossible to be devoured by a white shark and, according to scientists, the extremely rare cases when humans are attacked are ascribable to a fatal "mistaken identity." Basically, we're not attractive prey for them. These great predators – that, having remained unchanged for over 300 million years of evolution, are a kind of ocean dinosaur – are found at the top of the marine food chain and, therefore, have their choice in meals. The sea otters that populate the banks of Dyer Island's small archipelago, in the South African Cape Province, for example, are one of their favorite snacks, and this is why, during their annual ocean migration, the sharks love to hang around these parts. Actually, the narrow canal between these islands and the mainland has been baptized Shark Alley and the small coastal town Gansbaai, two hours from Cape Town, has made a formidable tourist attraction of it. It goes without saying, this is the world capital for adrenaline diving, called cage diving thanks to these very, very close encounters with white sharks safe inside a steel construction, in a kind of opposite marine zoo. Cage diving is a 100% safe sport, but finding yourself just 10 centimeters from the open jaws of a 5-meter long white shark is a thrilling experience. Try it to believe it.

Internet site www.gansbaaiinfo.com

NOT TO MISS

- SAYING THAT GANSBAAI IS THE "COAST OF CONTRASTS" SEEMS CLICHÉ, BUT IT'S TRUE. STARTING WITH THE NAMES OF THE LOCATIONS: **PEARLY BEACH** IS A SPLENDID VILLAGE ON A WHITE SAND BEACH, PERFECT FOR STROLLING, WHILE **DANGER POINT,** WITH ITS JAGGED COASTS AND UNDERWATER ROCKS, IS ONE OF THE MOST DANGEROUS PLACES IN THE WORLD TO SAIL. ADMIRE THE UNSETTLING PANORAMA GOING UP THE 100 STEPS TO THE TOP OF THE LIGHTHOUSE.
- KNOWN AS GANSBAAI'S "SHARK LADY," KIM MACLEAN IS THE ORGANIZER, IN OCTOBER, OF THE **WHITE SHARK FESTIVAL:** IT CELEBRATES THE END OF THE SEASON WITH SHOWS, GASTRONOMIC EVENTS, EXPOS AND CONFERENCES TO SENSITIZE THE PUBLIC ABOUT PROTECTING WHITE SHARKS.
- THE HEADQUARTERS FOR CAGE DIVING EXCURSIONS IS THE PICTURESQUE FISHING PORT OF **KLEINBAAI.** AFTER YOU ADVENTURE, REWARD YOURSELF WITH LOBSTER, MOLLUSK AND WHITE WINE AT THE GREAT WHITE HOUSE.

| **266** *A simple metal cage separates you from the white sharks.* | **267** *A white shark, an endangered species, shows its jaws.*

When to go *From June to September, in the austral winter.*

How long to stay *Cage diving lasts 3-5 hours.*

Organization *Of the tour operators in Gansbaai that organize cage diving excursions, we recommend Shark Lady Adventures and White Shark Projects: both are also active in study and conservation projects of the white shark, a species on the IUCN's Red List (International Union for Conservation of Nature).*

Advice *There are no obstacles for cage diving with white sharks, except for your courage: the dive never goes below 1 meter and the respirator is feed from a tank on the boat, so you don't need a PADI license.*

HOT AIR BALLOONING THE WADI RUM

Experience it from the inside, climbing its red rock walls. Then admire the wonders and oddities of the desert of Lawrence of Arabia from above.

When the English baptized the Arabian Desert as the Empty Quarter, they certainly didn't take into account tis northernmost offshoot. Compared to the great – and philosophic – emptiness in the very essence of the term "desert," the Wadi Rum is extraordinarily full. Part of the powerful system of geological shifts known as the Rift, its luminescent red sand (thanks to the presence of grains of quartz) lies between two mountain ranges, the Jebel Um Ishrin to the east and the Jebel Rum to the west, over 1000 meters high and characterized by a battery of enchanting spires, pinnacles, arches, narrow canyons that hide the mirage of perfect, little oases with date palms and tamarisks feed by waterfalls and springs that seem to bubble magically from the rock. Today, together with the nearby "lost city" of Petra, the Wadi Rum is Jordan's tourist destination par excellence, crowded with jeeps that travel uninterrupted along its paths, lined with typical Bedouin tents of heavy black wool (sipping the classic "desert tea" or eating lamb by moonlight are almost obligatory experiences) and with just as many excursionist tents. Besides, the Wadi Rum – and not only for the absolute beauty of its landscapes – is an literary icon, linked to one of the characters that helped create the legend of desert adventures: T.E. Lawrence, the charming secret agent

| 268 *A Bedouin bear a natural rock arch in the Wadi Rum.*

NOT TO MISS

- THE MOST FAMOUS ROCK FORMATION IN THE WADI RUM IS UNDOUBTEDLY THE ONE CALLED *THE SEVEN PILLARS OF WISDOM*, FROM THE TITLE OF T.E. LAWRENCE'S MEMOIRS. THEN GO TO **SIQ UM TAWAQI** AND, IN THIS NARROW CANYON, LOOK FOR INCISIONS THAT PORTRAY LAWRENCE'S HEAD, MADE BY THE BEDOUINS THAT WERE HIS COMRADES.
- **ASFANEH MOUNTAIN** IS A FANTASTIC ALBUM OF INCISIONS DATING TO THE NABATEA EPOCH, REPRESENTING FIGURES OF HUMANS, ANIMALS AND CAMEL CARAVANS. FROM ABOVE, FIND THE SUGGESTIVE REMAINS OF THE TEMPLE DEDICATED TO ALLAT, THE NABATEI'S MOTHER GODDESS.
- FOR CLIMBING ENTHUSIASTS, ON **JEBEL RUM** THERE ARE MANY COURSES THAT, ALREADY BY THEIR NAMES, INDICATE THE LEVEL OF DIFFICULTY: *FROM TOWERING INFERNO* TO *ALLAH FACTOR*. INSTEAD, YOU DON'T NEED MUCH EXPERIENCE TO GET TO THE SUMMIT OF THE SO-CALLED **ROCK BRIDGE,** MADE OF RED ROCK AND FROM WHICH YOU GET A PHENOMENAL PANORAMA OVER THE DUNES.

Internet site www.wadirum.jo

| 269 *On a hot air balloon, get a breathtaking panorama over the Wadi Rum.*

from Britain that made the Wadi Rum his home when, during WWI, he guided the Bedouin revolt against the Ottoman Empire. Before him, this desert was, thanks to the presence of water, a vital stop for caravans, exhausted from crossing the terrible emptiness of the Arabian Desert and, even before that, was populated by the Nabatei, the race of merchants that built Petra, who left behind many fascinating remains that can still be found readily scattered throughout the area today, from the ruins of an ancient temple to the thousands of paintings and rock incisions that make the multicolored stratified clefts a marvelous stone book of human history. Experience the Wadi Rum from inside: get one of the expert Bedouin guides to take you to discover its most hidden secrets, to climb up its natural cathedrals, to spend (at the very least) one night gazing up at the pristine desert sky to count stars, brighter than you've ever seen them before. But remember that you won't truly understand the poetry of the desert unless you have seen it whole, during a silent hot air balloon ride, gently floating over it on a trip that allows you to finally grasp the beauty of its complexity and majesty from above. In fact, from up here, you are ultimately able to realize how surprisingly close this great sand desert is to another "great empty": the shinning waters of the Red Sea that, tinting the port of Aqaba deep blue, stretch all the way to the infinite horizon.

When to go *From March to May and from September to November.*

How long to stay *The hot air balloon ride takes 1 hour, but spend at least 1 night under the stars of the Wadi Rum.*

Organization *Founded by decree of King Abdullah II Ibn Al Hussein of Jordan, the Royal Aero Sports Club of Jordan is located at the Aqaba airport and proposes hot air balloon rides and trips in flights on ultralights over the Wadi Rum. The adventure, that takes place early in the morning, can be booked through tour operators in the area, like Rum Stars. For a desert adventure on foot or on a camel, or climbing excursions, take a look at the proposals of the Bedouin guide's association Wadi Rum Mountain Guides.*

Advice *When you pack your bags for an adventure in the Wadi Rum, remember that here the thermic shift between the day and the night is extreme, going from above 30° C to 0° C (and, on a hot air balloon in the morning, it is really, really cold!).*

ON LAKE BAIKAL

An subzero adventure with record-breaking ice in the most fascinating destinations in Siberia's "Great Empty."

With 336 tributaries and only 1 outlet, Baikal is the oldest - at 25 millions year old! - and largest (23,000 cubic kilometers of water) freshwater lake in the world: only 6th in surface area due to its record depths, according to recent measurements, at 1741 meters. Add the fact that it is located 5500 kilometers east of Moscow, 3700 west of the Pacific Ocean, 250 north of the Mongolian steppes and south of nothing (meaning that it might as well be the moon, even if around 80,000 live there). Add to that the fact that most its 2000 kilometers of banks, steep and covered by dense conifer and birch forest, are inaccessible by land, that its waters are pure enough to be considered a Kantian category or that its surface freezes over, often in just one night, trapping the waves in a rough sculpture that lasts for five months, until slowly melting, then it is clear that it is also a place shrouded by a sacred mystique. Not by chance, some of Baikal's areas, like the Olkhon Island and the Svyati Nos Peninsula, are majestic settings for the Taiga nomadic population's shamanistic rites, while for Russians (who only discovered it in 1662), it is a profoundly important symbol, a place that reflects Mother Russia in its very waters: immense, powerful and able to overcome any adversity.

NOT TO MISS

- A BAIKAL ADVENTURE MERITS ANOTHER GREAT ADVENTURE: TO GET HERE, TAKE THE TRAIN, FROM MOSCOW, ON THE LEGENDARY **TRANS-SIBERIAN RAILWAY.**
- CONSIDERED THE PARIS OF SIBERIA, **IRKUTSK** IS BAIKAL'S UNOFFICIAL CAPITAL. STOP HERE A FEW DAYS TO ADMIRE THE 18TH CENTURY WOODEN ARCHITECTURE AND ITS MANY MUSEUMS.
- HOSTED IN PRIBAYKALSKY NATIONAL PARK, **OKHON** IS THE BIGGEST OF BAIKAL'S 26 ISLANDS. HERE, AT THE EDGE OF THE PICTURESQUE VILLAGE OF KHUZIN, YOU MUST PHOTOGRAPH **SHAMAN ROCK,** WHERE ELABORATE MAGICAL RITES ARE STILL PERFORMED TODAY.
- AFTER A LONG DAY ON THE ICE, TREAT YOURSELF TO A *BANYA,* A TRADITIONAL **RUSSIAN SAUNA:** THERE IS ONE IN EVERY VILLAGE. PUSHKHIN DEFINED IT "A SECOND MOTHER," FOR ANOTHER FOREIGNER IT IS "VOLUNTARY TORTURE." TRY IT TO FIND OUT!

Internet site www.baikal.ru

| **270 and 271** *Lake Baikal's frozen waters allow you to reach and explore remote corners, including ice caves.*

Surprisingly, however, not all of Baikal territory is actually in Russia: part of the eastern end of the lake is under the jurisdiction of the semi-unknown Republic of Buryatia, with its capital, Ulan-Ude. This lake is also a destination for epic adventures, absolutely to be taken – in order to remain faithful to its spirit – during the winter months, when the temperatures that drop far below zero are a small price to pay for the privilege of admiring the greatly suggestive icy landscapes. Paradoxically, it is precisely in the most frigid part of the year that Baikal seems to truly awaken: it is then that the surface, in its solid state, becomes a sort of highway that allows you to reach, on snowmobiles or riding jeeps with nail-studded tires, the most remote areas of its far banks and to explore its wondrous frozen caves, charming villages and surrounding forests, all with downhill skis on your feet. March and April, just before the spring thaw, are the best months to experience a trip over the lake aboard old Soviet sidecars to the cove named Maloyee More (Little Sea). This is the place where, after giving birth to its adorable cubs, the nerpa – the only freshwater seal in the world – gather every year. They have a lovely soft, white coat that perfectly camouflages them in the stark, frosty landscape and, in this place characterized by a fauna with an extremely high rate of endemism, are the animal species that best symbolically represent a winter adventure on Lake Baikal: these furry seals migrated here all the way from the distant polar seas, following the Yenisei, the great Siberian river, on an epic journey way back at the beginning of time.

| **272** *Crossing Baikal on skis takes training.*
| **272-273** *The lake freezes, usually in November, overnight, thus trapping the waves until the thaw.*

When to go *During the long Siberian winter, between November and April. The climate is more moderate (kind of), with temperatures between -15° C and -8° C, from mid-February to April.*

How long to stay *The adventures proposed by tour operators last 1 or 2 weeks.*

Organization *Many operators in Irkutsk propose extreme tours: among these, Baikal Nature distinguishes itself for their respectful approach to the fragile ecosystem and local populations. They propose snowmobile, jeep, downhill ski and sidecar tours with lodging in traditional villages and supply the technical equipment to protect yourself from the cold.*

Advice *Be careful when you chose your tour: the one that includes skiing is only adapted to those in optimal form and who have experience in this sport.*

Curiosities

In 2002, a network of non-profit organizations started a Baikal preservation project through sustainable tourism and the creation of the Great Baikal Trail, connecting the national parks along its banks. Since then, volunteer camps are organized to participate in its construction. Lasting two weeks, they are a fantastic occasion to experience the lake's natural environment.

Related to the trout, the omul *is at the base of the local diet. Among the peoples of the lake, the prize for gourmet cooking goes to the Evenki nomads, who cook everything that is possible to fish, hunt or gather in the forest. Their signature plate is* kulnin*, dried meat stewed with berries.*

The Siberian equivalent to the Amish, the Starovernyi (or "old believers," indicative of their break, in the 17th century, from the Russian Orthodox Church) live in the region of Zabalkaiye, in Buryatia. Their lifestyle hasn't changed in three centuries: in the villages of Tarabagatay and Desnyatikovo, they have set up cultural centers where banquets and traditional shows are organized.

Inhabited by peoples of Mongolian descent, the Republic of Buryatia is the keystone of Russian Buddhism. Here the most sacred site is Ivolginsky Datsan, a monastery that hosts a precious collection of sacred texts in Russian and Tibetan and a dense community of monks.

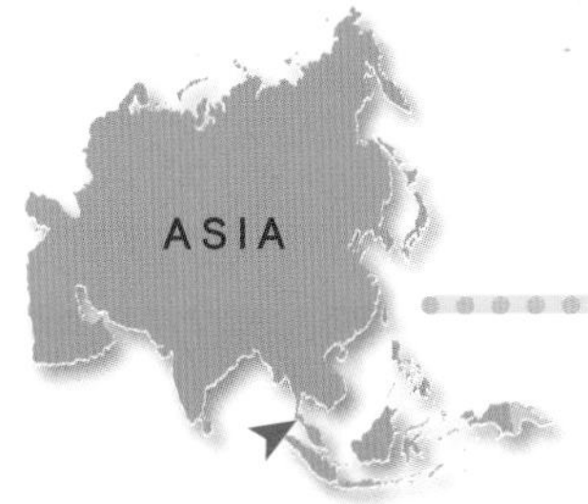

ROCKCLIMBING IN KRABI

Vertical emotions between the sea and sandstone pinnacles in Raily, the Asian capital of rock climbing. All in the magical setting of Southern Thailand.

NOT TO MISS

- ALONG THE COAST OF TON SAI, THE ROCK GYM OF RAILEY SPREADS OUT: THE HARDEST CLIMBS ARE **DUM'S KITCHEN,** PERFECT FOR A CLIMB AT SUNSET AND **EAGLE WALL,** ACCESSIBLE AFTER A BRIEF TREK THROUGH A PALM FOREST.
- IN RAILEY WEST, CLIMB UP TO **KHOA LUK CHOEE CAVE,** A CREVICE IN A WALL THAT OPENS BETWEEN 17 M AND 60 METERS ABOVE SEA LEVEL, OFFERING AN ENCHANTING PANORAMA OVER THE BAY'S TURQUOISE WATERS.
- TO RELAX, GO TO **CHICKEN ISLAND,** WITH ITS STRIPS OF WHITE SAND THAT CHANGE SHAPE ACCORDING TO THE TIDE.
- WHEN NIGHT FALLS, ALL THE ROCK CLIMBERS MEET TO EXCHANGE ADVICE AND TELL ABOUT THEIR EXPERIENCES AT **FREEDOM BAR** OR **SMALL WORLD BAR,** WITH BEER AND REGGAE MUSIC IN THE BACKGROUND THAT IS ANYTHING BUT DISCRETE.

When to go *From November to March.*

How long to stay *1 week.*

Organization *There are many rock climbing schools in Railey and on the beaches o Ton Sai that propose courses for beginners and guided itineraries. Among these, we recommend Hot Rock Climbing School that offers deep water soloing experiences and hospitality in rustic beach bungalows; it also has a the most furnished sports shop in the area.*

Advice *The touristic offerings in this Thai sport enclave is aimed at young visitors with tight budgets and is rather Spartan. The nearby locations of Ao Nang and Ai Pra Nang, just 20 minutes by boat from Railey, instead offer an ample choice of more confortable bungalows or even luxurious resorts.*

| **274 and 275** *The equipped walls in Hat Pra Nang, on the beaches of Railey, offer exciting challenges and breathtaking views.*

Also known as *psycobloc* (quite revealingly), deep water soloing is the adrenaline version 2.0 of rock climbing. It is practiced alone along the coasts during high tide, usually on high-level difficulty walls, without any help except for shoes and magnesium for increasing grip and with water below in case of a fall. In Krabi, a province in Southern Thailand, mostly protected in a national park and made up of around 80 little islands and a coast fraught with scenic sandstone pinnacles, there is even a deep water soloing circuit with a series of climbs with difficulty ranging between 5 and 8 degrees, accessible on a canoe itinerary. Here, Railey Bay, on the Pra Nang peninsula, is one of the most desired destinations for rock climbers all over the world. Although on the mainland, it is only accessible by sea from the famous Ao Nang Resory and has a beautiful white sand beach protected by mangroves and steep rock formations with around 70 climbs of every difficulty level traced up them. The most vertiginous is the Thaiwand Wall, dominating the western bay of Railey East, where the rocks hide caves transformed into temples. There is one that unites sports with romanticism: it's the "Princess Wall" that leads to a spectacular blue lagoon hidden in the rocks where, after your hard work, you can take a relaxing swim in a scene from *The Beach!*

Internet site www.krabi-tourism.com

| **276-277** *Clearwater Cave is 108 kilometers long.*

When to go *From July to September and from March to April.*

How long to stay *2-3 days.*

Organization *On Gunung Mulu National Park's official website, you can book cave excursions of varying levels of difficulty, defined Introduction, Intermediate and Advanced, with a minimum of three and a maximum of eight participants. To enroll in the upper two, you have to present a document that states you are a member of an internationally recognized speleological club or written documentation of at least three hours of previous experience in an unlit cave. Of the tour operators that organize speleological tours combined with trekking, boating and lodging in the longhouses of the native Dhalak in Sarawak, we recommend Kuching Caving and Borneo Ecotours.*

Advice *Treat yourself to the luxury of a nature stay at Royal Mulu Resort, the exclusive - and only - hotel structure inside the protected area.*

DOWN THE GUNUNG MULU CAVES

The celebrated Sarawak massif is the largest and most majestic underground system on the planet. Explore it armed with rope and flashlights.

Protected by a national park, the sandstone massif of Gunung Wulu stands out at an altitude of 2377 meters in the Sarawak forest, in Borneo, and its bowels host the largest system of underground caves on the planet. Going down opportunely lit paths, here everyone can admire Deer Cave – a hall so long that it could hold five gothic cathedrals or 20 Boeing 747s – or the impressive room of Good Luck Cave, the world's most sensational, or the curiously shaped stalactites in the imposing Clearwater Cave. But these are just a taste of the massif's over 300 kilometers of caves and tunnels explored up to now (estimated to be a third of the total) and, to really experience adventure, you have to participate in the speleological expeditions guided by park rangers. Exceptional in themselves, the cavities explored with the help of ropes and flashlights are only reached by boats that travel the plateau's rivers or along forest paths, in a labyrinth of palms and rock pinnacles forged by millenniums of erosion from tropical rains. And as sharp as razors.

NOT TO MISS

- TWELVE SPECIES OF **BATS** HAVE BEEN REGISTERED IN DEER CAVE, ONE OF WHICH, *CHAEREPHON PLICATA,* IS ESTIMATED TO HAVE OVER 3.5 MILLION EXEMPLARS IN THESE CAVES. BETWEEN 5:30 P.M. AND 6:30 P.M., FROM A SPECIAL PANORAMIC BALCONY, YOU CAN WATCH THE FASCINATING SPECTACLE OF THIS ANIMAL'S MASS EXODUS, WHILE THE ADJACENT STRUCTURE HAS GIANT SCREENS FOR OBSERVING THE BATS' ACTIVITIES UP CLOSE AND PERSONAL BY WEBCAM.
- PREPARE YOURSELF TO COME BACK FROM THIS ADVENTURE SOAKED AND DIRTY, BUT IT'S WORTH IT TO GO DOWN **DEER CAVE** ON AN UNDERGROUND RIVER TO THEN REEMERGE ON THE SURFACE, ENJOYING A SWIM IN THE POOLS FEED BY THE WATERFALLS OF THE SO-CALLED GARDEN OF EDEN, SURROUNDED BY SCENERY OF RARE GREEN BEAUTY.
- PAY ATTENTION TO THE RICH FAUNA OF THE FOREST AND IN THE CAVES, WHERE THE MOST POPULOUS COLONY OF SALAMANDERS ON THE PLANET LIVES, NUMBERING IN THE MILLIONS.

Internet site mulupark.com

THE UNDERGROUND RIVER OF PUERTO PRINCESA

Palawan Island is an exceptional laboratory for biodiversity. And, with forests and the sea, provides great excitement... in the dark.

| **278 and 279** *The underground river in Puerto Princesa National Park crosses a cave with stalactites and stalagmites before flowing into the South China Sea.*

Illuminated by a flashlight, the Sirenia fossils look almost alive. A mammal ancestor of the dugong that lived 20 million years ago, it got stuck in between these rocks forever. To keep it company, there are cathedrals of speleothems, stalactites and stalagmites and rock walls that hold, mounted like jewels, rare minerals like serrabrancaite with its sapphire-blue crystals. And these are only a few of the bizarre wonders of this subterranean river held in the underground cavity of Puerto Princesa National Park that, 8.2 kilometers in length, is the longest navigable subterranean waterway in the world. The experience of boating down it last just an hour, but simply arriving - along a trail through virgin forest, accompanied by the calls of macaques and colorful parrots - to the pond that signals the cave entrance is an adventure in itself. And, furthermore, this incredible place is in the south of the great Palwan Island (in turn included in the archipelago by the same name that includes 1700 islands and reefs), considered the Philippines' amazing biodiversity laboratory, an exceptional destination in insular Asia for those who love vacations that have the flavor of exploration.

Internet site www.puerto-undergroundriver.com

NOT TO MISS

- THE PARK'S VISITORS CENTER ORGANIZES SPELEOLOGICAL EXCURSIONS NEAR THE **KAWILI AND LION CAVES**. AND THE ADVENTURES AREN'T LIMITED TO THE DARK: THE **BABUYAN RIVER** RUNS THROUGH THE PARK, AND YOU CAN FLOAT DOWN IN ON A BAMBOO RAFT OR IN A TRADITIONAL WOODEN CANOE, ALL THE WAY TO THE MOUTH, ON A MAGNIFICENT WHITE BEACH OVERLOOKING THE SOUTH CHINA SEA.
- WITH WHITE SAND AND TRANSPARENT WATER -PERFECT FOR RELAXING AND SNORKELING - PUERTO PINCESA'S MOST BEAUTIFUL **BEACHES** ARE **SABANG, PANAGUAMAN AND MARTA FE.**
- ALTHOUGH THE CENTER OF TOURISM ON PALAWAN IS **EL NIDO,** A FISHING VILLAGE TRANSFORMED INTO A PICTURESQUE RESORT DESTINATION, THE WHOLE ISLAND OFFERS OPPORTUNITIES FOR TREKKING ENTHUSIASTS, INCLUDING PROTECTED RAIN FORESTS AND THE REMOTE VILLAGES OF THE TAGBANUA, PALAW'AN, TAU'T BATO AND BATAK ETHNIC GROUPS, EACH WITH ITS OWN CHARACTERISTIC BAMBOO ARCHITECTURE.

When to go *From January to May.*

How long to stay *The tour lasts 1 day, but you need 2 weeks to visit all of Palawan.*

Organization *The tour along the river is organized every day and costs 250 Philippian Pesos (46 Euro), including entrance to the park. To organize an adventure vacation on the island, staying in ecotourist structures, we recommend Tao Explore.*

Advice *Since 2011, when Puerto Princesa National Park was included in the list of the Seven (new) Wonders of the World, the number of visitors has increased exponentially, so it is necessary to book the subterranean adventure at least 1 week ahead of time (you can do it online on the protected area's official website).*

BUNGEE JUMPING IN QUEENSTOWN

In Vanuatu it was a traditional test of courage. In the mountains of South Island, this leap into the void has become the most popular extreme sport.

Queenstown has 7500 residents and the air of a quite town reflected in the blue waters of Wakatipu Lake, surrounded by pastures and the imposing "Antipodal Alps," on South Island. At first glance, it seems like the stereotypical *buen retiro* for older retirees. Instead, surprisingly, Queenstown has earned the name Adrenaline City, New Zealand's (although locals say: world) extreme sport capital, where the term "sport" is a bland euphemism for the most improbable, adrenaline-driven and breathtaking activities imaginable.
Among these, the one that has become famous on a planetary scale is bungee jumping. A couple of decades have now passed since Alan John Hackett proposed his adventure companion, Henry van Asch, to jump off the bridge over the Kawarau River, near their hometown, with a cord tied to his ankles: the idea came to him during a geography lesson, reading about a test of courage that the Vanuatu natives practiced. No sooner said than done. The experience was so exciting that it had to be shared, so the two kids decided to open a business: founded in 1988, AJ Hackett is the first and larges bungee jumping company on the planet, with branches on every continent.

NOT TO MISS

- AROUND HERE, CANYONING, RAFTING AND RAFTING ARE "NORMAL" ACTIVITIES; INSTEAD, **WHITE WATER SLEDGING** IS TRULY ORIGINAL: IT CONSISTS IN THE RAPID DESCENT OF THE SHOTEOVER RIVER ON A KIND OF SURFBOARD WITH HANDLES.
- IN THE WINTER, THE SOUTHERN MOUNTAINS ARE A PARADISE FOR WINTER SPORTS LOVERS. THERE IS A PARTICULAR ATTENTION TO SNOWBOARDING AND FREESTYLE SKIING DURING THE *100% PURE NEW ZEALAND WINTER GAMES*, IN AUGUST.
- MAKING GOLF EXCITING? HERE THEY'VE MANAGED TO DO IT: IN QUEENSTOWN GARDENS YOU WILL FIND THE ONLY **FRISBEE GOLF** COURSE IN THE WORLD, WITH FRISBEES INSTEAD OF BALLS AND BASKETS HUNG ON TREES AS HOLES.
- JUST 20 MINUTES AWAY BY CAR, VISIT **ARROWTOWN,** A PICTURESQUE VILLAGE FOUNDED IN THE DISTANT (AT LEAST FOR NEW ZEALANDERS) 1861, WHEN THE RIVER GOLD RUSH STARTED.

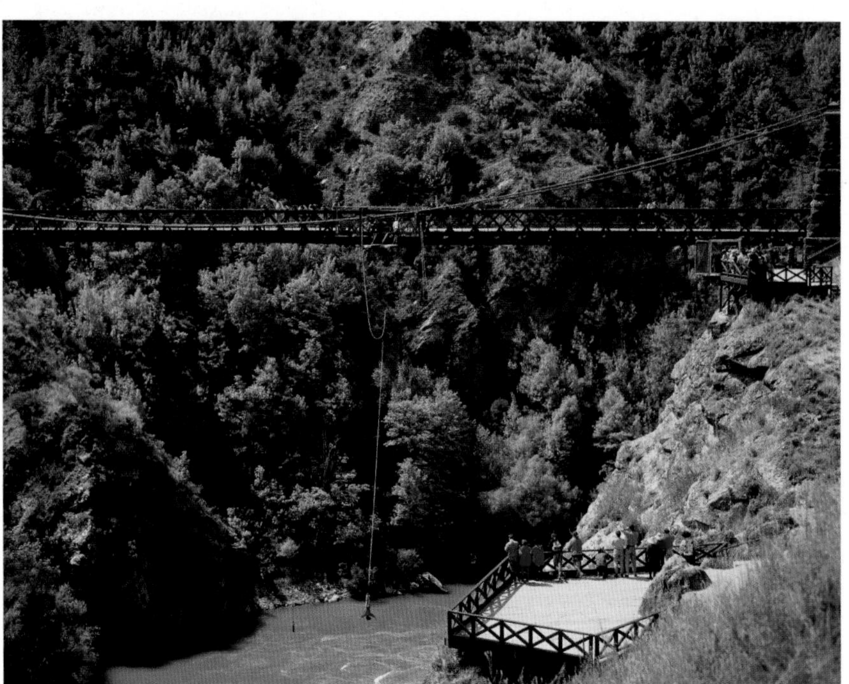

| **280** *Jumping off the Kawarau River Bridge.* | **281** *Jet boating down Shotover River.*

When to go *The antipodal summer, between December and February, is perfect for all the extreme sports, but Queenstown is pleasant year round and, in the winter (from June to August) bungee jumping is considered a perfect after-ski activity.*

How long to stay *A jump lasts just a few seconds, but you should stay in Queenstown for at least four days.*

Advice *If you've decided to come here for the thrill, that means you are already resistant to any wise council.*

SKIPPERS CANYON
SKIPPERS CANYON

| **282** *Rafting down the rapids of Shotover River.* | **283** *White water sledging, one of the adrenaline activities that Queenstown offers.*

For people who love this sort of thing, jumping into the void from 43 meters up off the Kawarau Bridge is *The Original,* and a shop with t-shirts and other souvenirs, a radio station, a studio with recordings of all the jumps done here every day (around 200, and every bungee jumper receives a DVD with the video of their efforts included in the price), as well as a series of panoramic platforms for the public. And it doesn't stop there, because since 2011 you can also jump from a launching station suspended 134 meters above the Nevis Gorge as well as a platform called Ledge Bungy, suspended 400 meters up at the end of the panoramic funicular above the city. Instead, or those who suffer from a fear of heights, another native here came up with a popular aquatic adventure, jet boating, that is based in the picturesque gorge of the Shotover River. Advertised as "the most exciting speedboat ride in the world," it consists in boarding a fireball equipped with two 700-horsepower turboprop engines and get shaken around by a pilot driving at breakneck speeds down the gorge, just barely missing the granite walls, slaloming between jagged rocks and exaggerating with a series of acrobatic spins that give a sudden shower to the curious spectators on shore. It's incredible to say, but this 100% New Zealand experience is very healthy: Thrill Therapy supposedly has the power to lengthen your life, nuroushing the heart and brain with a beneficial cocktail of oxygen, sugars, adrenaline and endorphins.

Internet site www.queenstownnz.co.nz

Curiosities

- *Between 1988 and today, over a million people have bungee jumped with AJ Hackett. The minimum age is 10 years; the oldest jumper was a 94-year-old man, the heaviest weighing in at 235 kilograms and the lightest an adolescent weighing 35 kilos.*
- *Queenstown's Ledge Bungy is one of the few locations on the planet where you can jump at night.*
- *Are you looking for something more extreme than bungee jumping? In Nevis Gorge and in Ledge, try the swing jump, a new technique that combines the effect of jumping with that of a roller coaster. And, for experts, AJ Hackett has perfected 10 different techniques for acrobatic jumping, from* Karate Kid *to* The Matrix, *from* Flying Squirrel *to* The Gainer.

HELISKIING THE ROCKY MOUNTAINS

The most gratifying experience for any skier comes from Canada. To be experienced in the Rocky's extreme wild nature, naturally!

Austrian-born Hans Gmoser was probably the greatest Canadian mountaineer. He scaled many peaks, climbing for the first time Wickersham Wall and Mount McKinley and the east wall of Mount Logan, respectively the first and second summits on the American continent, and was the founder of the Association of Canadian Mountain Guides. But he will be remembered in history above all for having invented heliskiing, the most gratifying and extreme experience for any skier. His first adventure of this sort dates back to 1965 and the Bugaboos, the range of granite peaks in the northwestern corner of the Canadian Rocky Mountains, was the setting. And, two years later, here in this area inaccessible if not by air, Gmoser himself built the Bubaboo Lodge, the first of a series of refuges dedicated exclusively to "helicopter skiers."

Internet site www.canada.travel

Spending a week (at least) on the Canadian Rocky Mountains skiing – either alone or with a select group of friends – on virgin slopes and with the helicopter doing the

| **284** *A helicopter is ready to pick up skiers from the Bugaboos' snows.*

| 285 *Helicopters allow skiers to reach numerous virgin slopes in the Rocky Mountains.*

work of a ski lift is to the classic white week on marked runs even in the vastest and most equipped ski areas on the planet like going to the zoo is to participating in a safari in the heart of Africa. No lines, no crowd: only you, the silence and the immenseness of what are among the most wild mountains in the world, and where every descent feels like an epic challenge (expect five of these per day...). You are the one creating your own runs, facing powder or corn snow, with large granular flakes that result from an incessant cycle of daytime surface melting and nocturnal re-solidification. Or, furthermore, a special slalom in limitless forests or on the surfaces of glaciers covered in fresh snow, admiring the enchanting panorama all the while. Even from above...

When to go *From November to April.*

How long to stay *1 week.*

Organization *There are many Canadian operators that offer heliskiing adventures, but we recommend Canadian Mountain Highways: this is the company Hans Gmoser himself founded and offers the widest range of adventures adapted to skiers of every level, or specific runs for snowboarders and free-riders, for all female groups and even for families with children starting at the age of 12 years.*

Advice *When organizing, inform yourself about the type of adventure to chose based on your strength and your ability. Off-slope downhill skiing (above all through forests) is physically quite demanding. If you are used to listening to music while you ski, forget about it! Mp3 players and cellphones are prohibited for safety reasons because they could interfere with the avalanche radio transmitter that you will be provided.*

NOT TO MISS

- THE ADVENTURE STARTS EVEN BEFORE YOU GET THERE IF YOU TAKE THE **ROCKY MOUNTAINEER TRAIN** TO REACH BANFF AND JASPER, THE QUEENS OF THE ROCKIES, ALONG ONE OF THE MOST SPECTACULAR RAILWAYS IN THE WORLD.
- THE DEPARTURE POINT FOR HELICOPTER ADVENTURES, SURROUNDED BY A NATIONAL PARK, IS **BANFF,** THE CANADIAN SKI CAPITAL. HERE, VISIT THE **WHYTE MUSEUM OF CANADIAN ROCKIES** AND PARTICIPATE IN THE SPORTING EVENTS THAT TAKE PLACE ALL YEAR.
- THE MOUNTAIN RANGES OF THE BUGABOOS, CARIBOOS, MONASHEES AND PURCELL ARE THE TOP FOR HELISKIING. HOWEVER, YOU SHOULD KNOW THAT DURING THE SUMMER YOU CAN ALSO PRACTICE **HELI-HIKING,** FOOTING IT INSTEAD OF SKIING.

| 286 *The Colorado River at the start of the Grand Canyon.*

RAFTING THE GRAND CANYON

NORTH AMERICA

Down the Colorado rapids, discovering the most celebrated gorge on the planet from an unusual (and spectacular) prospective... from below.

Looking down of the edge of the Grand Canyon for the first time, the naturalist Donald Culross noted having felt, in that moment, "God's will." And the writer J.B. Priestley described the spectacle of the Colorado River pushing its way between the rock walls as "Nature's Judgment Day." Although in the 1800s – i.e. when America discovered the aesthetic of nature – you couldn't escape metaphysical rhetoric to describe the magnificence of the Grand Canyon, even today the setting of what is one of the "cult" destination when traveling in the United States escapes definition. Deep 1500 meters, 447 kilometers long and between 549 meters and 30 kilometers wide, the gorge dug by the river's force (that here forms around 100 rapids) is a sort of geological Disneyland where even laymen can't help but be bewitched by the beauty of the forms and colors of rocks polished by millions of years of water erosion. Furthermore, there is a constant debate among visitors and tour operators as to what is the best way to experience the Grand Canyon: flying over in a small plane or helicopter, trekking – and in this case either down into it, on the South Rim or the North Rim – or, even preferring a visit during the winter, when there are fewer tourists and, every now and then, snow covers the rock walls. Those who have tried everything, however, are ready to swear that the Grand

Canyon is at its best if you admire it from the bottom up, navigating along the river aboard a raft. Most visitors participate in half-day rafting trips, but here the true adventure is traveling along the Colorado River for at least a week, sleeping in tents in the presence of this extraordinary rock cathedral. This is the only way to truly experience the wilderness of America's most legendary landscape.

Internet site www.nps.gov/grca/index.htm

When to go *From April to October.*

How long to stay *Tour operators specializing in rafting propose adventures that last between 3 and 18 days.*

Organization *There are about 15 tour operators specialized in rafting along the most spectacular part of the Grand Canyon (364 kilometers long between Lees Ferry and Diamond Creek). We recommend Aramak Wilderness River Adventures, Grand Canyon Whitewater and Oars.*

Advice *Among the many tailor-made rafting proposals, the most complete is without a doubt the one that combines navigation along the rapids and treks. You have to be prepared, however, to support the fatigue of steep slope and hot temperatures that become torrid in July and August.*

NOT TO MISS

- ABOVE ALL IN JULY AND AUGUST, WHEN TEMPERATURES SOAR, THERE IS NOTHING BETTER THAN DIVING INTO THE WATERS, LIMPID AND CALM, OF THE **LITTLE COLORADO,** WHICH CUTS OUT A SMALL, SUGGESTIVE SANDSTONE GORGE, CONSIDERED A SACRED PLACE BY THE NAVAJO NATIVES.
- IN ORDER TO PREPARE YOURSELF FOR THE EXCITEMENT OF RIDING THE TURBULENT **PRESIDENT HARDING RAPIDS,** TREAT YOURSELF TO A BREAK ADMIRING THE MAGNIFICENT **REDWALL CAVERN:** IT IS HUGE AND HAS A SOFT SAND "FLOOR" WHERE THE MOST POPULAR PASTIME IS PLAYING FRISBEE UNDER ITS ARCHS.
- NEAR PHANTOM BEACH, ONE OF THE ARRIVAL POINTS FOR RAFTING ADVENTURES, TAKE ON THE CLIMB (15 KILOMETERS) OF **BRIGHT ANGEL TRAIL:** BLAZED BY NATIVES AND DOTTED BY MULTICOLORED ROCKS RICH WITH ANCIENT PICTOGRAPHS, IT IS PROBABLY THE MOST PANORAMIC AND EXCITING TRAIL IN THE ENTIRE GRAND CANYON PARK.
- IN THE GRAND CANYON, AROUND 2000 SITES WITH THE REMAINS OF THE ANASAZI CULTURE HAVE BEEN FOUND. THE MOST SPECTACULAR IS THE **TUSAYAN PUEBLO** THAT, TOGETHER WITH THE ADJACENT MUSEUM, OFFERS A LOOK BACK AT THE ANCESTORS OF THE LARGEST NATIVE AMERICAN GROUPS.

| **287** *Colorado River rapids should be faced from April to October.*

| 288-289 *The Yucatan* cenotes *can be explored both scuba diving or simply snorkeling.* |

NOT TO MISS

ON THE ROAD BETWEEN TULIM AND COBÁ, THE **CENOTE CALAVERA** (OR "SKULL CAVE") IS THE ONE THAT REALLY GIVES THE IMPRESSION OF FINDING YOURSELF IN THE MAYAN AFTERLIFE. ABOVE THE WATER'S SURFACE, THE SANDSTONE WALLS ARE LITERALLY ENCRUSTED WITH FOSSILS, AND DURING A DIVE YOU CAN SWIM THROUGH THICK SCHOOLS OF A SPECIES OF BLIND CATFISH.

THEY NAMED IT **CENOTE TAJ MAHAL** AND THE COMPARISON TO THE INDIAN ARCHITECTURAL MASTERPIECE IS NOT EXCESSIVE. WITH MAJESTIC STALAGMITES AND STALACTITES, IT REALLY DOES SEEM LIKE A TEMPLE OR CATHEDRAL, WHILE GETTING HERE FROM PUERTO AVENTURAS, THE BUMPY ROAD THROUGH THICK FORESTS IS THE PERFECT START FOR AN UNDERWATER EXPERIENCE IN SEARCH OF LOST CIVILIZATIONS.

A SHORT DISTANCE FROM THE TULUM COAST, **CENOTE ANGELITA** IS THE DESTINATION FOR ONE OF THE MOST TECHNICALLY ADVANCED DIVES: IT DROPS DOWN TO 60 METERS AND, BETWEEN THE LAYERS OF FRESHWATER AND MARINE WATER, AT 35 METERS DOWN, THERE IS A LAYER OF HYDROGEN SULFATE, ORIGINATING FROM THE BACTERIAL COMPOSITION OF ORGANIC SUBSTANCES FROM THE FOREST. ABOUT 3-4 METERS THICK, IT IS DENSE AND MILKY, AND DIVERS SINK LIKE ANGELS THROUGH CLOUDS.

IN THE MAYAN CENOTES

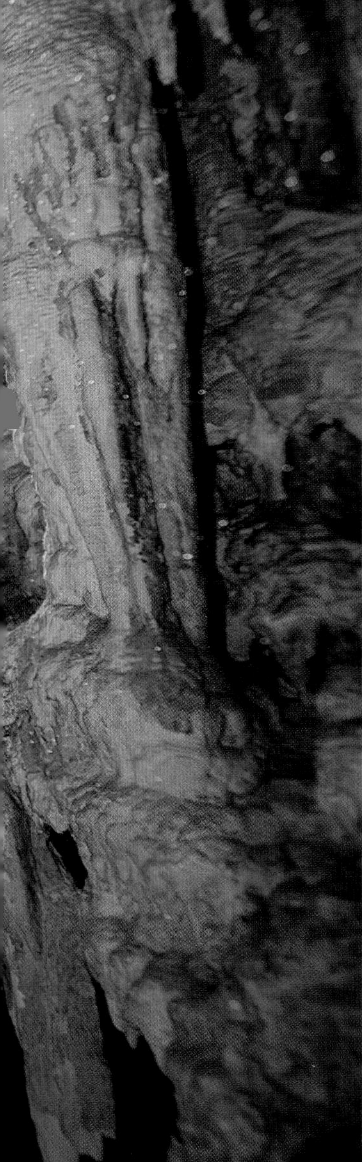

For the Mayan, these were the gates to the afterlife. Today, these caves rich with freshwater (and saltwater) are the Yucatán's most exciting underwater experience.

Sixty-five million years ago a 10-kilometer wide meteorite hit the Yucatán. The impact left an immense crater, immediately covered in water, and gave way to the climatic changes that provoked the dinosaur's extinction. Much later, a glaciation drew the sea back and a series of incredible geological phenomena called cenotes emerged, caverns with collapsed roofs due to erosion where the rainwater that falls stays perfectly separated from the saltwater due to their different densities. Interconnected by an enormous labyrinthine system of sinkholes and underground canals, the cenotes were a long guarded Mayan secret: they were their source for freshwater as well as the passage to Xibalba, the after-life for what was the most mysterious and complex pre-Columbian civilizations. A good portion of the *cenotes* has been explored over many decades now, first by scientists (like archeologists, since these cave were the theater of ritual human sacrifice) and then by cave diving enthusiasts, so today they have become the most exciting adventure activity in the super touristic Mayan Riviera. Distributed throughout the peninsula, they are magical right from the entrance, often hidden by tropical vegetation, and they offer experiences for every level of difficulty, from challenging underwater speleological explorations to simple dives to 10-18 meters in depth that, in any case, allow you to admire the splendid stalactites and stalagmites and experience the passage from the crystal clear freshwater in the first few meters to saltwater, where the setting is transformed, becoming a lacework of jagged white calcium rock formations.

When to go *From October to April.*

How long to stay *In four days you can dive seven* cenotes, *but leave a little time to experience the Caribbean and for exploring the Yucatán's archeological sites.*

Organization *All the dive centers on the Mayan Riviera (from Cancún, Playa del Carmen and up to Tulum) propose* cenote *immersions. We recommend Maya Diving, Phantom Divers and Tan-Ha Dive Center.*

Advice *Even if you don't have a PADI license, you can experience the magical adventure of the* cenotes. *Some of them are adapted for snorkeling and, on the road between Playa del Carmen and Tulum, you'll find Hidden Worlds: it calls itself a Family* Cenotes *Adventure Park and proposes a series of adrenaline activities in nature, including a visit to two* cenotes.

Internet site www.rivieramaya.com

"AIR TREKKING" IN MONTEVERDE

...And not only: the most ecological country in the world created zip-line adventures for experiencing the forest through Tarzan's eyes.

Hats off to a country that – in the turbulence of Central America – is a champion for political stability and decided, already in 1949, that it could easily do without an army and concentrate its efforts, this time vigorously, on protecting its natural heritage. And Coast Rica's environment is really exceptional: extending over a piece of land just over 250 kilometers between the Pacific and the Caribbean Sea, it represents just 0.03% of the planet's exposed terrestrial surface, but hosts 5% of its biodiversity. It is literally covered in forests, protected and cared for with love, and has developed its tourism based on the most rigorous environmental sustainability. Not by chance, right in Costa Rica, and precisely in the mountain forests of Monteverde, canopy tours were born, an adrenaline activity that allows you to experience the forest from Tarzan's perspective, launching yourself attached to cables 30 meters off the ground (and up to 700 meters long) between wooden platforms built in the canopy.

Internet site www.visitcostarica.com

290 *Canopy tours were created by Canadian biologists in 1992 to study the forest.*

| 291 *Zip-line technology was perfected in Costa Rica to minimize environmental impact in the forests.*

Don't think that this is merely a dreamy idea: zip-line technology (their technical name) was perfected in the 1970s by American biologists during a Costa Rican research project as to minimize the human impact on the virgin forest environments and to better study "aerial" species, from monkeys to birds, notably the colorful and majestic quetzal. And, today, you can discover the natural wonders of this country on a tour without every touching the ground, in foggy, dry or tropical forests. You can even cross canyons, rivers and waterfalls!

When to go *If you can't renounce constant sunlight, go between November and May, but perhaps Costa Rica is most fascinating in the other months, during the so-called "green season."*

How long to stay *Every canopy tour lasts half a day, but you need two weeks to enjoy Costa Rica's many areas.*

Organization *The Pacific coast of Costa Rica is perfect for do-it-yourself adventures, and you can participate in canopy tours any time you find one. If you prefer an organized trip, the main tour operators propose zip-line circuits in the forests. We recommend Anywhere Costarica, Ecotours Express and Go Visit Costarica.*

Advice *As pioneers of canopy tours, Costa Ricans are very careful about safety and always supply helmets and protective gloves. On your part, wear long pants, make sure your shoes are well-tied and remove watches and bracelets from your wrists: they could get caught up in the handles.*

NOT TO MISS

- IN THE PROTECTED AREA OF MONTEVERDE, **SELVATURA PARK** HOSTS THE COUNTRY'S FIRST AND LONGEST ZIP-LINES - THE AERIAL JOURNEY EXTENDS OVER 3 KILOMETERS, PLUS A SERIES OF PICTURESQUE SUSPENDED BRIDGES. AND HERE YOU CAN ALSO VISIT ONE OF THE RICHEST MUSEUMS IN THE WORLD DEDICATED TO INSECTS.
- THE CANOPY TOUR PROPOSED BY BUENA VISTA ECOLODGE, IN THE GUANACASTE REGION, CAN BE COMPLIMENTED WITH A **HORSEBACK RIDE TO THE RINCON DE LA VIEJA VOLCANO,** ONE OF THE PLANET'S MOST ACTIVE VOLCANOES, AS WELL AS THE EXPERIENCE OF A NATURAL SPA, WITH BENEFICIAL MUDS AND THERMAL WATERFALLS.
- FACING THE PACIFIC OCEAN, THE **LUSH MANUEL ANTONIO TROPICAL FOREST** IS EXTRAORDINARILY RICH WITH FAUNA AND IS THE HEADQUARTERS FOR TITI CANOPY TOURS THAT PROPOSE NOCTURNAL "AERIAL" ADVENTURES, WHEN ANIMALS LIKE LITTLE TITI MONKEYS, ANTEATERS, RACCOONS, OLINGOS AND KINKAJOUS ARE MOST ACTIVE.

SHARKS AT ISLA DEL COCO

A high-adrenaline dive safari in the remote Pacific outpost considered the capital of ferocious hammerhead sharks.

NOT TO MISS

- BOOK A **DEEP SEA SUBMERSIBLE TOUR** ABOARD A SUBMARINE WITH THREE SEATS TO DIVE DOWN TO 90 METERS, SURROUNDED BY MANTA RAYS AND GREAT PREDATORS, TO A SUBMERGED VOLCANO CRATER: LIKE EVEREST, THIS IS THE TOP FOR EVERY DIVER'S CAREER.
- THERE IS NO BETTER SPOT THAN **BAJO ALCYONE** FOR OBSERVING HAMMERHEAD SHARKS IN ACTION. AT 30 METERS DEEP, YOU WILL SEE THEM SWIMMING JUST ABOVE YOU.
- OFF THE ISLAND'S WESTERN COAST, **DIRTY ROCK** IS AN INCREDIBLY DYNAMIC DIVING SPOT: THE GREAT BIOMASS OF FISH ATTRACTS THE SHARKS, WHILE THE CORAL BETWEEN THE ROCK PINNACLES ARE THE IDEAL HABITAT FOR GREEN TORTOISES AND HAWKSBILL SEA TURTLE, THE NINJA OF THE ABYSSES.

| 292 *Isla del Coco's lush forests.* | 293 *The hammerhead shark, with its unmistakably oblong head, is a very aggressive predator.*

When to go *Close to the Equator, the island receives 7 meters of precipitation per year. From December to May the climate is dryer, the sea calmer and there is better visibility, but the best season for diving is from June to November, when there are more hammerhead sharks.*

How long to stay *10 days.*

Organization *Diving at Isla del Coco is only possible when participating in a dive cruise, organized by all the main operators specialized in underwater adventures. Among these, Undersea Hunter, an American operator based in Costa Rica, is known for their experience in adventure diving.*

Advice *Diving at Isla del Coco is for experienced divers because it is easy to panic during a head to head dive with sharks. Added to this, it takes 30-36 hours at sea to arrive here, with waves that are often anything but gentile. Bring comfort foods to resist the crossing.*

The best-selling author Michael Crichton was inspired by these landscapes for his novel Jurassic Park. Earlier, in 1889, the German adventurer August Gissler came here driven by his obsession that pirates had hidden "The Great Lima Treasure" here. He stayed here for 20 years, reducing the island to Swiss cheese, only finding a handful of Spanish doubloons. Instead, today its waters are every diver's obsession. 550 kilometers from Costa Rica's Pacific coast, the Isla del Coco – with its 2400 hectares covered in forest – is the world's largest uninhabited island, famous for having the high concentration of sharks on the planet. Rich in plankton, its waters are the habitat for whale sharks; here whitetip sharks laze in the "cleaning season" in ravines full of shrimp fond of the parasites that live on the rough skin of these great sea predators. But the Isla del Coco's superstar is the hammerhead shark, the most ferocious and intelligent of the ocean's great predators, living here in terrifying, colossal shivers: diving here to observe their behavior is the equivalent of an underwater cum laude, but you need a good dose of cold blood to do it.

Internet site www.visitcostarica.com

INTERNET SITES

ON FOOT

MONT BLANC TOUR
Not to miss
Spa Thermal du Mont Blanc: www.spa-thermal-mont-blanc.com
Barefoot trail in Morgex: www.comune.morgex.ao.it/it/men-barefoot.html
Alpage de La Peule refuge: http://lapeulaz.skyrock.com

Organization
Compagnie des Guides et Accompagnateurs de Chamonix Mont-Blanc: www.chamonix-guides.com
Guide Escursionistiche Naturalistiche in Valle d'Aosta Association: www.agenva.it
Les Guides de Verbier: www.guideverbier.com

THE MONTE ROSA TOUR
Not to miss
Glacier Express: www.glacierexpress.ch
La Montagna di Luce: www.montagnadiluce.it
Organization
La Compagnie des Guides de Champoluc-Ayas: www.guidechampoluc.com
Advice
Booking refuges: www.rifugimonterosa.it

ALONG THE KÖNIG LUDWIG WEG
Not to miss
Wieskirche: www.wieskirche.de
Neuschwanstein Castle: www.neuschwanstein.de
Fussen: http://fuessen-en.ictourismus.de
Organization
Alpenland Touristik: www.alpenlandtouristik.de/King-Ludwig-Way.htm

THE GRANDE RANDONNÉE IN CORSICA
Not to miss
Hotel Monte d'Oro: www.monte-oro.com
Organization
Corsica Adventure: www.corsica-aventure.com
Corsica Trek: http://corsicatrek.free.fr
Corsica Rando Evasion: www.corsica-rando-evasion.com

ON ETNA
Organization
Etna Avventura: www.etnanaturaavventura.it
Etna Experience: www.etnaexperience.com
Etna Trekking: www.etnatrekking.com

ALONG THE DOGON CLIFFS
Organization
Tourism Office: www.syndicattourismebandiagara.com
Mali Adventure: www.mali-aventures.com
AfricVision Tourism: www.africvisiontourism.com

VIRUNGA, THE GORILLA MOUNTAINS
Not to miss
Sabyinyo Silverback Lodge: www.governorscamp.com
Organization
Gorilla Expedition: http://gorillafund.org/travel

ON THE PEAK OF KILIMANJARO
Not to miss
Lake Chala Safari Camp: www.lakechalasafaricamp.com
Kiliman Adventure Challenge: http://kilimanjaro-man.com
Organization
Kilimanjaro Climbing Company: www.kilimanjaroclimbingcompany.com
Ultimate Kilimanjaro: www.ultimatekilimanjaro.com
Team Kilimanjaro: www.teamkilimanjaro.com
Advice
Kilimanjaro Porters Assistance Project: www.kiliporters.org.

WALKING SAFARI IN LUANGWA
Not to miss
Kutandala Safari Camp: www.kutandala.com
Bush Spa del Mfuwe Lodge: www.mfuwelodge.com
Organization
Norman Carr Safaris: www.normancarrsafaris.com
Robin Pope Safaris: www.robinpopesafaris.net

TREKKING IN TIEN SHAN
Organization
Asia Outdoor: www.asiaoutdoor.com
Central Asia Travel: www.centralasia-travel.com
Dostuck Trekking: www.dostuck.com.kg
Tien Shan Travel: www.tien-shan.com

PILGRIMAGE ON MT. KAILASH
Organization
Karnali Excursions: www.kailashtrekking.com
Himalaya Kailash Travel&Tours: www.himalayakailash.com
Tibet Explorer Tours: www.tibetexploretour.com

THE ANNAPURNA CIRCUIT
Not to miss
Muktinath: www.muktinath.org
Organization
National Trust for Nature Conservation: www.ntnc.org.np
Trekking Agencies Association of Nepal: www.taan.org.np

TAKTSANG MONASTERY
Organization
Adorable Brothers Adventure: www.aba.com.bt
Happy Bhutan Adventures: www.happybhutan.bt
Shangri-La Bhutan Tours & Treks: www.bhutanonline.net

AT THE SPRING OF THE GANGES
Organization
Peak Adventure: www.gangotri-tapovan-trek.com
Snow Leopard Adventures: www.snowleopardadventures.com

ON THE JAPANESE ALPS
Not to miss
Matsumoto: http://welcome.city.matsumoto.nagano.jp
Organization
Club Alpino Giapponese: www.jac.or.jp/english/jac_e.htm
Quest Japan: www.hikejapan.com

PILGRIMAGE TO KOYASAN
Organization
Maps of the trails in Kuman Kodo Region: http://tb-kumano.jp/en
Japan Tourism Board: http://www.japanican.com/tours/list.aspx

AMONG THE PAPUA NATIVES
Organization
Trek Papua: http://trek-papua.com
National Tourism Board: www.papuanewguinea.travel/touroperators

THE GREAT OCEAN WALK
Not to miss
Otway Fly Treetop Walk: www.otwayfly.com
Helicopter flights: http://acahelicopters.com.au.
Organization
Booking campgrounds: http://parkweb.vic.gov.au/
Great Ocean Walk Holidays: www.greatoceanwalkholidays.com.au
Walk 91: www.walk91.com.au

IN FIORDLAND
Not to miss
Fiordland Cinema: www.fiordlandcinema.co.nz
Helicopter Tours: www.fiordlandhelicopters.co.nz
Organization
Booking refuges on the Great Walks (40 excursionists per day): www.doc.govt.nz
Ultimate Hikes: www.ultimatehikes.co.nz
Trips & Tramps: www.tripsandtramps.com
Fiordland Nature Observations: www.natureobservations.com
Curiosities
GPS coordinates for *The Lord of the Rings* shooting locations: www.doc.govt.nz/parks-and-recreation/places-to-visit/lord-of-the-rings-locations

AMBRYM, THE BLACK ISLAND
Organization
Air Vanuatu: www.airvanuatu.com
Wrecks to Rainforest: http://wreckstorainforest.com

Advice
News on volcanic and seismic activity from Vanuatu Geohazards Observatory: www.geohazards.gov.vu

THE JOHN MUIR TRAIL
Not to miss
Devils Postpile National Monument: www.nps.gov/depo
Organization
Information: www.hikejmt.com e www.jmt-hiker.com
Map of the trail: http://johnmuirtrailmap.com
National Parks Service: www.nps.gov
Curiosities
Ansel Adams: www.anseladams.com

ATOP CORDILLERA BLANCA
Organization
Casa de Guias: www.huaraz.com/casadeguias
Andean Kingdom: www.andeankingdom.com
Pony's Expeditions: www.ponyexpeditions.com

TREKKING IN PARQUE NACIONÁL LOS GLACIARES
Organization
Hielo y Aventura: www.hieloyaventura.com
Morresi Viajes: morresi@cotecal.com.ar
Mil Outdoor Adventure: www.miloutdoor.com

ON THE ROAD

FROM CAIRO TO GILF KEBIR
Organization
Badawiya Expedition Travel: www.badawiya.com
Zarzora Expedition: www.zarzora.com
Advice
Ecolodge Adrère Amellal: http://adrereamellal.net

IN THE OMO VALLEY
Not to miss
Lumale Tent Camp: www.lumaletoursandcamp.com
Organization
Origins Safaris: http://www.originsafaris.info
Ethio Guzo Tour and Travel: http://ethioguzo.com
Curiosities
For more information on the Mursi culture: www.mursi.org

THE GREAT WILDEBEEST MIGRATION
Not to miss
Hot air balloon safari, Serengeti Baloon Safaris: www.balloonsafaris.com
Organization
Grumeti Camp: www.grumeti.com
Governors' Camp: www.governorscamp.com
Advice
To follow the great migration:
http://wildebeestmigration.blogspot.it

ON THE FIANARANTSOA-CÔTE EST RAILWAY
Not to miss
Lac Hotel: www.lachotel.com
Canal des Pangalanes: www.pangalanes.net
Organization
List of tour operators approved by the Association des Tours Opérateurs Réceptifs de Madagascar: www.top-madagascar.com

ALONG THE KARAKORUM HIGHWAY
Not to miss
Shandur Polo Festival: www.shandur.com

AMONG THE ETHNICITIES OF LUANG NAM THA
Not to miss
Guided trekking, Ecotourism Laos: www.ecotourismlaos.com
Organization
Nam Ha Eco Guides: www.namha-npa.org
Lao Youth Travel: http://njsj280.wix.com/laoyouthtravel
Exotissimo: www.exotissimo.com
Tiger Trail Laos: www.laos-adventures.com

IN THE LAND OF GENGHIS KHAN
Not to miss
Erdene Zuu: www.erdenezuu.mn
Factory store Gobi Cashmere: www.gobi.mn
Organization
Mongolia Tourism Association: www.travelmongolia.org
Open Tour Around Mongolia: www.otamecotours.com
Steppe Nomad Travel & Tours: www.lookmongolia.com
Advice
Trans-Mongolian, CITS: www.cits.net or www.chinatraintickets.net

IN THE KINGDOM OF THE LUGU HU WOMEN
Organization
Yunnan Adventure: www.yunnanadventure.com

WILD HOKKAIDO
Not to miss
Lake Akan: www.lake-akan.com
Organization
Japan Rail Pass: www.japanrailpass.net
Hokkaido Rail Pass: www2.jrhokkaido.co.jp/global/index.html
BFH Tours: www.bfh.jp/tour/en

ON KODIAK ISLAND
Not to miss
Alutiiq Museum: www.alutiiqmuseum.org
Remote Lodge: www.raspberryisland.com
Organization
Era Aviation: www.flyera.com
Alaska Airlines: www.alaskaair.com
Kodiak Adventures: www.kodiakadventuresunlimited.com
Kodiak Wild Side: www.kodiakswildside.com
Advice
Alaska Department of Fish and Game: www.adfg.alaska.gov

IN CHURCHILL, WITH POLAR BEARS
Not to miss
Wapusk National Park: www.pc.gc.ca/eng/pn-np/mb/wapusk/index.aspx
Organization
Calm Air: http://www.calmair.com
Kivalliq Air: www.kivalliqair.com
Churchill Wild: www.churchillwild.com
The Tundra Buggy Adventure: www.tundrabuggy.com

A TRAIN RIDE THROUGH THE BARRANCAS DEL COBRE
Not to miss
Copper Canyon Sierra Lodge and Riverside Lodge in Batopilas:
www.coppercanyonlodges.com
Posada del Hidalgo:
www.hotelposadadelhidalgo.com
Organization
Tarahumara Tours: www.tarahumarastours.com
Viajes Dorados de Chihuahua: www.coppercanyon.com.mx

IN THE SALAR DE UYUNI
Not to miss
Palacio de Sal: www.palaciodesal.com.bo
Organization
Tupiza Tours: www.tupizatours.com
Ruta Verde: www.rutaverdebolivia.com
Tayka Hotel: www.taykahoteles.com

BY SEA

IN THE ILULISSAT ICEFJORD
Organization
World of Greenland: www.worldofgreenland.com
Ilulissat Tourist Nature: www.ilulissattn.com
Arctic Adventure: www.arctic-adventure.dk
Aqua-Firma: www.aqua-firma.co.uk

CRUISING TO SPITSBERGEN
Not to miss
Fossil-finding tours, Green Dog: www.greendog.no
Kayak expeditions: www.wildlife.no
Organization
Hurtigruten navigation company: www.hurtigruten.com
Spitsbergen Travel: www.spitsbergentravel.com
Advice
Jazz music, Svalbar: www.svalbar.no

FISHING IN LOFOTEN
● *Not to miss*
Polar Light Center: http://polarlightcenter.com
● *Organization*
Nusfjord: www.nusfjord.no
Lofoten Fisherman Adventures: www.lofoten-rorbuopplevelser.no
Aqua Lofoten Coast Adventure: www.aqualofoten.com
Information on World Championship Cod Fishing: www.vmiskreifiske.info

KAYAKING THE OUTER HEBRIDES
● *Not to miss*
Fèis Barraigh Festival: www.barrafest.co.uk
Dunard Lodge: www.dunardlodge.com
Real-time orca and whale sightings on Hebridean Whale & Dolphin Trust: www.whaledolphintrust.co.uk
● *Organization*
Clearwater Paddling: www.clearwaterpaddling.com
● *Advice*
Beginner kayaking courses: www.monkeysee.com/play/454-kayak-fundamentals

DIVING CRUISE IN PORT SUDAN
● *Organization*
Don Questo Sudan: www.sudandiving.it
Felicidad II Sudan: www.felicidad.it

KAYAKING MASOALA
● *Not to miss*
Masoala Forest Lodge: www.masoalaforestlodge.com

IN THE MERGUI ARCHIPELAGO
● *Organization*
Ayuda Myanmar Travel: http://ayudamyanmartravel.com
Asia Whale: www.myanmarasiatravel.com

KOMODO, THE ISLANDS OF DRAGONS
● *Not to miss*
Komodo Resort: www.komodoresort.com

DIVING SAFARI IN RAJA AMPAT
● *Not to miss*
Birdwatching: www.papuabirdclub.com
● *Organization*
Raja Ampat Homestays: www.rajaampathomestays.com

ON THE RING OF FIRE
● *Organization*
Aurora Expeditions: www.auroraexpeditions.com.au
Kamchatka's Vision: www.kamchatka.org.ru
Kamchatka Lost World Tour: www.travelkamchatka.com

THE HUMPBACK WHALES OF FREDERICK SOUND
● *Not to miss*
Petersburg: www.petersburgalaska.com
Tongass National Forest: www.fs.usda.gov/tongass
● *Organization*
Alaska Marine Highway System: www.dot.state.ak.us
Alaska Sea Adventures: www.yachtalaska.com
Gastineau Guiding Company: www.stepintoalaska.com
● *Advice*
Snorkel Tours: www.snorkelalaska.com

ALONG THE COASTS OF BAFFIN ISLAND
● *Not to miss*
Great Adventure Company in Edmonton: www.adventures.ca
Alianait Arts Festival: www.alianait.ca
● *Organization*
Adventure Canada: www.adventurecanada.com
The Great Canadian Travel Company: www.greatcanadiantravel.com
Compagnie di Ponant: www.ponant.com
● *Curiosities*
Stories, legends and the scientific mysteries of the narwhal: www.narwhal.org

WHALE WATCHING IN EL VIZCAÍNO
● *Not to miss*
Desert excursions, Baja Outback: http://bajaoutback.com and Baja Wild: www.bajawild.com
Ecoresort Prana del Mar: http://pranadelmar.com
● *Organization*
Searcher Natural History Tours: www.bajawhale.com

DIVING THE GREAT BLUE HOLE
● *Not to miss*
List of diving spots: http://ambergriscaye.com/pages/town/divesites.html
● *Organization*
Aqua Scuba Center in San Pedro: www.aquascubabelize.com
Turtle Inn Resort in Placencia: www.coppolaresorts.com/turtleinn

GALÁPAGOS CRUISE
● *Organization*
Enchanted Expeditions: www.enchantedexpeditions.com
Row Adventures:
www.rowadventures.com/galapagos-islands.html
Natural Habitat Adventures: www.nathab.com/galapagos
● *Advice*
Dive the Galápagos!: www.divethegalapagos.com

CARGO BOATING THE MARQUESAS ISLANDS
● *Organization*
For information and booking: www.aranui.com

SAILING THE WHITSUNDAY ISLANDS
● *Not to miss*
Ngaro Sea Trail:
www.nprsr.qld.gov.au/parks/whitsunday-ngaro-sea-trail
● *Organization*
Air Whitsunday: www.airwhitsunday.com.au
GLS Aviation: www.whitsundayscenicflights.com.au
Whitsunday Escape: www.whitsundayescape.com
Queensland Yacht Charters: www.yachtcharters.com.au
Whitsunday Sailing Adventures: whitsundayssailingadventures.com.au
ProSail: www.prosail.com.au
● *Advice*
Book 100 Magic Miles: www.100magicmiles.com

DIVING CRUISE THROUGH ROCK ISLANDS
● *Not to miss*
Etpison Museum: www.etpisonmuseum.org
● *Organization*
Sam's Tours: www.samstours.com
Neco Marine: www.necomarine.com
● *Advice*
Divers Alert Network: www.diversalertnetwork.org

CRUISING ANTARCTICA
● *Organization*
Antarpply Expeditions: www.antarpply.com
Quark Expeditions: www.quarkexpeditions.com

ON 2 WHEELS AND 4 PAWS

MOUNTAIN BIKING GEYSERS AND VOLCANOES
● *Organization*
Icelandic Mountain Bike Club:
http://fjallahjolaklubburinn.is/content/view/112/104/
Opus Adventures: www.opusadventures.is
Blue Lagoon: www.bluelagoon.com

ALONG THE RALLARVEGEN
● *Not to miss*
Rallar Museet: http://rallarmuseet.no
Nærøyfjord: www.naeroyfjord.com
● *Organization*
Haugastøl Station: www.rallarvegen.com
Hotel Finse 1222: www.finse1222.no
Norwegian Railways - Norges Statsbaner AS: www.nsb.no

PYRENEES TOUR
● *Not to miss*
Parc Pyrenees: www.parc-pyrenees.com
Bagnères-de-Luchon: www.luchon-bien-etre.fr
Vall de Boí: www.centreromanic.com
Interesting villages for landscapes and culture, see the Midi-Pyrénées section on: www.les-plus-beaux-villages-de-france.org

Organization
Vélo Loco: www.veloloco.com
Best of the Pyrénées: www.bestofthepyrenees.com

ON HORSEBACK IN FISH RIVER CANYON
Not to miss
Fish River Lodge: www.fishriverlodge-namibia.com
Organization
Namibia Horse Safari Company: www.namibiahorsesafari.com
Chameleon Holidays & Travel: www.chameleonholidays.com

ON THE ALTAI MOUNTAINS
Not to miss
Rafting: www.rusadv.com/English/Russia/Altai/tour_Russia_Altai_rafting_English.html.
Organization
Altai Expeditions: www.altaiexpeditions.com
Blue Wolf Travel: http://bluewolftravel.com
Kazakh Tour: www.kazakhtour.com
Mongolia Horseback Riding: www.mongoliahorseriding.com
Ecotours Russia: www.ecotours-russia.com
K2 Travel: www.adventuretravel.ru

IN THE TAKLAMAKAN DESERT
Organization
Adbul Wahab Tours: www.kashgartrip.com
Uighur Tours: www.uighurtour.com

WITH ELEPHANTS IN THE GOLDEN TRIANGLE
Not to miss
Chiang Dao Elephant Training Camp: www.chiangdaoelephantcamp.com
Organization
Elephant Nature Camp: www.elephantnaturepark.org
Advice
Anantara Golden Triangle Resort & Spa in Chiang Saen: http://goldentriangle.anantara.com

ALONG THE HO CHI MINH TRAIL
Organization
Activetravel Vietnam: www.activetravelvietnam.com
Explore Indochina: http://exploreindochina.com

THE BICENTENNIAL NATIONAL TRAIL
Not to miss
Imperial Hotel, Ravenswood: www.heritageaustralia.com.au/search.php?region=93&state=QLD&view=1234
Grand Parade, Kilkivan: http://tourism.southburnett.com.au/townkilkivan.htm
Section 8, Discovery Rangers: www.wildwildworld.com.au
Alpine Walking Track: www.australianalps.environment.gov.au/walktrack/index.html
Organization
State of Victoria: www.visitvictoria.com
Curiosities
Scone horse stalls: www.horsecapital.com.au

WESTERN AUSTRALIA BY MOTORCYCLE
Not to miss
Gibb River Road: www.gibbriverroad.net
Coral Coast: www.australiascoralcoast.com
Southwestern itineraries: www.australiassouthwest.com
Organization
Kimberley Trail Bike Tours: www.kimberleytrailbiketours.com.au
Down Under Motorcycle Tours: www.harleytours.ws

IN MONUMENT VALLEY
Not to miss
Monument Valley Safari: http://monumentvalleysafari.com
Hotel The View: www.monumentvalleyview.com
Organization
Sacred Monument Tours: www.monumentvalley.net
Black's Tours: www.blacksmonumentvalleytours.com
Discover Navajo: http://discovernavajo.com

THE FAR WEST OF PINAR DEL RÍO
Organization
Pinar del Río Province: http://vinalescuba.org
Mototouring: www.mototouring.com
Cuba Motorcycle Tours: http://motorcycletourscuba.com
Advice
Climbing: www.cubaclimbing.com

IN THE PAMPA WITH THE GAUCHOS
Not to miss
San Antonio de Areco: www.portaldeareco.com
Estancia Santa Catalina: www.santacatalina.info
Estancia Dos Lunas: www.doslunas.com.ar
Organization
Estancias: www.estanciasargentinas.com
Argentina Exeptión: http://en.argentina-excepcion.com
Riding Argentina: www.ridingargentina.com
Welcome Argentina: www.welcomeargentina.com
Advice
For information on Feria de Mataderos: www.feriademataderos.com.ar

FRESH WATER JOURNEY

IRELAND'S WATERWAYS
Not to miss
Belvedere House & Gardens, Mullingar: www.belvedere-house.ie
Lough Allen: www.loughallenadventure.com
Organization
Irish Boat Rental Association: www.boatholidaysireland.com

IN THE LABYRINTH OF THE SUNDARBANS
Not to miss
Southern Health Improvement Samity - Visitors and aid information: www.shisindia.org
Organization
Tour de Sundarbans: http://tourdesundarbans.com
India Beacons Sojourn: www.sundarbans.net
Bengal Tours: www.bengaltours.com

IN THE MEKONG DELTA
Organization
SinhBalo Adventure Travel: www.sinhbalo.com
Viet Bamboo Travel: www.cruisemekongdelta.com
Blue Cruiser: www.bluecruiser.com

WITH THE ORANGUTANS OF KALIMANTAN
Organization
Adventure Indonesia: www.adventureindonesia.com
BorneoEcoTour: www.borneoecotour.com
Orangutan Foundation International: www.orangutan.org/orangutan-eco-tours

ON THE NAHANNI RIVER
Organization
Canadian River Expeditions: www.nahanni.com
Black Feather: www.nahanniriver.ca
Advice
Wolverine Air: www.wolverineair.com
Simpson Air: www.simpsonair.ca

IN THE OKAVANGO DELTA
Not to miss
Delta Rain Safaris: http://www.deltarain.com
Golden Okavango: www.golden-okavango.com/heli.html
Kavango Air: www.kavangoair.com
Organization
Information on various safaris, lodges and tent campsites: www.okavangodelta.com
Polers Trust Seronga: www.okavangodelta.co.bw
Khwai River Lodge: www.khwairiverlodge.com

SAILING THE RÍO DULCE
Not to miss
Hacienda Tijax: www.tijax.com
Organization
Caribbean Experience: www.sailing-diving-guatemala.com
Exotic Travel Agency: www.bluecaribbeanbay.com

IN A CAYUCO AT LA MOSKITIA
Organization
La Ruta Moskitia: http://larutamoskitia.com
Omega Tours: www.omegatours.info
La Moskitia Ecoaventuras: www.honduras.com/moskitia

CANOEING SALTO ÁNGEL
Organization
Orinoco Tours: www.orinocotours.com
Venezuela Eco-adventures: www.adventurevenezuela.com
Angel Eco Tours: http://angel-ecotours.com

ON RIO NEGRO
Not to miss
Pescamazon: www.pescamazon.com
Organization
Discover Brazil: www.discoverbrazil.com
Southern Cross Tours & Expeditions: www.amazon-travel-brazil.com
Amazon Riders: www.amazonriders.com

IN THE PANTANAL
Not to miss
Araras Eco Lodge: www.araraslodge.com.br
Organization
Pantanal Nature: www.pantanalnature.com.br
Pantanal Trackers: www.pantanaltrackers.com.br

ADRENALINE

CROSS-COUNTRY SKIING THE NORTH POLE
Not to miss
UVU North Polar Marathon: www.npmarathon.com
Organization
Polar Expeditions: http://polar-expeditions.ru/eng
Global Expedition Adventures: www.northpole-expedition.com

EMOTIONS IN LAPLAND
Not to miss
Lumi Linna: www.snowcastle.net
Arctic Husky Farm: www.huskysafaris.com
Sami Ecomuseum, Siida: www.siida.fi
Syötteen Eräpalvelut: http://en.lammassammal.kotisivukone.com
Organization
Book cruises at: www.sampotours.com
Links to all specialized local operators: www.laplandfinland.com
Curiosities
Haparanda and Tornio: www.haparandatornio.com
Finish saunas: www.sauna.fi

AT THE PORTES DU SOLEIL
Not to miss
Rock the Pistes: www.rockthepistes.com
Morzine: www.morzine-avoriaz.com
Les Gets: www.lesgets.com
The Stash: www.thestash.com

ŠKRAPING IN DALMATIA
Not to miss
Škraping Race: www.skraping.hr
Organization
Zara Adventure: www.zara-adventure.hr

RAFTING THE ZAMBEZI
Not to miss
Steam train: www.steamtraincompany.com
Organization
Safari par Excellence: www.safpar.net
Global Descents: www.globaldescents.com/expedition/zambezi-river-expedition
Water by Nature: www.waterbynature.com
Zambezi Safari & Travel Company: www.zambezi.com

CAGED UP IN SHARK ALLEY
Not to miss
White Shark Festival: www.whitesharktrust.org
Great White House: www.thegreatwhitehouse.co.za
Organization
Shark Lady Adventures: www.sharklady.co.za
White Shark Projects: http://whitesharkprojects.co.za

HOT AIR BALLOONING THE WADI RUM
Organization
Royal Aero Sports Club of Jordan, for bookings: www.royalaerosports.com
Rum Stars: www.rumstars.com
Wadi Rum Mountain Guides: www.rumguides.com

ON LAKE BAIKAL
Not to miss
Trans-Siberian: http://eng.rzd.ru
Organization
Baikal Nature: www.baikalnature.com
Great Baikal Trail: www.greatbaikaltrail.org

ROCKCLIMBING IN KRABI
Organization
Hot Rock Climbing School: www.railayadventure.com
Basecamp Tonsai: http://basecamptonsai.com

DOWN THE GUNUNG MULU CAVES
Organization
Kuching Caving: www.kuchingcaving.com
Borneo Ecotours: www.borneoecotours.com
Advice
Royal Mulu Resort: www.royalmuluresort.com

THE UNDERGROUND RIVER OF PUERTO PRINCESA
Organization
Information for traveling independently: www.palawan.gov.ph
Tao Explore: www.taophilippines.com

BUNGEE JUMPING IN QUEENSTOWN
Not to miss
White water sledging on Shoteover river: www.frogz.co.nz
100% Pure New Zealand Winter Games: http://wintergamesnz.com
Arrowtown: www.arrowtown.com
Organization
List of all (not only extreme) activities in Queenstown: http://experiencequeenstown.com
AJ Hackett: www.ajhackett.com
Jet boating: www.shotoverjet.com

HELISKIING THE ROCKY MOUNTAINS
Not to miss
Rocky Mountaineer Train: www.rockymountaineer.com
Whyte Museum of Canadian Rockies: www.whyte.org
Banff: www.banff.ca
Organization
Canadian Mountain Holidays: www.canadianmountainholidays.com

RAFTING THE GRAND CANYON
Organization
Aramak Wilderness River Adventures: www.riveradventures.com
Grand Canyon Whitewater: www.grandcanyonwhitewater.com
Oars: www.oars.com/grandcanyon

IN THE MAYAN CENOTES
Organization
Maya Diving: www.mayadiving.com
Phantom Divers: www.phantomdivers.com
Tan-Ha Dive Center: www.tankha.com
Advice
Hidden Worlds: www.rainforestadventure.com/hidden_worlds_mexico

"AIR TREKKING" IN MONTEVERDE
Not to miss
Selvatura Park: www.selvatura.com
Buena Vista Ecolodge: www.buenavistalodgecr.com
Titi Canopy Tour: www.titicanopytour.com
Organization
Anywhere Costarica: www.anywherecostarica.com
Ecotours Express: http://ecotoursincostarica.com
Go Visit Costarica: www.govisitcostarica.com

SHARKS AT ISLA DEL COCO
Undersea Hunter: www.underseahunter.com

INDEX

PHOTO CREDITS

123RF.com: pp. 150-151
Peter Adams/Getty Images: p. 59
Alaska Stock Images/National Geographic Stock: pp. 156-157
Alexandrite/iStockphoto: p. 257
William Albert Allard/National Geographic Stock: p. 211
Steve Allen/Getty Images: p. 166
Stephen Alvarez/Getty Images: p. 67
Johnathan Amperstand Esper/Getty Images: p. 42
Anders Peter Amsnæs/iStockphoto: pp. 136-137
Galyna Andrushko/iStockphoto: p. 60
Noriyuki Araki/Getty Images: p. 62
Jon Arnold/Getty Images: pp. 184-185
Yann Arthus-Bertrand/Corbis: pp. 223, 238
Art Wolfe/Getty Images: p. 168
Antonio Attini/Archivio White Star: pp. 28-29, 30, 34, 182-183, 210, 212, 213, 264
Stefan Auth/Getty Images: p. 51
Patrick Aventurier/Gamma-Rapho/Getty Images: p. 116
Axiom/DanitaDelimont.com: p. 260
Fiona Ayerst/iStockphoto: p. 192
Manfred Bail/Imagebroker/Agefotostock: p. 292
Barcroft Media/Getty Images: p. 175
Tim Barker/Getty Images: p. 281
Ben Blankenburg/iStockphoto: p. 287
Per Bergsbo/iStockphoto: p. 123
Marcello Bertinetti/Archivio White Star: pp. 24-25, 61, 95, 96, 110, 148, 159, 163, 170, 171
Nikki Bidgood/iStockphoto: p. 128
Daniel Boang/Getty Images: pp. 202-203
Massimo Borchi/Archivio White Star: p. 269
Brytta/iStockphoto: p. 235
Buena Vista Images/Getty Images: p. 201
Bruno Buongiorno Nardelli/iStockphoto: p. 172
Franck Caillet/iStockphoto: p. 188
Robert Caputo/Getty Images: p. 245
David Caravias/Alamy/Milestone Media: p. 266
Fabio Cardano/123RF.com: p. 286
Mark Carwardine/Getty Images: p. 162
Franck Charton/Getty Images: p. 57
Chelovek/iStockphoto: p. 270
William Chu/Getty Images: p.119
Rafal Cichawa/iStockphoto: pp. 149, 231
China Photos/Getty Images: p. 50
John Coletti/Getty Images: p. 291
Robert Cope/123RF.com: p. 267
Mark Cosslett/National Geographic Stock: pp. 240-241
Crossi/iStockphoto: pp. 194-195
Ian Cumming/Getty Images: p. 33
Ed Darack/Science Fiction/SuperStock: pp. 80-81
Deb22/iStockphoto: p. 172
Ricardo De Mattos/iStockphoto: p. 46
Grant Dixon/Getty Images: p. 70
Andre Dobroskok/iStockphoto: p. 204
David Doubilet/National Geographic Stock: pp. 152-153
Dziikus/iStockphoto: p. 49
John Eastcott and Yva Momatiuk/National Geographic Stock: p. 177
David Else/Getty Images: p. 190
Steve Estvanik/123RF.com: p. 261
Suzi Eszterhas/Minden Pictures/National Geographic Stock: p. 103
Andy Farrer/Getty Images: p. 256
Focus on Nature/iStockphoto: p. 290
FotoVoyager/Getty Images: p. 21
Josef Friedhuber/iStockphoto: p. 139
Romeo Gacad/AFP/Getty Images: p. 279
Alfio Garozzo/Archivio White Star: pp. 84, 85
Gcoles/iStockphoto: p. 87
M. Gebicki/Getty Images: p. 72
Henry Georgi/All Canada Photos/SuperStock: p. 284
Gianni Giansanti/Immaginazione: pp. 98, 99, 100, 101
Peter Giovannini/Getty Images: p. 32
Goinyk/iStockphoto: p. 176
Michael Gounot/Godong/Corbis: p. 105
Tom Grundy/123RF.com: p. 81
Bobby Haas/National Geographic Stock: p. 246
Tim Hall/Getty Images: p. 229
Chuck Haney/DanitaDelimont.com: pp. 252-253
Bill Hatcher/National Geographic Stock: p. 205
Christian Heeb/Marka: p. 243
Hemis.fr/SuperStock: pp. 36-37, 215
Tom Horton, Further to Fly Photography/Getty Images: p. 107
Matej Hudovernik/iStockphoto: p. 230
Richard I' Anson/Getty Images: p. 56
Image Asset Management/Marka: p. 242
Imagebroker.net/SuperStock: p. 53, 165, 259
P. Jaccod/De Agostini Picture Library: p. 43
Pierre Jacques/Getty Images: p. 23
Matthias Jenter/iStockphoto: p. 187
Mark Jones/Minden Pictures/National Geographic Stock: p. 293
JTB Photo Communicati/JTB Photo/SuperStock: p. 65
Jaume Juncadella Olivares/iStockphoto: p. 114
Koichi Kamoshida/Getty Images: p. 118
Oytun Karadayi/iStockphoto: pp. 110-111
Torsten Karock/iStockphoto: p. 234
David Klein/iStockphoto: p. 122
Iris Kuerschner/Getty Images: p. 20
Tim Laman/National Geographic Stock: p. 66
Frans Lanting/DanitaDelimont.com: p. 167
Jason Larkin/Getty Images: paggg. 92-93
Todd Lawson/Getty Images: p. 83
Andre Lebrun/Agefotostock/SuperStock: p. 228
Elisa Locci/iStockphoto: p. 48
Enrique Lopez-Tapia/naturepl.com: pp. 18-19
Alfredo Maiquez/Getty Images: p. 236
Piero Malaer/iStockphoto: p. 150
Richard Manin/Hemis/Corbis: p. 189
Marka/SuperStock: pag: 44
Peter Mather/First Light/Corbis: pp. 232-233
René Mattes/Hemis.fr/Getty Images: pp. 227, 268
Claus Meyer/Minden Pictures/National Geographic Stock: p. 244
John Miles/Getty Images: p. 82
Paul Miles/Getty Images: p. 186
John Miller/Getty Images: p. 31
David Min/Getty Images: p. 54
Minden Pictures/SuperStock: p. 154
Bobby Model/National Geographic Stock: p. 263
Colin Monteath/Hedgehog House/Getty Images: pp. 72-73
Colin Monteath/Marka: p. 282
Bruno Morandi/Getty Images: p. 196
Bruno Morandi/Hemis/Corbis: p. 272
Luciano Mortula/123RF.com: p. 109
Paolo Mudu/iStockphoto: p. 127
Josef Muellek/123RF.com: p. 113
Josef Muellek/iStockphoto: p. 112
Jon Mullen/iStockphoto: p. 79
Matt Mylon/iStockphoto: p. 138
Andrey Nekrasov/imagebroker.net/SuperStock: p. 255
Paul Nicklen/National Geographic Stock: pp. 160, 161, 288-289
Olive/Getty Images: p. 104
Randy Olson/Getty Images: p. 144
Per-Gunnar Ostby/Getty Images: p. 47
Borge Ousland/National Geographic Stock: p. 254
Panoramic Images/Getty Images: pp. 97, 208
Leonardo Patrizi/iStockphoto: p. 69
Nigel Pavitt/Getty Images: pp. 220-221
Doug Pearson/JAI/Corbis: p. 191
Carsten Peter/National Geographic Stock: p. 155
Christopher Pillitz/Getty Images: p. 214
Andrea Pistolesi/Getty Images: p. 278
Andrey Plis/iStockphoto: p. 275
Ingolf Pompe/Getty Images: p. 27
Prisma/SuperStock: p. 174
Olivier Renck/Getty Images: p. 271
Rest/iStockphoto: p. 129
Nicolas Reynard/Getty Images: p. 149
Jim Richardson/National Geographic Stock: p. 142
Robert Harding Picture Library/SuperStock: pp. 58, 237
Luciano Romano/De Agostini Picture Library: pp. 37, 38
Eric Rorer/Getty Images: p. 169
Jenny E. Ross/Corbis: pp. 120-121
C. Sappa/De Agostini Picture Library: p. 94
Sami Sarkis/Getty Images: pp. 74, 76
Kipp Schoen/iStockphoto: p. 78
Setimino/iStockphoto: p. 115
Dmitriy Sharov/123RF.com: pp. 272-273
Robbie Shone/Getty Images: pp. 276-277
Patrick Shyu/iStockphoto: p. 63
Robin Smith/Getty Images: p. 206
Jordi Solé Marimon/iStockphoto: p. 64
Antony Spencer/Getty Images: p. 140
Martin Strmko/iStockphoto: p. 145
Keren Su/Getty Images: p. 106
Giovanni Tagini: p. 222
Luiz Eugenio Teixeira Leite/iStockphoto: p. 86
Alan Tobey/iStockphoto: p. 126
Roy Toft/National Geographic Stock: p. 247
Raul Touzon/National Geographic Stock: p. 75
B. Trapp/Agefotostock: p. 239
Jasmina Trifoni: pp. 71, 283
R. Tyler Gross/ Getty Images: p. 22
Mark Van Aardt/Getty Images: p. 193
Glenn Van Der Knijff/Getty Images: p. 274
Sandro Vannini/De Agostini Picture Library: p. 41
Jennifer Vaughn/iStockphoto: p. 52
Giulio Veggi/Archivio White Star: pp. 26, 141
Peter Walton Photography/Getty Images: p. 207
Linda Wang/iStockphoto: p. 198
John Warburton-Lee/Getty Images: p. 45
Andrew Watson/Getty Images: p. 200
Feng Wei Photography/Getty Images: p. 199
Gordon Wiltsie/National Geographic Stock: p. 108
Konrad Wothe/Getty Images: p. 125
Alison Wright/National Geographic/Getty Images: p. 197
Michael S. Yamashita/Getty Images: p. 226
David Yarrow Photography/Getty Images: p. 39
Antonio Zanghì/Getty Images: p. 35

Via G. da Verrazano, 15 - 28100 Novara, Italy
www.whitestar.it - www.deagostini.it

Translation: Free z'be – Paris

ISBN 979-88-544-0755-8
1 2 3 4 5 6 17 16 15 14 13

Printed in Italy